Wake Up!

Wake Up!

Survive and Prosper in the Coming Economic Turmoil

Al Chalabi & Jim Mellon

CAPSTONE

This edition published in the UK by Capstone Publishing Ltd (a Wiley Company) The Atrium, Southern Gate, Chichester, West Sussex, PO19 8SQ, England. Phone (+44) 1243 779777

Email (for orders and customer service enquires): cs-books@wiley.co.uk
Visit our Home Page on www.wiley.co.uk or www.wiley.com

Other Wiley Editorial Offices

John Wiley & Sons, Inc. 111 River Street, Hoboken, NJ 07030, USA

Jossey-Bass, 989 Market Street, San Francisco, CA 94103–1741, USA

Wiley-VCH Verlag GmbH, Pappellaee 3, D-69469 Weinheim, Germany

John Wiley & Sons Australia Ltd, 42 McDougall Street, Milton, Queensland 4064, Australia

John Wiley & Sons (Asia) Pte Ltd, 2 Clementi Loop #02–01, Jin Xing Distripark, Singapore 129809

John Wiley & Sons Canada Ltd, 22 Worcester Road, Etobicoke, Ontario, Canada, M9W 1L1

Wiley also publishes its books in a variety of electronic formats. Some content that appears in print may not be available in electronic books.

Library of Congress Cataloging-in-Publication Data

A catalog record for this book is available from the US Library of Congress

British Library Cataloguing-in-Publication Data

A catalogue record for this book is available from the British Library

ISBN 13: 978-1-84112-691-3 (PB)
ISBN 10: 1-84112-691-8 (PB)

Typeset in Baskerville by Sparks (www.sparks.co.uk).
Printed and bound in Great Britain by TJ International Ltd, Padstow, Cornwall.
This book is printed on acid-free paper responsibly manufactured from sustainable forestry in which at least two trees are planted for each one used for paper production.
10 9 8 7 6 5 4 3 2

Contents

Protect Your Business and Investments

' **I** t can't happen to me' – a phrase all of us either say or think with regularity. Every human being, when confronted with the problems of others, has a tendency to downplay the likelihood of the same thing happening to him or to her, whether it is being in a car accident, or seeing a colleague getting laid off, or finding out that a friend or acquaintance has fallen seriously ill. Mixed in with the sympathy, there is often a little internal calculation – 'what are the chances of the same event befalling me?' or 'could it happen to me or my nearest and dearest?' Usually, the answer is 'no, surely not'.

We all view ourselves as being somewhat immune to the catastrophes that happen to others and this survival instinct makes sense. If we didn't take that view, we probably wouldn't leave our homes or get out of bed for fear of being run over or of dying in a plane crash. All of us assess risk as it affects us personally on a daily basis and, in most cases, without much conscious thought.

Every person on this planet takes risks, knowing that the chances of the worst happening to them as individuals are low – and all the while chanting the internal mantra 'it can't happen to me'. It is a universal form of complacency, which allows the world to function and for life to go on.

This brings us to the subject of our book – it is about a specific risk – that of an economic meltdown in many so-called 'rich' societies. It is a risk that is staring us in the face and where the odds are hugely against our favour. And yet, it is a risk where the instinctive, self-absorbed complacency of 'it can't happen to me' continues to be the attitude of many.

Let's look at this scenario: the major economies of the world are growing, some robustly, some not so well. New technologies are fuelling productivity growth; consumers in most economically advanced countries are buying like never before, quite often using credit to do so. Trade between countries is at record levels, stock markets are buoyant, and money is relatively easy to come by. There is speculation in some parts of major economies – namely in real estate and in share prices, but governments are aware of this. The major economy – the United States – is starting to deal with creeping inflation and the speculative elements in its economy by raising interest rates. Countries everywhere do their best to maintain the competitiveness of their traded goods by keeping their currencies at lower levels against those of their competitors.

All in all, a fairly benign economic backdrop, don't you agree? Not perfect, but people in the richer parts of the world are generally feeling fine about their economic lives.

So, are we talking about today? Sounds like it, doesn't it?

Actually, no. We are referring to about 80 years ago, the late 1920s, just prior to the Great Depression. In fact, we are describing the 'world economy', in general terms, between 1928 and 1929.

Electricity was the major economic theme of the period, with other technologies, including those of the motor car and of the airplane, also coming in to their own. Credit, particularly in the United States – then, as now, the world's largest economy – was easy. Lending to buy stocks 'on margin', was prevalent. Real estate prices were booming, and trade, particularly with the newly opening markets of the Far East, was booming. The Jazz Age – for those living in the US and in other fortunate countries – was a good one.

Then something went wrong and it went wrong quickly. Hope and optimism were replaced by despair. Between 1929 and 1932 the income of the average American family fell by 40%. Germany and Italy replaced their democracies with dictatorships. In the United States, spending on imports fell by more than two-thirds in just three years. National production fell in each of the three years from 1929 to 1932 and total output in the United States fell from $104 billion in 1929 to $59 billion in 1932. Unemployment in the US rose from 1.6 million to 13 million in 1933. Also in that year, the percentage of people unemployed in the US rose to over 25%. Agricultural prices fell by half, and just about every country in the world suffered a similar contraction in national output to that of the US. The Great Depression, as it became known, bottomed out in 1933 and engulfed the world's economies almost simultaneously like a great tsunami.

It wasn't until the United States entered World War II that the Great Depression finally came to an end after a period of economic bleakness that lasted for more than a decade. In fact, it wasn't until the 1980s that trade was once again a significant part of the world economy – a full half century after the Great Depression.

But surely the events of the Great Depression couldn't happen to me or us today?

Yes they can, and they may well do so *soon*. Dear reader, we have written this book not to scare anyone, but to provide practical solutions to demonstrate how 'we' can survive what is going to be a very difficult situation in the world economy. The Great Depression was not anticipated by those who lived through it. People in the 1930s were totally shocked at the speed with which their economies imploded.

Those of us fortunate enough to be a part of the one-fifth or so of the world's population, we who live in relative comfort, had better beware. Change – radical, complete and awful change – is on its way. This change will affect the way that all Rich World businesses operate and it will create huge pitfalls for unwary investors – and indeed just about everyone who relies on money for daily living. The good news is that opportunities will be created for those who are prepared for change and nimble in their reactions to it.

Our book is about this coming change and how investors and business people can cope with it and profit from it. These changes will affect everyone, not just people from richer nations, but also the people of less developed economies who will also feel the cold draughts of the Rich World's economic difficulties.

This book is about the reasons why the United States and the other nations of what we call the 'Rich World' are in for a rude awakening. By unfortunate proxy, all other nations will be affected too. Our book is not a polemic that puts blame for this coming economic debacle on any one country, institution or individual. Rather, we examine dispassionately the failing structures that have supported two very different worlds for the past half a century or so: a 'Rich World', and a much larger 'Poor World'. This traditional structure is crumbling – and fast. The invisible but effective walls that have kept those of us in the Rich World several steps away from the penury of the Poor World are coming down rapidly – and we had better be ready for the consequences.

The changes that are going to impact our lives will be more radical and far reaching than anything experienced in just about anybody's living memory. Writing about these changes is one thing, but the main purpose of this book is to set out some simple, practical principles for investment and business preservation. In other words, we think that we can provide a measure of protection to those that follow our simple steps for financial survival – and we hope that many do. Most importantly, this book seeks to give its readers – who we imagine to be business people and investors – specific advantages that they can use in the deployment of their capital. These advantages will be vital in dealing with the changes that are going to take place in the next decade or so and are going to make the cost of buying this book seem like a trifle in comparison to the savings and profits that can be made by following our advice.

First, however, we must set the scene. Nothing we write about will be new to readers of newspapers or magazines. What may be new is the sensible collation of the swirling mass of stories and opinions which assault us daily into a cohesive business-orientated view of why this coming decade is more important than any since World War II.

The time for action is now!

The past fifty years have been ones of unparalleled prosperity for the rich, industrialized world. Economies have grown more or less continuously, technology has advanced at an astonishing pace and the Pax Americana has confined conflict and unpleasantness to the more remote and generally poorer parts of the world.

Almost everything has gone right for those of us who live in rich nations: health has improved, educational standards have risen, goods have become abundant and leisure time has increased. However, a confluence of events and factors is going to interrupt that seemingly verdant horizon. This will cause upheaval on a scale unimaginable to those of us living in our cosseted parts of the world. Possessions will be lost, lifestyles altered beyond recognition, and for some, existence imperilled. Businesses will topple like ninepins and 'traditional', 'safe' investments will crumble to the dust of theory paper remnants.

Such change, of course, will not be new to students of history. Mankind has a brilliant record of making things worse for itself. When things are too good – and they are – something bad inevitably will come along. This will turn prosperity into economic collapse, peace into carnage and settled political systems into dictatorship or anarchy.

The principal reasons for holding these pessimistic and strident views should be evident to anyone who reads the newspapers. However, the difference between us and other commentators is that we see a pattern in these well-reported international developments, a pattern that will lead to ominous consequences. We believe that these consequences are probably inevitable and as a result we have written this book as an aid to navigating through the rough waters that lie ahead.

It is going to happen – and within this decade

The momentum behind the changes leading to coming hardship is too strong to reverse; the best we can do is to minimize its impact on our lives. We need to prepare ourselves for these events because of three fundamental factors, which we analyse in detail in this book. These three factors overlap, they are not distinct – they also intertwine with a number of other issues that we weave into our analysis. Our modern world is complex and there is no easy way to understand the many strands that make up its economic and political structures. However, we do believe that by attempting to distil certain key issues into the following themes we will help to put what is occurring and likely to occur into a more understandable perspective:

1 *The Widening Rich–Poor Divide.* The world is currently partitioned into a small(ish) rich part, and a much larger poor part. The population of the world today is three times its level of just forty years ago and the populations of the poorer parts have grown far more rapidly than those of the rich.

   The failure of the Rich World to halt destructive agricultural subsidies and to fully extinguish crippling levels of debt for the Third World further widens the gap between the rich and poor nations.

   Disaffection, anti-Western sentiment and religious fundamentalism are all symptoms of that widening economic divide. Terrorism is the child of fundamentalism and it is a child that is growing daily – both in terms of capability and in terms of reach.

The events of September 11, 2001 foreshadow continuing and expanding attempts by a small minority to destabilize the world order through the use of terror tactics. In itself, this will not work, but allied to declining confidence levels in the economies of the major nations of the world, terrorism will contribute to the coming depression in the economies of rich countries.

2 *Unsustainable Behaviour in the Global Economy.* The use of terror as an economic weapon is only now being appreciated. People can and do lose confidence in travelling, in spending and in going out after major terrorist acts. Terrorism may well be the straw that breaks the economic camel's back – Iraq excluded, terrorism has abated in the immediate past, but no one should doubt that it lurks in the shadows, awaiting its deadly call. Meanwhile, the key factors that will contribute to the future depression in the world's economy continue to mount. The huge debt burden that is a feature of many major nations: consumer debt, government debt and corporate debt combined is at record levels in most large countries. This debt is the major impediment to the effective use of monetary and fiscal policy in reviving sluggish economies – even if from time to time it appears that the major economies are gaining traction. On top of this unappetizing cake is the cherry of a vast imbalance in international trade and capital flows – and all of these are examined in detail in this book. Sadly, it means that the world is perched on a precipice of deflation, recession and possibly depression. But, for our readers, there is positive news: profits can and will be made during this period and those that are prepared for a rough ride will come out of the difficult period well placed to prosper in a renewed golden age. In the meantime – brace yourselves for serious economic turbulence.

3 *The Impact on the West of China's Unrivalled Competitiveness.* The now dominant deflationary tendency in the world today is, in part, the result of a huge shift in the relative production capacities of the large nations of the world. Yes, you read right – we do say deflationary tendencies despite a recent resurgence in commodity price inflation. This is because we believe ultimately that deflation will be the hallmark of the economic period

ahead. China's phenomenal growth since 1978 has resulted in an abundance of cheap goods, the effect of which is literally to hollow out many areas of Western and Japanese manufacturing.

The rapid dissemination of technology – through the Internet and foreign capital transfers – has meant that China's catch-up to the West will be more rapid and more destructive than any other industrial revolution in history. Its impact will be felt in a variety of ways: environmental, other countries' industry and employment, and to the financial balances between nations. This is not a bad thing, and the Chinese cannot be blamed for wanting to grow their way out of poverty, but it is likely to cause serious and potentially lethal tensions between the West and China, which will last for some considerable time.

Since labour costs – as most business people know – are generally a much more important cost than commodities or anything else, the continuing pressure of lower labour costs from China and other Third World competitors will lead to persistent deflationary pressures. These will be exacerbated by a rise in Rich World 'real' (i.e., inflation adjusted) interest rates, designed to slow down and control the pace of debt accumulation.

Already, China is the world's sixth largest economy; by 2006 it will be the world's fourth largest and by 2010 is likely to be world's second largest. There are already 100 million Chinese middle class and that number is expanding rapidly. There are a similar number of Chinese Internet users. In the early 1990s three-quarters of the world's construction cranes were in China, a quarter of them in Shanghai.

Within only a few short years China will rank as an economy to rival the United States in its productive capacity; as it catches up with the US, two things will happen:

- China will continue to accumulate large reserves of foreign exchange as it sells more goods overseas than it buys from others – and this is particularly the case in its trade with the United States. In addition, the Chinese Central Bank persistently and aggressively intervenes in foreign exchange markets to maintain the value of the yuan at a fixed rate against the US dollar – and this means that it keeps on buying more and more US dollar assets. These foreign exchange reserves are largely held at the moment in US dollars and in US government bonds – and thus China will increasingly be a swing, and potentially a dangerous factor in US capital markets.

- China will continue to increase its military expenditures, counterbalancing the one-sided hegemony of US military strength that has been a feature of geopolitics for so long. As China's military might expands, so too will the potential for conflict with the United States and its allies. This may appear to be a fanciful view, especially as US military power on paper is at least ten times greater than all other militaries combined, but we urge readers to look at the arguments we make in this book – and then judge for themselves. China's regime is not wholly benevolent – either in its actions towards its own people or towards its nearest neighbours, especially Taiwan, and there is an agenda which must be examined and taken into account.

Before events unfold, investors must do all they can to protect themselves from their financial impact. This book outlines measures that can be undertaken now, such as debt reduction and portfolio shifts. These are selfish measures; we want to protect our readers and so we seek to give them advantages through advice that others will not have or will not be taking. At the same time, we recognize that the problems of the so-called Rich World are likely to exacerbate those of the poorer countries of the world. The gap between rich and poor may even widen, and this is not only wrong, but also a factor which will contribute to the coming turmoil.

The world that we know is in serious trouble. There is no escaping the facts that confront us. All we can and must do is prepare ourselves so that we do not lose everything – investments, homes and businesses.

Exaggeration? Please read on … No one should doubt the severity of the crisis that is looming. The lessons of history – genocides, wars, plagues, famines, and upheavals of every sort – are those that we should all be familiar with, if only for self-preservation.

Time after time in the past, comfortable lives have been shattered because people did not recognize the signs of change until it was too late to avoid the steamroller of destruction heading towards them.

*part*ONE

Global Tensions

There is no doubt that the world we live in is becoming increasingly crowded. Never before have so many human beings inhabited our small green planet.

Naysayers may view this talk of overpopulation as 'alarmist guff'. There are many who believe that we have nothing to worry about; they point to Thomas Malthus's essay *On the Principles of Population*, written in 1798, which (wrongly) predicted that the world's overpopulation was about to eat up available food supplies. Yet here we all are – over six billion of us – all nice and cosy on planet earth, and our numbers are still growing. As amazing as this accomplishment is, its consequences will forever change our lives.

We continue to industrialize in the name of progress at the cost of upsetting Mother Nature. Yes, it's true, we have been rather irresponsible guests on this planet and earth just isn't able to cope with the rate at which we are pillaging it, and it's really starting to show. We are depleting our planet of its finite resources, all raw materials, from oil to wood, is in record high demand, and we continue to pollute our rivers and oceans. And with our population at such high levels, it means we need more energy, food and water, as well as more manufactured 'stuff' (more often than not, made in China).

Unfortunately, our population has not grown responsibly as a human race, rather we have done so selfishly, protecting our own interests – and so the rich–poor divide continues to widen, both inter and intra-nation. The rich continue to concentrate their wealth whilst, at the same time, the number of people joining the ranks of the poor is increasing every day.

Not only are there more humans alive today than ever before, but we're also hanging around a lot longer thanks to advances in medicine. The average age is also the highest it has been and this trend is set to continue well into the 21st century. That's great news for us as we get older, but at what price?

With the world economy more interdependent and interconnected than at any other time in history, these factors and trends have consequences and knock-on effects – socio-economic, political and environmental. Thus, it is important to analyse these shifts to figure out how they are related and what it means for us as investors, both professional and non-professional. To study only the economic aspects of long-term investing is to ignore the big picture.

In mathematics there is a branch of study called chaos theory in which there is a phenomenon known as the 'butterfly effect', where one small and apparently insignificant event in a complex system can trigger a substantial event elsewhere in that system. It gets its name from a frequently used example, where a butterfly flapping its wings in Africa triggers a series of events that result in a tornado forming in Texas. In this section we take a look at the butterflies that we believe have the potential to trigger big tornados …

Global population growth

If, like us, you are fortunate enough to live in the rich West, you will certainly have noticed the trend to 'population compression' over the past decade or so, probably in your home town or city. Notice those people who keep bumping into you on the pavement – notice that public transport seems ever more crowded, that airports are full to capacity, that every tourist destination is bursting at the seams. Not surprising really, when you think that the global population has increased threefold in half a century … yes, three times! It's worth pausing for a second on that particular statistic. Frightening, or what? The trouble is, it's going to get much worse.

The population growth we have experienced in the West is negligible compared to that of the developing world. While populations everywhere are increasing, another significant and irreversible global trend has already started – one that will have far-reaching consequences: there are an unprecedented number of people living today who are over 60. This older group of people is growing not just in absolute numbers, but also, and more importantly, as a percentage of the world's total population.

The last 50 years has seen the highest rise in population growth in mankind's history. It is a fact that any number that grows by just 3% per annum will more than double in 25 years.

The population of our world therefore quadrupled during the 20th century. In the past, nature has controlled populations with droughts, famines and disease, assisted by man's propensity for armed conflict. For example, the Black Death in the 14th century reportedly killed 25 million people in Europe alone – and this was in a time when the entire population of the continent was only 75 million.

Another example occurred as recently as 1918, when the flu pandemic occurred. This is often cited as the most devastating epidemic of disease ever recorded. 'Spanish Flu', as it was also known as, killed 20 to 40 million people – many more than the number of people who died in the Great War itself.

Since the end of World War II, however, we in the Rich World have been living in relative peace and prosperity. With these positive factors, our ability to combat disease has become unparalleled. Combine this with the development of sophisticated and efficient farming techniques, and the world's human population has kept on rising, almost unchecked.

In 1999, the world welcomed its 6 billionth human inhabitant; by 2050, the UN projects a world population of 9.4 billion. It's going to get rather crowded on this planet, to say the least. Consider it another way – if in 1950 two people lived in a room, then by 2050 nearly 10 people will be in that same room!

Importantly, as our population continues to grow over the coming decades, this expansion will come almost exclusively from the developing world. Indeed, the Rich World's population will barely grow. Figures provided by the United Nations (Figure 1.1) illustrate the distribution of the world's population growth across the various continents. This also demonstrates the relative significance of the developing world's population – and its projected growth.

Between 1998 and 2020, the world's population is expected to rise by 1.74 billion, with 1.7 billion of that growth coming from the developing world and only 40 million from the developed world. To put it another way, by 2020, 84% of the world's population will live in the developing world, and populations of

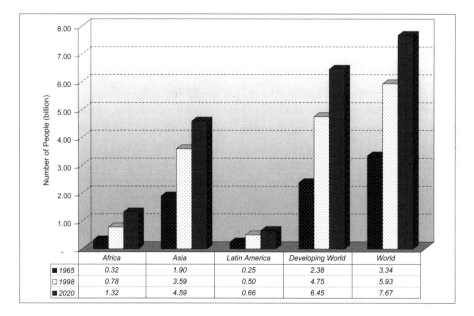

Figure 1.1 World population growth and distribution
Source: United Nations Secretariat, Department of Economic and Social Affairs, *World Population Prospects: The 1996 Revision* (New York, 1996).

several European countries (such as Germany, Spain and Italy), as well as that of Japan, are expected to fall.

It is difficult to really comprehend the full consequences of this demographic trend, but we can certainly expect increasing tensions between the rich and the poor nations – the so-called 'haves' and 'have-nots'.

We will also see an increasing strain on our planet as we strive to provide sufficient energy, food and water for the increased numbers in our population. This may seem obvious – but what is rarely appreciated is the *scale* of the increase in numbers of voracious human beings.

Although Malthus – a clergyman and political economist – predicted disaster for the world as population growth outdid economic and agricultural capacity, he was wrong. However, he wrote his treatise in an era before modern agricultural methods, before genetically modified (GM) crops and before refrigeration and efficient logistics. All of these have served to massively increase food output and allowed billions of extra human mouths to be fed.

Limitless expansion of food supplies is simply not possible because the earth's mass is finite and, similarly, providing heat, power and clothing to our greatly expanded numbers will become more and more difficult as supplies of energy begin to run out. The effects of a limited global supply of oil became evident in 2004 with the rise in oil prices. It is our belief that oil prices will remain high and volatile for some time to come – we're talking years, not months, with the Middle East/OPEC controlling the majority of the supply side, and China driving much of the increase on the demand side. There is also a global water shortage that could cause nations to act in their self-interest, with unpredictable consequences. The supply constraints on these vital commodities are discussed later in the chapter.

An ageing population in the Rich World

It will be no surprise to readers that as a result of medical advances, abundant food supplies and a relatively safer society, we are all also living longer. Most of the developed world has an average life expectancy of over 70. In the US, UK and Germany, for example, life expectancy ranges between 76 and 79, and people in some countries such as Italy and Japan can expect to enjoy even longer average life spans.

It is in the US, the world's largest and most influential economy, that the true impact of the phenomenon of longer life expectancy will be most apparent. This is because we are going into a period when 'baby boomers' (those born in the immediate post-World War II years) enter retirement age. This has started to occur for the first wave of older baby boomers. But the vast majority will reach retirement age over the next decade.

Here are some pertinent facts on the ageing of the world's population:[1]

- Two-thirds of all people who have been fortunate enough to live to 65 or older in the history of the world are alive today!
- More than 50,000 Americans are over 100 years old.
- Advances in medicine have raised life expectancy in the United States from 46 to 75 in just 100 years.
- Prior to AD 1000, the average life expectancy was 18 years.

The last two points may seem hard to believe, but they are largely due to the dramatic decline in infant mortality.

But it's not just the Rich World that is ageing; it's happening all over the world. A report published by the United Nations Population Division (DESA)[2] uncovered four major findings relating to the ageing of the global population:

- The current trends in population ageing are unprecedented in the history of humanity. By 2050, older persons (defined as those older than 60) will outnumber the young (those 18 or younger). In the more developed world, this point was already reached in 1998.
- Population ageing is a global phenomenon and will affect all members of society.
- Population ageing will have major consequences and implications for all facets of human life – economically, socially and politically.
- Population ageing is an irreversible and important trend. For example, in 1950, the old represented 8% of the world's population; this number increased to 10% in 2000 and is forecast to rise to 21% by 2050.

In Japan – an indicative microcosm of what is happening in most rich nations – there are now over 20,000 centenarians, with the Okinawa chain of islands boasting the highest concentration of people over 100 – 34.6 per 100,000 of the population. (It must be something in the seaweed!) The number of centenarians in Japan has increased one hundredfold since 1963.[3] The oldest woman in the country is around 117 and the oldest man about 115. The ratio of female to male centenarians in Japan, and indeed around the world, is about 4 to 1. Japan has the world's highest average life expectancy at 78 years for men and 85 for women.

Japan also has an extremely low birth rate. Currently it stands at below 1.3 births per woman, less than the replacement rate (2.1 children per woman) and this is adding to further concerns that pension burdens will become unmanageable for the country in the not-too-distant future. Already a fifth of the Japanese population is over 65 – and this is estimated by some commentators to rise by the year 2025 to a ratio which will leave only two workers for every pensioner.

Japan's problems in respect of the ageing population are amongst the worst, but it is only one country among many in the rich part of the world which suffer from this deteriorating ratio of young/old.

An ageing Rich World population will also mean a decline in aggregate savings which could have a significant impact on the financial sector; this is because as people age they tend to use up their financial savings and are less inclined to invest in higher risk assets such as growth stocks. For instance, Japanese savers are estimated to have about $7 trillion in savings – mostly deposited in post office savings accounts and risk-averse vehicles such as government bonds. The reluctance of consumers to apply this pool of savings to expenditure has been a key reason why the Japanese economy has been mired in the doldrums for so long.

So the world's population is ageing – and rapidly

The implication of this is that the 600 million older persons in the world at the start of the 21st century will have grown in number to 2 billion by 2050.

Today, the median age[*] of the world's population is 26 years. The country with the lowest median age is Yemen, 15 years, and the highest is Japan, at 41 years. By 2050, the median age of the world's human population will have risen to 36 years. By then, it is projected that Nigeria will have the youngest median age, 20 years, while Spain will have the oldest, 55 years[4] – yes really!

If the world's population is getting older, with a future majority in what are now considered to be retirement years, then who is going to be left in the workplace to grow economies? And who will provide retirees with their pensions now that many of them are living for 20 years plus after retiring? This added financial burden poses a huge financial burden and liability to many rich nations – its cost represents a ticking time bomb that should scare readers, perhaps more than any terrorist threat. The coming pension crisis is something that will affect everyone who is currently in their working life and is discussed in more detail in Part Two.

It doesn't look promising for most of us, so don't expect to retire early unless you are very lucky or work for the government. The retirement age in most rich countries will *have* to rise; retirement for a Rich World person at 65 is a dated

---

[*] Median is a type of average found by arranging a series of numbers in ascending order and selecting the one in the middle of the series. For example, if we take the series 10, 10, 11, 14, 18, 19, 22 – the median is 14. It is a useful average because it tells us that there are as many numbers below the median as there are above it. In the case of the world's population, the median age is 26, i.e. there are the same number of people living above this age as there are below it, roughly 3 billion of each.

notion and belonged in a time when people were very lucky just to reach that age. Now anyone who *doesn't* live to that age is considered to have died young.

Think about this: people start in the workforce in rich countries at an average of about 20 years old; they typically work to an average of 65 then retire. That means they are only working for half their lives. It's not long enough and the economic unreality of this situation will soon become apparent. Increases in productivity, robotic technology and so forth will not be enough. There just won't be enough people of working age in the Rich World to provide for the dribbling and ageing majority.

As if all that wasn't burdensome enough on the State, there's another consequence of having an ageing population that has governments equally concerned: older people require more health and long-term care. Some governments are already straining to meet their pension obligations; now they have to prepare their nation's healthcare system for the coming surge in geriatric patients. Alzheimer's/dementia, arthritis, diabetes, gastrointestinal disorders and osteoporosis are just a few of the many diseases that the elderly suffer from. (Governments also need to brace themselves for the coming surge in illnesses associated with obesity – a Rich World disease – but that's another story.)

The environmental consequences of our 'footprint' on earth

Certainly, it takes a huge amount for man to change the natural environment that he lives in – but there are many more of us today than at any time in history, and we *are* having an effect. Thankfully, mankind's destructive power is not yet as great as that of Nature herself; in this respect consider as an example the eruption at Krakatoa, in Indonesia, in 1883. This one volcanic explosion caused more destructive force to be unleashed on the earth than man has ever managed in all of his existence. Much of Asia was dark for three days after this event – the explosion was heard 2200 miles away in Australia, and one single tidal wave killed 36,000 people in South America.

More recently, an even greater natural disaster emanated from Indonesia on December 26, 2004. It is believed that around 300,000 people died as a result of the tsunami that was unleashed by an undersea earthquake. The visual impact of this event highlighted for many of us in the Rich World the tremendous and appalling gap that characterizes our way of life with that of the billions who have but a fraction of what we have.

The tsunami was a natural disaster – it was not man-made, but its destructive effects were in a sense compounded by man-made factors: overpopulation on the coastlines of vulnerable areas, lack of warning systems and shoddy building – all symptomatic of poor countries. Flooding and other natural disasters have nowhere near the impact in rich countries.

So, yes, man has not yet conquered the forces of Nature, nor yet changed them to the extent that the more radical environmentalists would have us believe. But the pace of change is accelerating and it is not being helped by the huge growth in population – and by the longevity of this increasing number of human beings. It goes without saying that these demographic changes will affect our lives in a number of ways – and not just because more people will be buying hair dyes and going on cruises.

Due to industrialization and the growing human population, we as people are having more of an impact on the earth than ever before. With the world's population already threefold what it was only 40 years ago, man is leaving a disproportionately large footprint on Mother Nature's tender flesh. What are the ramifications of this and how will the environmental change affect our everyday lives? Will the impact of global warming be felt in our lifetime? Will we be prepared? Scientists believe a global temperature increase of only a few degrees could have a significant, i.e. mostly negative, impact on much of the world's population.

Global warming – it's getting hot in here!

Human beings have high energy needs, ones that severely impact on the environment. This impact usually translates into increasing carbon dioxide levels in the atmosphere (which is one of the main so-called greenhouse gases). These carbon dioxide emissions trap heat near the planet's surface (by reflecting heat back towards the earth rather than dissipating into space) and change the earth's climate (Figure 1.2). The by-products of industry across the world are also fouling the air with other chemicals, as well as polluting land, rivers and oceans.

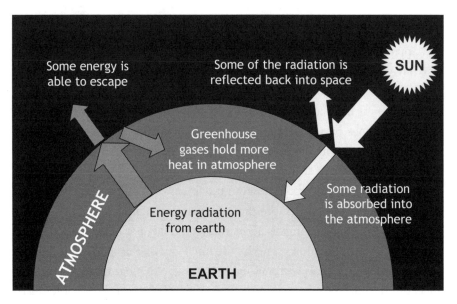

Some energy is able to escape

Some of the radiation is reflected back into space

SUN

Greenhouse gases hold more heat in atmosphere

ATMOSPHERE

Energy radiation from earth

Some radiation is absorbed into the atmosphere

EARTH

Figure 1.2   Global warming

According to the Intergovernmental Panel on Climate Change (IPCC), there is indisputable evidence that earth's surface temperature is on the rise.[5] The IPCC believes that the global average temperature has increased by about 1° Fahrenheit or 0.47° Celsius over the past 100 years and that the 1990s were the warmest decade in the last thousand years (Figure 1.3).

If this increase in temperature does not seem very significant to you, consider this also: between the years 1000 and 1900, the earth's temperature increased by only a few tenths of a degree.[6] In fact, the average global temperature difference between the end of the last ice age and today is only about 5°C (10.6°F). So if a small drop in the earth's temperature can send us into an ice age, imagine what a small increase can do.

It is rare for a week to go by without learning of new scientific results evidencing global warming – from rising carbon dioxide levels to the melting of the polar ice caps to the rapidly melting Himalayan glaciers. Given the overwhelming evidence supporting global warming, it is truly baffling how some governments and interest groups still refuse to acknowledge it as a phenomenon and a threat to our global ecosystem. It sounds rather similar to the tobacco companies of the past that claimed there was no evidence linking smoking to cancer.

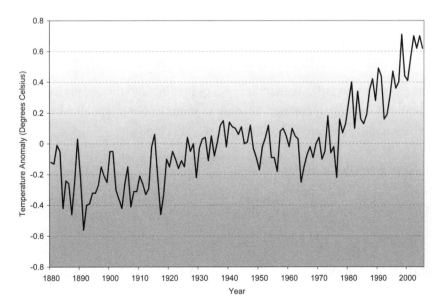

Figure 1.3   Global temperature changes 1880–2003
Source: NASA Goddard Institute for Space Studies.

Rising sea levels

Higher temperatures will lead to more melting of the polar ice caps. A rise of only a few metres would redefine significantly the world's coastlines. Some of the countries at risk are:

- The Maldives – with its 1200 or so islands and a population of around 250,000, it is believed that 80% of its land area is less than one metre above sea level.
- The Marshall Islands – the highest point on these islands is less than two metres.
- Bangladesh, China and Egypt – according to a report by the United Nations Food and Agricultural Organization, a one metre rise in sea level could affect over 90 million people living in these countries.
- In Africa: Angola, Cameroon, Gabon, Gambia, Nigeria, Senegal and Sierra Leone would be affected, according to the IPCC.
- In Europe: the coasts of Germany, the Netherlands, Russia and the Ukraine would be affected, according to the IPCC.

- The Japanese coastline – where 50% of its industrial production is located.

Some studies also indicate that the ice caps melting into the oceans would disrupt the global ocean currents, leading to more El Niño-type phenomena or perhaps a more catastrophic shift in the world's climate.

Changes in weather patterns

As we continue to disrupt our planet's delicate balance, we will begin to notice more consequences of climate change. Regions that become warmer will be become new havens for disease. For example, mosquitoes will begin to thrive and with them will come malaria and dengue fever, both life-threatening diseases but extremely rare in the Rich World at the moment.

Other effects of global warming include:

- The early arrival of spring – which would have an unknown impact on ecosystems.
- More extreme weather – more heavy rain and snow and hence more flooding. Hurricanes will be stronger and more frequent, as will other extreme weather systems.
- Heatwaves, droughts and consequently fires are expected to occur more frequently – a lack of rainfall in the summer months combined with extreme heat will result in droughts and fires, destroying crops and forests.

What is El Niño?[7]

El Niño was originally observed by Peruvian fishermen who noticed at a certain time of year an unusually warm current in the Pacific Ocean where they fished. Today, its effect is more far-reaching, significantly disrupting the ocean–atmosphere system in the tropical Pacific. It has important consequences for weather and climate around the globe and is believed to be the cause of some of the world's serious droughts, floods and bleaching of coral reefs. It is called El Niño, Spanish for 'the little boy' or 'Christ child', because it usually occurs just after Christmastime.

Its counterpart is called La Niña (little girl), also known as El Viejo, which refers to an unusual cooling of the tropical Pacific.

Some scientists believe that the climate anomalies associated with El Niño and La Niña may increase in severity with global warming.

Evidence of climate change can already be found throughout the world. Here are just a few examples specific to Europe and the United States evidencing the changing weather patterns across the world: [8]

Europe
- United Kingdom – August 2003 saw the hottest temperature since records began (38.1 °C).
- Spain – half the glaciers that were present in 1980 are now gone.
- Caucasus Mountains, Russia – half of all glacial ice has disappeared in the past 100 years.
- Denmark and Germany – 2001 was the warmest October on record.
- United Kingdom – birds are shifting northward. Over a 20-year period, many birds have extended the northern margins of their ranges by an average of about 12 miles (19 km).

North America
- An unprecedented series of hurricanes that battered the US coastline in August and September 2004 (Charley, Frances, Ivan and Jeanne).
- New York City – record heat, July 1999. New York City had its warmest July on record, the temperature remained above 95°F (35°C) for 11 days straight.
- Edmonton, Canada – warmest summer on record, 1998. Temperatures were more than 5.4°F (3°C) higher than the 116-year average.
- Monterey Bay, California – shoreline sea life is shifting northwards.

Additional examples can be found on the Internet by visiting: http://www. climatehotmap.org – if you like a good, scary read. The website is run by a 'Union of Concerned Scientists' based in Cambridge, Massachusetts, and has extensive references from all over the world of abnormal climactic events and related phenomena.

Changes in food output
As a result of the changes in the global climate, agricultural yields may fall and fertile regions will become barren. Western Europe may see agricultural yields *rise* while Africa will likely see yields *fall*. As most developing countries

are already in the borderline fertile regions, they will be particularly hard hit. The irony here is that most of the developing countries have not contributed significantly to greenhouse gas emissions (and hence global warming) yet they will end up being its the biggest victims. The timescale of the effects of global warming remain uncertain – there is one school of thought that believes once the earth's natural balance is destabilized, it will set off a series of events that will result in adverse weather changes around the globe and a new global weather system, as per the 2004 film *The Day After Tomorrow*. Other scientists believe that the effects of global warming will manifest themselves slowly (plenty of evidence of it today) and can be reversed if we reduce our greenhouse gas emissions. Either way, within 50 years, if we don't act collectively to reverse our emissions levels, the effects of global warming will transform the weather all over the world.

Increasing demand for energy, food and water

As populations increase and economic activity expands in many parts of the world, the appetite for vital materials will grow quicker than nature can accommodate.

For the first time in history the world is bumping up against the limits of potential human expansion. As a result, there will be recurring and increasing shortages of key materials. We will experience difficulties in meeting our demand for energy, food and water. *Please do not underestimate the capacity of this situation to create trouble for us all.* It is a serious and ultimately overwhelming problem, which will lead to old-style land grabs and conflicts.

Energy – alternative supplies are not sufficient

As the world continues to develop and its population rises, the thirst for energy grows insatiably. Energy is required primarily for industry, transportation and domestic consumption (heating, cooling, lighting, etc.).

Experts predict that the world will be consuming over 40% more energy per annum in just 20 years' time (see Figure 1.4).

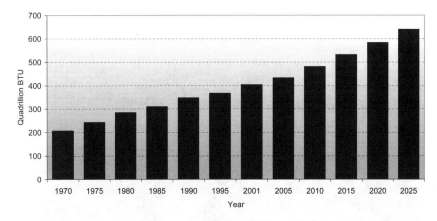

Figure 1.4 World energy consumption 1970–2025
Source: History: Energy Information Administration (EIA), *International Energy Annual 2001*,
DOE/EIA-0219(2001) (Washington, DC, February 2003), web site www.eia.doe.gov/iea/.
Projections: EIA, *System for the Analysis of Global Energy Markets* (2003).
Note: The y-axis reference to 'quadrillion' is one followed by 15 zeros

Where does all this energy come from at the moment and where will it come
from in the future? Petroleum remains the primary source of our energy.

As can be seen in Figure 1.5, petroleum and natural gas combined have,
for the past ten years or so, consistently provided us with around 60% of the
energy we consume. The breakdown of energy sources over the past decades
looks pretty stable, implying that we are likely to continue to consume energy
from these sources in similar percentages over the course of the next decade
or two.

Oil
So how much oil is there in the world?

It is expected that 670 billion barrels of oil will be consumed between now
and 2020 which accounts for about two-thirds of the world's currently proven
reserves. The pressure on global oil supplies is likely to prove especially severe.
According to the US Department of Energy, global oil consumption is expected to rise from about 77 million barrels per day in 2000 to 110 million in
2020 – an increase of 43%.

So where is the world's oil located?[9] Fully 65% of the oil reserves are in the
Middle East, a region that remains troubled and never far from news headlines.

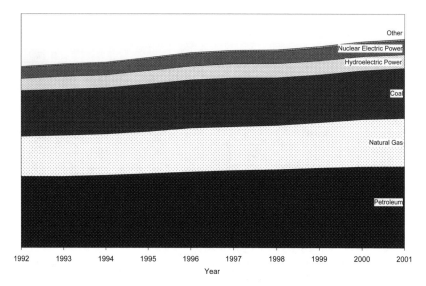

Figure 1.5 The raw materials of world energy consumption 1992–2001
Source: US Energy Information Administration, *International Total Primary Energy Consumption (Demand) and Related Data.*

Figure 1.6 shows the breakdown of known (so-called 'proven') oil reserves, by region.

As a very rough guideline, the reserves of natural gas are found in the same regions as those with the oil reserves. The exceptions are Russia (which has only 5% of the world's oil reserves but a much more impressive 29% of the natural gas reserves) and, in reverse, Saudi Arabia (which has 25% of the world's oil reserves, yet its natural gas reserves make up a little under 4% of the world's total).[10]

Table 1.1 lists the top ten countries with the largest oil reserves:[11]

The United States' oil reserves are a little over 22 billion barrels, accounting for a mere 2% of the world's reserves (but it still ranks twelfth in the world), yet the US is the world's number one consumer of oil, guzzling 20 million barrels per day, *one-quarter* of the world's oil demand, of which about half is accounted for by transport – and in particular, automobiles.

The second largest consumer of oil, China, consumes around 6.5 million barrels per day. Fortunately for the US, just under half its oil needs are pro-

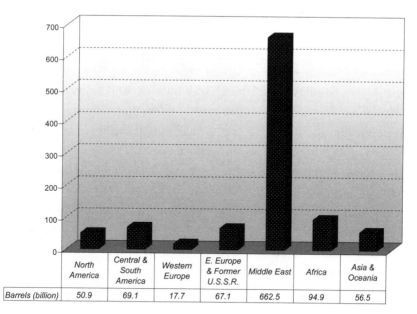

Figure 1.6   World oil reserves by region
Source: Gulf Publishing Co., *World Oil*, Vol. 223, No. 8, August 2002.

Table 1.1   Distribution of oil reserves

	Country	Oil Reserves (Billions of Barrels)
1	Saudi Arabia*	261.7
2	Iraq*	115
3	Iran*	99.1
4	Kuwait*	98.9
5	United Arab Emirates*	62.8
6	Russia	53.9
7	Venezuela*	50.2
8	Libya*	30
9	Nigeria*	30
10	Ch ina	29.5

* OPEC member states

duced domestically. But the other half has to come from oil exporting countries, many of whom are part of an oil cartel known as OPEC (Organization

of Petroleum Exporting Countries). OPEC meets regularly to try to agree on oil production levels so that oil prices remain profitable for all member states.

OPEC has 11 member states: Algeria, Indonesia, Iraq, Iran, Kuwait, Libya, Nigeria, Qatar, Saudi Arabia, United Arab Emirates and Venezuela.

OPEC exists to try to prevent the large oil exporting nations from competing with one another in a price war. By agreeing beforehand oil production levels, the supply is supposedly controlled – though OPEC members are notoriously difficult to control and output agreements are rarely honoured in full. As demand is more or less already known, OPEC can have a pretty accurate prediction of what the oil price will be, based on the agreed production levels. OPEC's member states sit on approximately 80% of the world's oil reserves, so their influence can be immense. Saudi Arabia alone has 25% of the world's oil reserves, and is thus by far the largest oil state, followed by Iraq, then Iran. In our section on geopolitics, we discuss in more depth the power plays associated with securing supply of precious commodities such as oil.

Figure 1.7 shows from which countries the US imported its oil for the first six months of 2003 and 2004.

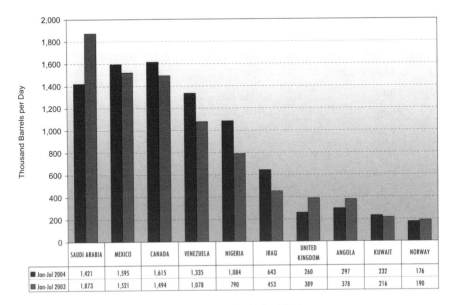

	SAUDI ARABIA	MEXICO	CANADA	VENEZUELA	NIGERIA	IRAQ	UNITED KINGDOM	ANGOLA	KUWAIT	NORWAY
Jan-Jul 2004	1,421	1,595	1,615	1,335	1,084	643	260	297	232	176
Jan-Jul 2003	1,873	1,521	1,494	1,078	790	453	389	378	216	190

Figure 1.7 The top ten suppliers of crude oil to the United States
Source: Energy Information Administration.

Electricity: an increasingly scarce commodity
With the world's energy demands likely to rise dramatically over the next two decades, the Rich World's ageing electricity infrastructure will be pushed to its limits to keep up with demand. Yes, even in the West, there are countless examples of power outages in recent years. It is highly probable that all of us will be the victims of increasingly frequent power disruptions in our homes and places of work.

In developing nations this may not be anything new. However, here in the West we have become entirely dependent on getting our power 'on tap' 24 hours a day, 7 days a week. We need electricity for trains, lighting, cooling, heating, lifts, computers, air traffic control, Automatic Teller Machines (ATMs), televisions, pumping water – in fact electricity is the invisible backbone of our daily lives.

Few of us question our supply of electricity, even though some regions, such as California, have already experienced the great inconvenience – to put it mildly – of power outages. Just imagine for a moment how one of *your* days would play out without electricity.

A power outage could be triggered by any number of things – a hot summer's day, for example, that causes people to use extra air conditioning, in turn heavily overloading the power grid. A dramatic power outage affected some 50 million people in North America in August 2003. The antiquated power grid collapsed under heavy summer-related use, but fortunately, power was restored to most homes within 48 hours.

A further cause of disruption to power supplies could be the result of a terrorist attack which would probably put power stations out of operation for months, possibly years. This could mean power 'rationing' until supply can once again meet demand.

Food – abundance but in the wrong places

In a world which appears to have an abundance of crops and livestock, it would seem reasonable to assert that famines are a thing of the past. However, famines still do occur and are not simply the product of failed crops but also the result of explosive population growth and of a failure to distribute produce efficiently.

Additionally, in many Western countries, as well as in Japan, farmers have been heavily subsidized for decades and, as a result, produce unnecessary crops. These subsidized crops compete unfairly with those produced in less developed countries, making it economically unviable for the farmers of poor countries to produce to their full potential. This in turn can lead to famine or food shortages in many less developed countries. Many African nations would jump at the opportunity to sell to the Rich World but cannot possibly compete with Western farmers and their government subsidies.

Additional factors which might cause future famine include:

1　Failure of power supplies, leading to incapacity of the distribution system.
2　Contamination of crops through the use of biological agents in warfare.
3　Drought due to overuse and misuse of the world's fresh water supply.
4　Drought as a result of global warming, rendering formerly fertile growing areas barren.

Famines have been a frequent visitor to mankind throughout history. Below are examples of four prominent famines from the past 200 hundred years.

The Great Potato Famine, Ireland, 1845–49
In the 1800s, potatoes were the staple diet of almost all Irish people. Potatoes had become the mainstay of Ireland and, because they were abundant, the population of Ireland grew rapidly. Unfortunately, in 1845, the potato crops were struck with blight (a crop-killing fungus) and, as the crop failed, people began to starve. As the blight lasted for three harvests, the situation became desperate, not helped by the failure of the British administration to take effective action. The over-dependence on one type of crop meant that there was no alternative food to turn to. In the end the famine claimed 1.5 million lives and resulted in another 1 million or so moving to America and parts of the British Colonies. Almost half of Ireland's population was either displaced or died as a result of this particular crop failure.

Famine of the Great Plains, US, 1930s

This occurred after the longest drought in the US of the 20th century. The great 'dust bowl' created by the drought spanned 50 million acres, from New York to the California coast. Wind created dust storms as the dry topsoil was easily blown away. Welfare programmes prevented mass starvation but combined with the Great Depression in the US economy, the rural community was devastated for a number of years.

Famine of China, 1959–61

Undoubtedly the deadliest famine of all, this killed an estimated 30 million people in China. Again the famine was caused by severe drought followed by crop failure. As people starved, disease and cannibalism became widespread. Maoism and the inefficiencies of the communist systems of distribution and agriculture were largely to blame. China kept this disaster secret from the rest of the world for 20 years!

Famine of North Korea, 1995–1999

North Korea is one of the few remaining communist countries in the world. Its oppressive leader, Kim Jong Il, keeps the nation isolated from the rest of the world and has been aspiring to make his country self-sufficient. However, two successive years of floods in 1995 and 1996, followed by a typhoon and a drought in 1997 destroyed much of the country's crops and resulted in widespread famine. According to aid agencies, this modern day disaster resulted in 3 million people starving to death and left 5 million malnourished out of a population of 24 million. Rationing was down to 600 calories a day – a third of the daily minimum requirement! North Korea remains on the brink of famine today despite ongoing food aid from the UN and other organizations.

Most readers will be familiar with the tragic famines that occur from time to time in North and Sub-Saharan Africa. In addition, intermittent shortages of food elsewhere in the world also make the headlines.

No one in the Rich World seriously believes that famine could affect them. However, it surely could, either through an actual food shortage or as a result of a disruption in the food distribution mechanism. Many of us live in cities and towns that are physically very distant from where the food is grown or reared and so, effective and frequent distribution of food to the towns and cities is vital – but not certain.

Water – a critical shortage is emerging

In 1992 the UN General Assembly designated 22 March of each year as the World Day for Water. The UN also declared 2003 as the 'International Year of Fresh Water'. The supply of water is a major geopolitical concern and one which is only now receiving the attention it deserves. Here's why:

Of all the water on earth, 97.5% is salt water, found primarily in the oceans. The remaining 2.5% is fresh water but almost all of it is stored in the ice caps of the Antarctic, Arctic and Greenland or as fossil groundwater. The most accessible freshwater resources are in lakes, reservoirs, rivers and streams. These resources amount to only 0.26% of the total amount of fresh water in storage, or 0.007% of all water on earth that is renewable and available for use on a sustainable basis.[12]

As the global population of both humans and domestic animals continues to grow, beyond levels once considered to be unsustainable, it is only a matter of time before our water supply becomes a major constraint on mankind's ability to survive.

Indeed, in many parts of the world this is already a reality. Just think that by 2020 there will be an extra 1.5 billion or so thirsty mouths drinking from the same limited water supply. These thirsty mouths will also want to eat, so there will be additional water required for irrigation. They will also require water for sanitation.

According to the World Health Organization, as many as 5 million people die each year from poor quality drinking water, poor sanitation or a dirty home environment, often the result of a lack of water.

It may come as no surprise that Americans are the world's biggest consumers of water, consuming 1,688 cubic metres per person per year. Table 1.2 illustrates how other countries compare.

There are a number of factors that determine the per person water consumption in a nation. These include industry (it takes approximately 150,000 litres to make a car, for example); power plants; farming (agriculture and livestock); climate and sanitation.

Table 1.2 The top ten consumers of water

Country	Cubic metres of water consumed per person per year (estimate 2000)
United States	1,688
Canada	1,431
Australia	945
Japan	723
Germany	712
India	497
Finland	469
China	431
South Africa	288
Britain	201

Source: The World Water Council

In 2003 the United Nations released the *World Water Development Report* which is the first global evaluation of water resources. The report warns that the decreasing water supplies in the world could lead to epidemics and international conflict. The report also mentions that as many as one in three people do not have enough water for proper hygiene and one in five do not have enough to drink. These are worrying numbers indeed.

The picture looks bleaker for the future: over the next 20 years, the average global water supply is expected to drop by one-third. By 2050, 2 billion to 7 billion people will be severely short of water.

Gordon Young from the University of Waterloo, Ontario, Canada, the report's compiler, said that 6000 people already die from diarrhoea *every day* and that health problems in the future are likely to worsen.

Young identifies two regions in the world that could become sources of conflict over water:

- the Indus River, which runs between India and Pakistan; and
- the Tigris and the Euphrates rivers, which both rise in Turkey and flow through Syria and Iraq.

China, the world's most populous nation, is 'the one area worrying most people most of the time,' according to Marq de Villiers, author of a book entitled *Water*. In it he states that the water table is dropping one metre per year due to overpumping and the Chinese admit that 300 of their cities are running short of water.

Alternative sources?

One could argue that natural market forces will divert demand to alternatives and relieve the pressure on the world's limited supply of currently vital materials, i.e. as demand rises and prices increase, the private sector would be sufficiently motivated to develop new materials and processes that will allow demand and supply to once more be balanced. This might include cost effective desalination in the case of water, for example. However, the fact is that the negative demographic and environmental trends affecting the planet are irreversible – and even new technologies cannot and will not keep up with the drain on water supplies. Water politics – indeed wars – will be an increasing feature of geopolitics.

The growing divide between rich and poor

Mass migration – the yellow brick road and perils thereon ...

First, let's trace the history of man's early movements. The foundation of Western civilization dates back to around 8000 BC in the Middle East's 'Fertile Crescent'. It is believed that agriculture was first developed in this crescent. In today's terms, this area spans from just south of Jerusalem, and up and across parts of Syria then down through Iraq along its two main rivers, the Tigris and the Euphrates.

Wheat and barley grew wild and abundantly in this highly fertile land; in time nomads and herders began to settle along the lush banks of the rivers and became the world's first farmers, giving up their nomadic ways. This was arguably the most fundamental milestone in the history of our civilization as it began a series of subsequent evolutionary steps which altered the nature of man's existence on earth.

As farming techniques developed, larger scale farming gave rise to an early form of social planning. Groups of nomadic tribes settled down and joined co-operative forces. It wasn't long before irrigation techniques were developed as the need to feed and support rapidly growing populations increased. Artefacts and other remains from this period point to a culturally sophisticated people, moving rapidly from hunter–gatherer to organized cultivation.

Soon after the emergence of farming, towns began to be built as central gathering places, providing protection for their inhabitants.

By around 4000 BC in this Middle Eastern region, the first *larger* towns or cities started to emerge, along with supporting social infrastructure. The populations of these towns became known as Sumerians. These Sumerians transformed civilization in many ways; for instance, they brought to mankind the invention of the wheel, as well as rudimentary mathematics. In addition, the Sumerians developed one of the world's first systems of monarchy; the early states they formed needed new forms of government in order to govern larger areas and diverse peoples. These Sumerian territories were the very first states or 'nations' in human history. They were ruled by a type of priest-king, whose duties included leading the military, administering trade, judging disputes, and engageing in the most important religious ceremonies.

The priest-king ruled through a series of bureaucrats, many of them also priests – and these surveyed the land, assigned fields, and distributed crops after harvest. This institution of monarchy required the invention of a new 'legitimization' of authority beyond the tribal justification of chieftainship. Thus was developed the justification of a monarch's authority based on a sort of divine selection, taking the form of anthropomorphic gods. These gods were deemed largely responsible for natural forces such as the sun and rain, with the weather being an important factor in the Sumerians' livelihood, as their crops depended upon favourable growing conditions.

A further invention of the Sumerians, the first civilization, was the rule of law, i.e. a written and administered form of conflict resolution and retribution that did not feature revenge.

Today's civilizations all originate from three distinct branches: *Sumerian* (the granddaddy of Western civilization, as outlined above), as well as the *Indic* and *Sinic* branches.

It is from these three strands that contemporary civilized societies, in their various forms, all stem:

- **Sinic** – this includes the cultures of China, Korea and large parts of South East Asia.
- **Japanese** – originally part of Sinic culture, the Japanese are now sufficiently distinct to warrant their own category.
- **Hindu** – covering the Indian subcontinent.
- **Islamic** – although a distinct culture, Islam also exists as a subculture within other cultures.
- **Orthodox** – much of what was once the Byzantine Empire (the Eastern Roman Empire), including Russia and many parts of Eastern Europe and Central Asia.
- **Western** – includes Europe, North America and Latin America, although some commentators argue that Latin America should be classified separately.
- **African** – North Africa belongs to the Islamic civilization and South Africa was formerly a Western colony, but the rest of Africa's culture is distinct.

The origins of Western civilization's rise to global supremacy in the 20th century can be traced back to the spread of Christianity in Europe.

Christianity began to extend throughout the European continent following the Roman Empire's adoption of the religion and the establishment of the Catholic Church in Rome. Indeed, for many centuries in modern history, Christianity was the major reason – or at least excuse – in the expansion of nation states and empires emanating from Europe. This began with the First Crusade in 1095, spurred by Pope Urban II's call to arms after the capture of the Holy City of Jerusalem by the Muslim Seljuk Turks. As a result, a huge army from all parts of Christian Europe started the long trek to reclaim the lost Christian lands of the East. These 60,000 or so Crusaders were generally motivated not by territory or plunder but by Christian piety, bolstered by what one author has called the 'talismanic detritus' of Christianity – bones, relics of the Cross, etc. This worship of the relics of saints and other icons of the Catholic religion meant that by medieval times, large percentages of populations throughout Europe made pilgrimages, be it to Santiago de Compostela in northern Spain, to Rome in Italy, or, most worthy of all, to the Holy Land itself.

Europe was, generally speaking, successful in the intermittent Crusades, gradually recapturing the entirety of the territories occupied by the Turks, including Jerusalem, the spiritual home of Christianity and Judaism, as well as being the third most holy site in Islam.

For those of us in the West who cannot comprehend the religious motivation of the Islamic hardliners today who preach jihad (holy war) against us, we have only to look to our own ancestors to see how powerful a draw – perhaps even drug – religious fanaticism can be. After all, is the annual pilgrimage to Mecca (the hajj) by millions of Muslims any different from the long walks to the shrines of Christianity undertaken in previous centuries by millions of Christians?

The rise of Europe – the European hegemony
Despite military success in the campaigns against the Islamic invaders, as well as other incursions by tribes from the East, it wasn't until the 1500s – during the period known as the Renaissance – that European culture began to dominate. This was particularly the case after the voyages of discovery, first by the Portuguese and then by Christopher Columbus. These voyages laid the groundwork for what were to become international empires – much further flung than those of the relatively limited Roman imperial territories. The empire of Spain and the colonies of Portugal were soon supplanted in importance by the expansionist successes of the greater powers of Europe, most notably the British and the French.

The successive European imperialists were able to achieve dominance in comparatively inhospitable regions of the world as a result of their superior skills in organization, discipline and military power. The latter strength was largely due to the development of better weaponry, medicine, logistics, engineering support and transportation.[13] Through these means, Europeans occupied large parts of the rest of the known world, giving rise to important changes in global trade and commerce throughout the 15th to 19th centuries inclusive.

It is important to remember that as we face a period of instability in world order, the history of European colonization and occupation is one not lightly forgotten by its victims/subjects. The tactics of the occupying powers through-out what was once the colonized world still resonate. There remains continued resentment even today, particularly in Africa and in Asia, about the perceived exploitation and oppression of the colonial period.

Another factor which is worth considering is that the idea of a 'country' is a Western concept. The European empires carved up areas of the world by drawing borders based on their own Western interests and then by appointing leaders to rule them, without particular regard to regional or tribal nuances. For example, until European intervention, the whole of 'Arabia' was an amorphous land mass, spanning from the Mediterranean Sea to Iraq. This came under the rule of the Ottoman Empire before being taken over by the West, and then subdivided like plots on a housing estate. In the main, it was the British and the French who decided where to draw borders, how many countries to create and whom to appoint to rule them. This interference with the Middle East's own natural course of development and evolution is now coming back to haunt the Western interlopers, and the chaos and violence on the streets of Baghdad are just one symptom of this.

Colonized areas around the world have, in virtually every case, gained independence. Of course, many of these countries have retained diplomatic and commercial ties with their former colonial power. In quite a few former colonies the language of the former power is widely spoken, albeit often as a second language. Indeed, countries such as the United States, Canada, Australia and New Zealand are all largely populated as a result of mass migration from Europe. The effects of this migration now largely define the de facto culture of those particular countries, including their dominant language and religion, i.e. English and Christian.

In Africa, the Middle East and Asia there are many former colonies of the great powers of the 19th century in which resentment, alienation and even downright hatred characterize the attitudes of locals to their former occupiers.

Migration levels soar – today's world is mobile

In the past, the small numbers of people who migrated to foreign lands were forced to integrate with their new surroundings, particularly in inhabited lands, out of a need to survive. These people had to speak the local language in order to earn a living, to interact with local society and to conform to local laws and traditions. Their children, as a result, tended to become assimilated into the new society with greater ease.

However, something happened in the 1800s that changed all that: migration reached a threshold level in that the arriving groups of people, for instance into the United States, became significant enough in numbers to influence and impose their own cultures and traditions upon indigenous peoples.

The most noteworthy of such migrations started in 1815 and continued for a hundred years. This migration was catalysed in particular by the potato famine of Ireland in 1845, as well as by a generally expanding European population. During this particular period, from about 1840 to 1880, some 50 million Europeans headed for the 'new' worlds of the United States, Canada, South America, Australia and New Zealand, to start their lives afresh.

Cobh

The little town of Cobh, near Cork City, was one departure point for this mass exodus. It was from this port that millions of Irish, driven by poverty and despair, embarked on uncomfortable and uncertain journeys to the New World in the 19th and 20th centuries.

Flanked by hills rising into the Irish mist, this bay of great beauty was, for most, their last sight of home. Pathetic and tearful farewells took place in the cheap boarding houses of the town as families parted for the last time. Priests came from villages to bless the departing.

Cobh is an evocative location from which to empathize with the plight of the economic migrant. With little concept of what awaited them, and even less hope of surviving by staying at home, they prepared to say goodbye to loved ones and embarked on very difficult journeys. The scale of this movement was massive: about half of Ireland's population is estimated to have left (mostly for the United States or for Britain) in the period of greatest emigration. It is only recently that Ireland's population has recovered to 19th century levels.

The modern equivalents of this Irish exodus exist today, potentially in even greater numbers: the wetbacks of Mexico, seeking entry to the United States; the Afghans clinging to the sides of Eurostar trains trying to get into Britain having travelled across Europe, are just a couple of examples of the many desperate people around the world seeking a better life. The welcome that the Irish and others got in the America of the 19th century as they arrived in Ellis Island, i.e. generally easy entry, is not one that is typically extended to the many who wait for entrance to the US or to Europe today.

A revolution in travel ...

Since the advent of affordable air travel in the second half of the 20th century, global migration levels have grown more rapidly. This time, people from all corners of the world came in droves to the West for a better life.

Today, ethnic minorities make up a significant population in just about any Western country; some areas are so well known to be hospitable to certain minorities that new migrants often prefer to move to these specific places to make their integration into their new host society smoother. For example, Greeks moving to Australia tend to live in Melbourne, which has the largest Greek community outside Greece. Poles tend to move to Chicago, Illinois, if they are emigrating to the United States. Miami, Florida, has an enormous Cuban community, whilst Bradford, England, has a large Pakistani community and Germany has over 2 million Turks.

From an economic perspective, countries undoubtedly benefit from receiving waves of hard-working and sometimes well-educated, overseas immigrants looking to build new lives for themselves. From a societal perspective, the picture is less clear: how compatible is the culture of the immigrant with that of his new homeland, in particular language and religion? How willing is the immigrant to embrace and adopt his new homeland and, conversely, how prepared is society to welcome this immigrant? Aren't racial tensions inevitable if immigrants choose to live amongst their own people instead of fully integrating with their new society?

With victims of political, religious and ethnic conflicts numbering in their millions around the world, many look to the West as their only hope of a better life. The primary target regions for these refugees tend to be the United States, the European Union and Australia. Legally or illegally, these refugees seek entry into these lands of apparent plenty, often with the help of people smugglers who, for substantial sums (certainly great amounts of money for people from poorer nations), will assist in migrants' journeys. In terms of the actual number of people who succeed in gaining entry into their target country illegally, it is possible to draw parallels with drug trafficking to find an answer: we tend to hear about the operations that go wrong; i.e. the large majority of (successful) operations go unnoticed.

In recent times the West has apparently embraced immigration but, at the same time, it fears and restricts it.

September 11, 2001 served as a turning point for many nations' immigration policies, particularly those of the United States, a country that is almost entirely made up of immigrants or their descendants. The US is now making things much harder for certain types of would-be immigrants.

Here is a *true story* of someone who fell victim to America's tightening immigration laws:

During a recent visit to Egypt, the authors met an Egyptian man (early 30s) who had recently returned to Cairo after living in New York City. He had studied in the US and subsequently taken a job in New York, where he had been living for the past four years. However, when it came to renewing his visa, a routine procedure turned out to be anything but that for this young, innocent man. The authorities told him that his visa was not going to be extended and that he was to leave the country upon its expiry.

He was forced to abandon his job, his friends, his apartment, his girlfriend – his entire life came to an abrupt halt for no good reason. We're going to dismiss wild speculation that being an Arab had something to do with it, but the real irony of his case is that he is a Christian (around 10% of Egyptians are Christian) yet the US authorities did not seem to understand the implications of this rather important detail and sent him back to Egypt anyway. Obviously, the al-Qaeda network is a radical organization that claims to be acting under the Islamic faith (although virtually all Muslims denounce al-Qaeda's acts of violence); Christians would certainly not be welcome in such an organization. Our Egyptian friend was unfortunately an innocent victim of the war on terrorism.

Today, the most contentious and difficult political issue centring on migration is that of Muslims in Europe. There are about 12 million Muslims spread across Europe, and most of them have melted successfully into the societies which they have either been born in or migrated to. Muslims represent about 7.5% of the French population, in Germany it is about 5%, and in the UK about 2%. However, the events of September 11, 2001 and other related Islamic or quasi-Islamic issues have also served to heighten tensions among marginalized Muslims in Europe and the societies in which they live.

Migration – the story of two families

The Mellon family

There are a relatively small number of Mellons in the world – relative that is to Smiths, Singhs, and Lees, etc. In numerical terms, perhaps about 5000 Mellons exist on the planet, so schoolyard jokes about the name thankfully are not too abundant!

The Mellon family originated in Scotland, but settled in the 17th century in Ulster, the northern part of Ireland, where they were 'planters' (or Presbyterian colonialists) on behalf of Oliver Cromwell's regime in England.

The tradition of Protestantism in Northern Ireland remains strong even today and, in part, was the cause of civil war and also what is known as 'The Troubles'. These have gone on for a long time, with violence only ending quite recently. The antipathy of the Irish Catholics and of the so-called Scots-Irish towards each other is legendary. By the 19th century, many Scots-Irish had already left for the United States, the new Promised Land. They were to be followed much later by as many as 1.5 million victims of the great famine that blighted the whole Irish island in the 1840s, when the vital tuber crop failed three times in a row, leading to mass starvation. This famine caused the exodus of my own branch of the Mellon family – but sadly, they travelled the wrong way – back to Scotland – about which more will be explained later.

The Mellons who left Ireland for the US in 1818 were joined by one Thomas Mellon, then a five-year-old boy travelling with his parents. He went with his family to frontier Pennsylvania, close to the town now known as Pittsburgh. The story of his life is depicted at the Ulster American Folk Park in Campbell Hill in Omagh in Ireland, the largest such park in the world and partly funded by the Mellon family.

Thomas Mellon became a judge as well as a successful banker – his trick was to take stakes in the companies that he lent money to. His son Andrew then took the banking business inherited from his father in the late 1800s and built it into one of the greatest fortunes ever made. He founded the Union Trust Company, Gulf Oil, Pittsburgh Coal and the Aluminium Company of America (Alcoa). It was a Mellon company that funded the Waldorf Astoria Hotel and the Panama Canal Locks, and Andrew Mellon also became Secretary of State to the Treasury through three Presidential Administrations (1921–1932).

Andrew Mellon's great wealth was in turn passed on to his son, Paul, whose trick was to put it all into professional hands, where it grew mightily, while he pursued philanthropy, *art collecting and hedonism. He and his father co-founded the National Gallery of Art in Washington DC, where an immense Mellon collection of art is housed. Paul Mellon was a noted horse breeder, winning three Triple Crown races in his lifetime. His art collecting ability and racehorse eye, combined in his now immensely valuable collection of equestrian paintings by George Stubbs, resides at the Yale Centre for British Art. He died in 2000 at the age of 91. Sadly, I was not in his will and am unable to pursue the hedonistic lifestyle at a refined level. Not only did my great-great grandfather emigrate from Ireland back to Scotland, but his son – my great grandfather – converted to Catholicism. This was not a good idea in the bigoted Scotland of the late 19th century, where his budding career as a doctor was halted by a decree banning Catholics from practising medicine.*

So the Mellons of Scotland have been making a gentler – if not genteel – ascent of the proverbial ladder than their American counterparts. My grandfather was a teacher, and my father, Sir James Mellon, got the nomadic bug and became a successful diplomat. I am firmly of the view that emigration is best – I left the UK as soon as I graduated and went to Hong Kong. I'm hopeful that if enough people buy this book and if I follow its advice on finances, I might one day rival the monetary wealth of the American Mellons!

The Chalabi family

The Chalabi family name originated in Iraq from the time of the Ottoman (Turkish) Empire; hence the family name itself is Turkish and not Arabic.

When Iraq was a monarchy (after independence from Britain in 1921, and until 1958) my grandfather, Ahmad Chalabi (related to but not the same Ahmad Chalabi of the post-Saddam Iraqi governing Council), was a member of the Democratic Party of Iraq and a doctor by profession, working for the state in the mornings and at his private clinic in the evenings. After the monarch was deposed, Ahmad worked at the Ministry of Health. In the mid 1960s he bought some land and built a large house on the River Tigris where he intended to live with his wife, six sons and their spouses and children.

My father was the eldest son and in 1959 he went to the Soviet Union to study engineering. He eventually returned to Baghdad in 1966 and two years later was married to my mother, whereupon they decided to move into the family house that my grandfather had built. They had their quarters furnished and then went off on their honeymoon to Egypt. 1968 was also the year that the now infamous Ba'ath Party came to power in Iraq. (Although very influential from the start, Saddam Hussein would not become the official Iraqi President for another decade.)

When my parents returned to Baghdad after their honeymoon, they were greeted at the airport by relatives and driven home – or so they thought. On the way home, they were told that my grandfather, Ahmad, had been arrested and nobody knew why. A week later, Ahmad called his wife and told her that the government wanted possession of their house and unless it was vacated, he would not be released. Clearly there was little choice but to move all the furniture out and to vacate the house as per the government's orders. He was then released and the house was taken over by the Ba'ath Party – even Saddam Hussein lived in it for a while.

About a year later, the Ba'ath Party informed Ahmad that they would pay some rent for the house and a few months after that, they decided to pay for the house they had effectively 'nationalized' – obviously the price was non-negotiable for fear of another kidnapping or worse! They had lost their home.

My grandparents and parents had to rent houses elsewhere. As the Ba'ath Party grew stronger over the subsequent years, more citizens' lives were endangered by even the slightest criticism of the government. My parents decided that things were only going to get worse and my father used his connections to arrange for a student exit visa to the UK for the family. Initially, my parents moved to Oxford along with two of my siblings, but after a couple of years settled in the outskirts of London, where they still live today.

One of my uncles, Adnan, had to escape quickly from Iraq once the Ba'ath Party started to exterminate anyone who was a possible threat to it. He and his friends fled to Czechoslovakia. From there they made their way to northern Iraq, where they fought against the Ba'ath regime with the Kurds during the Iraq/Iran war. However, when Saddam started to drop chemical weapons on the resistance fighters, they became too traumatized by its horrendous effects and many gave up the cause, returning to their nations of exile.

Today, all of my five uncles (father's brothers) have long since left Iraq, living either in the US, Canada or the UK.

The decision by my family to flee Iraq early on (in the 1960s and 1970s) has undoubtedly saved the lives of many family members as they might well have perished under the cruel dictatorship of Saddam Hussein in the subsequent decades.

Mind the gap!

Of more immediate consequence than the expanding and ageing population is the dramatically widening gap between those who live comfortable existences – assumed to include the readers of this book – and those who merely subsist.

Currently, approximately 80% of the world's population is from a developing country.[14] Within 20 years, this percentage is expected to increase to 84%, and will rise even further to 87% by 2050. This expanding gap between the 'haves' and the 'have-nots' has terrifying consequences for the continued stability of the world, the extent of which has not been fully appreciated by most people living in the Rich World.

Within the wealthy nations themselves, this gap between the 'haves' and 'have-nots' is vast and widening. A similar disproportionate distribution of wealth appears to have been one of the reasons behind the severity of the Great Depression of the late 1920s and early 1930s. This was because in that period, as is the case now, increases in productivity were not fully shared by the average household and as a result there simply weren't enough affluent consumers able to buy the newly emerging surplus of goods that, in particular, the United States was producing.

Today, in the United States, the wealthiest 1% of the population controls an incredible 33% of the total national wealth, while the bottom 80% control a mere 17%. This represents a significant and continuing concentration of wealth. Stories abound about how the wealth of one or two individuals is equivalent to the output of many of the countries of the United Nations – and these stories are true.

The ownership of stocks is also unevenly distributed, with the top 1% of US stock owners holding about 50% of all stocks by value. Yet, at the same time, 12.1% of Americans are currently living below the poverty line (an annual income below $18,392 for a family of four), according to the most recent US Census Bureau figures. That's 34.6 million people living in poverty in the world's wealthiest nation! Other rich nations have similar, although less extreme, wealth distribution.

Another frightening fact: the world's rich nations, currently encompassing 20% of the global population, account for 86% of private consumption; the poorest 20% account for just over 1%. The raw effect of this is that a child born in an industrialized country will add more to consumption and pollution over his or her lifetime than between thirty to fifty children born in developing countries.[15]

If you think you've had a hard life, think again ... go on and read the following passage, which tells of a day in the life of a young African boy. His situation – which is pitiful by our standards – is shared by billions of others living on this planet. Perhaps a few of our readers will have experienced true hunger, thirst and poverty – but we doubt it.

A day in the life of Njoroge, a seven-year-old from Kenya, Africa

Njeri, Njoroge's mother, wakes up at five in the morning to another new day, feeling tired and far older than her 25 years. Remembering she must walk with her son 7 kilometres and back in search of water, her voice sounds sharper than she intends when she calls to him.

'Njoroge! Njoroge! Wake up! Wake up! You must walk with me to Githanji Dam to draw water for breakfast and for washing your face so your teacher will see you as smart at school.'

Seven-year-old Njoroge stretches and whimpers, thinking of the long walk on an empty stomach, the hours before his thirst is quenched, and his stomach stops growling. He thinks of his father at work as a shop attendant in Nairobi, which seems far away to Njoroge. It has been a month; father should be home soon for a visit. Most of the other children have fathers who must always be gone working too. But this doesn't fill the empty feeling he gets when his father is away from home.

Last month, his mother had been very sick from bad water, the visiting doctor had said. Njoroge had to carry water by himself and take care of his mother, and so missed a lot of school. Now he was behind again, and his mother was determined that he do well in school.

The only seasonal river where people draw water is 5 kilometres away and it runs for only three months a year. It is now dry, so the women and children must walk even further to find water. Njoroge's mother hands him a 5-litre plastic can that he will carry his water in. She throws a 30-litre jerry can on her back and pushes Njoroge on his shoulder. 'You lazy bones, let's hurry or you will get late for school and your teacher, Mr Kamau, will thrash you thoroughly!'

They hurry off to the dam and as she walks, Njeri hums a Christian chorus, 'yesu anapamba.' Oh Lord, help me to be strong today, she thinks.

At the dam, already scores of other people are drawing water. Some have bicycles to carry water with while others have donkeys and 'mikokoteni' (carts). Some have left their donkeys to stray inside the dam where they drink the water and then urinate.

'Mother!' calls our Njoroge, 'why doesn't the owner of the animal chase it out of the water? It's dirtying the same water that we are drawing. This is very awful, Mother.' As if it understood him, the donkey ambles slowly out of the water.

Njeri fills both their containers and hands Njoroge his. She calls for a young man nearby to help her place the 30-litre jerry can on her back.

As they start toward home, the sun is now rising and the houses far away seem to be awakening from the morning mist that had covered them. 'Oh, God,' she mutters to herself, 'when shall we get out of this mess? If only we could have a bore hole (well) or a big water tank as I have heard some villages have. Then we would have clean water nearby and not walk, walk all day long.' Njoroge looks down as he walks and says nothing.

They finally get home and she makes a fire while Njoroge goes to his room to put on his school uniform. 'Njoroge! This is the end of the month and your father has not come home from Nairobi. Why? He promised to buy me two water drums for harnessing clean rain water from our roof. I hope God will make him remember.' Njoroge tries not to listen, for his mother's fretting about his father makes him feel angry.

'This man is not serious with life,' she mutters. She pours the water in a bigger container and adds a chemical to clear the dirt. She stirs it, and the sediments settle to the bottom. She draws water in a small pan and puts it on the fire to boil. Meanwhile, she rushes off to milk her one cow.

'Fendu, you old cow. Come, I get something out of you.' The area has been hit hard by a drought and Fendu gives only a cup of milk to Njeri. 'Thank you, Fendu,' she whispers. 'And now to make Njoroge a cup of tea.' She hurries back to the kitchen.

'Njoroge! You mean you have not yet readied yourself for school? You lazy bones!'

'I can't find my shirt or my books, Mother,' says Njoroge, tired from too little sleep, the long walk for water, and not enough food.

'Look at you! I have always told you to keep your belongings together where you can find them easily, but you never listen. Am I to prepare breakfast for you or look for your books?'

Njoroge finds his things and drinks his tea quickly. His mother hands him a piece of last night's ugali to go with the tea.

'I am ready, Mother,' says Njoroge.

'Then hurry to school!' replies his mother, impatiently.

Njoroge walks to school very tired, knowing that he will now walk another 5 kilometres and definitely will be late for school. It is eight fifteen in the morning, and the other children are far ahead of him. He hurries on, a bitter child. Meanwhile, his mother continues with her daily chores, not forgetting that she will have to walk again to draw water when Njoroge returns from school.

(Extract from the Children's Water Fund website – www.childrenswaterfund.org)

This experience seems a million miles away from our own daily routine. In the life we lead, most of us never really stop to think about what a typically good life we actually have. It provides us with unlimited water for washing and drinking, comfortable beds, heated or cooled rooms, a large refrigerator and a pantry full of food and drink, effortless private/public transportation (well, kind of) to school/work/shops. Education, healthcare and vacations are available to most of us. Just imagine that these poorer people lived next door; would you be indifferent to their situation? Equally importantly, do you think that they would allow you to forever live in a way that was so superior to theirs while they watched? It is only the lack of proximity that protects the rich from the poor in this world; that, and lack of organization. Let's face it – most of us engage in shoulder shrugging when confronted by the very real images of poverty and destitution that, from to time, adorn our TV screens. We may engage in some palliative giving but we are mostly politically and economically inactive when it comes to alleviating the plight of those who are the least fortunate of us on this planet. This state will change – by force perhaps – unless we help to change it ourselves. Platitudes, adopting a child for a month and putting a few coins in a famine relief box will not do it. Political action other than the temporary fixes of sending over food is required but sadly unlikely to come.

Mismatch between rich–poor populations and other worrying facts …

The world's five most populated countries are home to half the planet's population (see Table 1.3). This is despite the presence of more than 200 nations on earth, 146 of which participated in the failed talks on world trade liberalization in Cancun, Mexico, in 2003, followed by similar forlorn and fruitless discussions in the 'Doha' round in Qatar.

Table 1.3 The world's most populous countries

Country	Percentage of the world's population
China	21%
India	16%
United States	5%
Indonesia	4%
Brazil	3%

The world's five wealthiest countries account for around 60% of the world's gross domestic product (GDP) (Figure 1.8). The five most populous countries contain almost half of the world's population.

Now compare the two lists of countries; only one of those countries – the United States – is in both league tables with only 5% of the world's population and 27% of its wealth. In other words, world wealth is highly concentrated and that concentration is getting worse. Putting aside the ethics of the issue, it is dangerous for those who have so much to allow the vast bulk of humanity to struggle on so little. The sandal-wearing woolly-jumper brigade are right – at least in this respect – that the Marie Antoinette attitude adopted by most in the wealthy world will lead us to the same fate as that which befell the infamously indifferent queen.

This gap between rich and poor nations has worsened over the past fifty years. Although some countries, notably China and the so-called Asian 'Tigers' have done amazingly well in terms of economic growth, other areas have been left trailing far behind, at least in economic development terms.

Half of the world's population lives on less than $2 per day[16] – roughly the price of our lattes as we finish off the proofing of this document. Contrast this lousy level of income with the fact that the average US citizen spends $15 per day on imported goods *from other nations* alone. In addition, the growth of agriculture in developing nations has been severely dented by the huge subsidies paid to Western farmers by their rich country governments. Agriculture, for

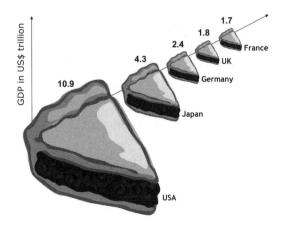

Figure 1.8   The world's wealthiest countries
Source: The World Bank Group, 2003.

many of these nations, represents their only source of comparative advantage, i.e. the industry that they are most competitive in compared to the rest of us. But they are priced out of even this one small place of opportunity by the effective and crippling burdens that we impose on them by subsidizing our own farm products. This subsidization of Rich World farming is a near universal policy – Japan does it, the Europeans do it and the United States does it – in spades.

The collapse in 2003 of the Cancun round of trade talks, which took place under the auspices of the World Trade Organization, was a direct result of this unfair trade in agricultural products. For the first time ever, poor nations have come together to call for an end to this appalling system, which serves in many ways to perpetuate poverty among their farming populations. This farming inequality, protectionism or whatever you want to call it is one of the biggest problems facing the world. Of course, the poor countries have a fairly weak hand – they are trying to hold up the rich man's stagecoach with a squirt gun. But they are making a serious point in their protest – and one that should be acted on.

On a positive note, some progress has was made in the 2004 discussions of the WTO – key member states (the US, EU, Japan and Brazil) accepted proposals to cut subsidies to their farmers for exports. A small step in the right direction, but implementation will be another thing.

The retiring President of the World Bank, James D. Wolfensohn, has accused wealthy countries of 'squandering' $1 billion a day on farm subsidies![17] This subsidization leads to overproduction in the West. The resulting surplus is then sold in competition to the output of the unsubsidized farms of the developing world. This depresses prices and ruins the chances for these countries to use agriculture as a means of growing out of poverty.

Even poor nations which are rich in natural resources tend to be stuck in a rut, despite a long-standing belief of some branches of economic science that such resources are keys to future national prosperity. According to the economist Jeffrey Sachs,[18] ownership of natural resources interestingly depresses growth rather than stimulates it. His contention is that in a survey of world economies, he can find no correlation between countries rich in natural resources and those that are prosperous other than Canada, New Zealand and Australia.

The most extreme examples of the point made by Sachs are Japan – the world's second richest nation – and Brazil, a much poorer one. The former is an incredibly wealthy country (GDP of US$4 trillion) with almost no natural resources in its 378,000 square kilometre land mass; Brazil, on the other hand, is enormous (8.5 million square kilometres), abundant in natural resources but has a GDP that is one tenth of Japan's. Measured another way, Japan's GDP per square kilometre is about 200 times that of Brazil!

Further bad news from the stats: the rapid development of new technologies in the world is only serving to accentuate the rich–poor divide. What we mean by this is that there is a *new* 'have' and 'have-not' gap developing: those who have *knowledge* and *technology* and those who do not. Entire regions risk being kept in a kind of feudal state as a result of this divergence. This will eventually contribute to disaffection, unrest and social upheaval among some populations and regions, and it will pose another significant risk to those of us who live in the Rich World.

Concerned by this widening gap between the rich and poor, the UN's Secretary General, Kofi Anan, warned member nations back in 1999 of the growing 'digital divide':

> 'People lack many things: jobs, shelter, and food, health care and drinkable water. Today, being cut off from basic telecommunications services is a hardship almost as acute as these other deprivations and may indeed reduce the chances of finding remedies to them.'

The digital revolution will almost certainly exacerbate the gap between the 'haves' and the 'have-nots'. What this means in a global context is that whole regions risk becoming irrelevant to the world economy.

At greatest risk is Africa, where many countries, for instance the Congo, Burundi, Burkina Faso, Uganda and Zimbabwe, find themselves almost completely detached from the global economy.

Of course, some nations are able to embrace and to take advantage of the digital age by rapid adoption of the latest technologies. China is perhaps the best example of this and is in the process of establishing an infrastructure using the most modern fibre optic and wireless technologies, leapfrogging much of the West's relatively aged telecommunication infrastructure.

While this may mean that major cities in China will rival cities in the West in terms of competitiveness, the issue of developing the vast rural regions of China is a different one altogether. These agricultural hinterlands remain largely undeveloped and should be causes for continuing concern. This is particularly the case because, as many Chinese move from farm-based lives to the cities, they depopulate the countryside of relatively young people, leaving the rural areas with a significantly reduced workforce, both in terms of absolute numbers and as a percentage of the rural population.

Likewise, India is in many ways at the vanguard of new technology – yet the majority of its population remains mired in dreadful poverty and economic growth has historically not been high enough to address this fundamental issue. The success stories of 'off-shoring' – the transfer of low wage jobs from the West to India and elsewhere, e.g. call centre, basic software development and customer service positions – create an exaggerated view of the reality of India's economic position. While Bangalore may be adorned by the gleaming buildings of its technical success, much of India is still the muddy, chaotic and poor place that it has always been. Many, many more Bangalores are needed – and they are unlikely to be forthcoming anytime soon.

Even in the rich nations of the West, there is a real danger of the formation of a similarly two-tiered society: one that is taking advantage of new technologies and the other remaining largely disengaged.

The big concern for us is where that dividing line will fall and to what extent it will create social tensions, possibly even unrest.

As we have noted before, in the United States an estimated 34 million people live in poverty; they struggle to maintain a basic standard of living and don't generally have access to the Internet or the latest advances in technology.

The wealth consolidation going on in the United States – and very much abetted by the George W. Bush administration – means that the average American is not really benefiting from the country's nominally high growth and consequently will not be able to keep spending in the long run. Since the spending of US consumers makes up almost 70% of America's GDP, the absence of this engine will surely lead to a stalling of the whole machine.

In Part Four, we analyse the lessons we believe that can be learned from the experience of the Great Depression and highlight the many parallels that we see in today's economy.

Egypt – a poor nation with a rich past

During the trip to Egypt, the authors found it hard to believe that this country was once home to the world's first empire. The cacophony of Third World horn-tooting that greets new arrivals to Cairo, the extensive use of donkeys, horses and camels in farming and in transport, and the near feudal conditions under which the large (70 million) population live are hardly reflections of the capabilities of once great Pharaonic dynasties.

The Egypt of today is a kind of mirror to the problems of the developing world. Its population continues to grow at the expense of overall living standards. The country, like many in the developing world, spends a disproportionately large amount on defence and security and it is burdened by a creaking and corrupt economy.

The major assets of Egypt are in fact, and ironically, its temples, monuments, pyramids, and the other artefacts of its prime period – one that took place three to four thousand years ago.

Although the Suez Canal is a major foreign currency earner for the country, it is tourism that is the true lifeblood of this economy. Every 'baksheesh'-seeking tourist guide, hotel and restaurant employee, provides the means for many members of his or her extended family to live.

Harping back to a well-known theme of ours, Egypt suffers because of the farm subsidies which prop up Western agricultural output. As a result, the country's principal natural asset, its fertile Nile valley, cannot be exploited to the full benefit of the nation's economy.

Egypt has little in the way of comparative advantages over, say, China in terms of manufacturing or anything else; the result is that the country can neither afford to adequately educate its population nor to provide it with adequate health benefits. The exile of the bulk of the intelligentsia during the Nasser years (in the 1950s and 1960s) has left a gaping hole in the country's management ranks. Bloated, monopolistic state enterprises weigh down economic performance, and the Egyptian pound – the local currency – is a dud.

The obvious contrast between the overfed camera-laden tourists and the grimy children emerging from mud-baked shacks, in which most of them live, could not be greater. No wonder festering resentment is evident behind the fixed smiles of the souvenir touts who follow foreigners everywhere.

*part*TWO

The Global Economy is Under Threat

The general outlook

The outlook for the world economy is uncertain at best – and dire at worst. In the period 2005–2015, the chances of a positive outcome for economic growth in the rich part of the world are low.

Please don't get us wrong: neither of us is a backwoodsman holed up in Wyoming or some other remote location, waiting for the end of the world. We are not struck with fantasies that foresee some sort of second coming or religious event which will submerge all but the righteous in a sea of lava. We don't have a crystal ball and, by nature, we are optimistic people. But facts are facts and those that are staring us in the face indicate a dark period ahead for the world economy.

Ignore grandstanding statements about the prospects of recovery from prominent world figures. Discount, as well, liquidity-induced rallies in stock markets as false dawns.

Figures indicating economic recovery since 2003 in the United States and elsewhere are the direct result of aggressive monetary stimulation. This stimulation is the equivalent of giving a credit junkie one last and potentially fatal fix. This injection of liquidity – credit – leads to a temporary upsurge in economic statistics but the reality is that these statistics are the result of short-term palliative care for Western economies that are in a deep long-term crisis.

This crisis is the result of staggering imbalances that have built up over a long period of time and therefore cannot be 'cured' with a simple dose of further credit. After all, that was one of the main factors which led us to the problem in the first place.

Let's fast forward to the reasons why we wrote this book, and why we are so gloomy. Of course, we would like to be writing a sunny, optimistic book about the wonders of technology, the opportunities in developing economies as they grow to rival the Rich World and the chances that we will live to a ripe old age because of improved healthcare. We can't though – unless we were to write a work of fiction. This is because the world as we know it is in need of a serious structural adjustment before we can expect to see any good times ahead. In the process of that adjustment there will be *dislocation, depression and severe difficulties* for the Rich World in which most of our readers live.

Headline figures indicating strong growth in countries such as the United States should be dismissed as dangerous to the naked eye. The underlying reality is very different: things are going to get worse and people had better prepare for it. Yes, we know that this sounds alarmist and we know that some will dismiss us as cranks for taking this view. But remember, did people in 1928 in Europe and the United States expect a depression? Did the Japanese in 1989, riding high in their 'bubble economy', expect more than a decade of stagnation? Of course not! Yet all the warning signs were clearly visible for the objective eye to see, as they are today.

But people's viewpoints are easily clouded by window-dressed statistics that don't show the full, frightening picture. No one wants bad news, and very few have the foresight to recognize that underneath the relatively calm exterior of our modern economic world there are seismic shifts occurring. These shifts will change the balance of power in the world in all sorts of ways and it is important to be aware of these developments, to recognize them and to embrace them because by doing so we firmly believe that you will not only survive the times ahead but perhaps even prosper.

Economic theories

How economies work and why ours aren't working any more

This book has as its central thesis that the rich industrialized world is entering a hazardous phase, one which is likely to lead to depression, social unrest and possibly global conflict.

There are several reasons contributing to this negative view of the future: debt; imperilled free trade; relatively free capital; and technology transfers are among the most important of these. Our negative outlook does not stem from a belief that there is an inherent fault with free markets – far from it. The free market is the most effective way of operating an economy. A capitalist system wins hands down when stacked up against a communist one. Think United States versus Soviet Union in the post-war period and think relative standards of living in, say, Singapore versus Vietnam.

The problem is that, notwithstanding the 'magic' of men such as Alan Greenspan, chairman of the Federal Reserve in the United States, there is ultimately no escaping the fact that economies are cyclical and move from time to time into recession and possibly depression.

There is no escape from the power of the cycle – there is no secret formula to create forever-and-a-day growth. Indeed, a series of Faustian pacts – consumers with lenders, Asian central banks with the US Treasury – have conspired to create conditions that will *accentuate* the down phase of the natural cycle.

We who live in the rich part of the world have experienced unprecedented levels of growth and prosperity, but the cracks in our edifice of affluence are becoming too visible to ignore. Elsewhere in this book these cracks are examined in some detail. Put in a nutshell they encapsulate the following: record amounts of debt which will become harder and harder to service; huge imbalances in global trade, particularly between the US and China; and slowly rising levels of unemployment in major economies which put further pressure on governments' budgets as tax revenues fall and welfare payments increase.

In short, the world is entering a period in which the so-called trade cycle is becoming adverse, and severely so. The 'trade cycle' is economist-speak for the passage of an economy through boom, recession, slump and recovery. Longer term, rich economies have, of course, grown at rates which naturally and gradually slow down as they get larger. It is obviously easier for developing countries, starting at low base levels, to grow more rapidly than larger mature economies.

In the post-war years there have been a number of recessionary periods in the major economies, mostly synchronized in depth or in timing. So, for instance, if the US has been in recession, then the economies of Western Europe have tended to be also in that state. These recessionary periods have been of varying severity but, generally speaking, only one of them – the recession of the early 1970s which coincided with a so-called 'oil shock' – has been seriously damaging. This is because there has emerged in rich societies a belief that the code by which a smoother long-term economic cycle can be managed has been cracked. Gone, it is thought by many, are the days of the boom–bust cycle, so characteristic of the pre-war days and best exemplified by the Great Depression of the 1930s.

The view that extremes in the trade cycle are not inevitable stems, in large part, from the work of John Maynard Keynes, whose seminal work *The General Theory of Employment, Interest and Money* was published in 1936. Keynes debunked the classical view that low levels of demand in an economy were self-correcting. This was because, according to the classical view, what happened in a *depression* was that wages would keep on falling as labour competed for the few jobs available until employers found it attractive to employ workers again.

Keynes explained that it was entirely possible for low levels of aggregate demand to persist in an economy for a long period of time, unless the central government took action to rectify this. Thus, he advocated that when an economy was in or likely to go into recession, central government engaged in *deficit spending*. This meant borrowing money to *spend* on public works and other government expenditures, thereby expanding overall demand. In addition, he advocated expansionary monetary and fiscal policies at times of incipient or actual recession. By this he meant the use of *expanding* money supply and credit, and *lowering* taxes to stimulate economic activity.

Keynes's thinking was the basis of a great deal of the conduct of post-war economic policy in rich nations. Indeed, Keynes himself was instrumental in the formation of such agencies as the World Bank and the International Monetary Fund after World War II, which have been valuable vehicles in the coordination of economic policy among nations.

Keynesian thinking has been the subject of much debate since the war but particularly since the early 1990s when some of its central tenets were challenged by the so-called *monetarist* school of economics. This monetarist viewpoint takes a somewhat different line to Keynes, who was an advocate of the management of demand, in part, to maintain full employment in an economy.

Monetarists take the view that the control of inflation in an economy is much more important than the goal of reducing unemployment. In practice, in their view, interest rates are supposed to rise to counteract any threatened or actual increase in inflation, even at the price of starting a recession. The increased costs of borrowing will cause consumers and businesses to cut back on their spending and to reduce borrowing, resulting in what is known as a *downward multiplier* in the economic system, i.e. that all factors in the economy are made to act at a slower pace.

All of this may be (a) obvious to those who have a grounding in economics (b) boring or (c) both a and b. But the development of economic theory in the past few decades is very important for understanding why the global economy is where it is at today. It also explains why the current languid prosperity of the Western world and of Japan is about as real as an illusion performed by David Copperfield.

John Maynard Keynes (1883–1946)

The most influential economist in recent history, John Maynard Keynes was born on 5 June 1883 in Cambridge, England. The son of Cambridge economist John Neville Keynes, John Maynard was educated at Eton College and in 1902 went to King's College, Cambridge, on a scholarship in mathematics and classics. In 1906, he entered the British civil service but found it dull and returned to Cambridge in 1909 after he was elected to a Fellowship to teach economics there.

From 1914 to 1918, John Maynard was called to the UK Treasury to assist with the war financing effort, at which he excelled. At the end of the war, he was part of the British delegation to the Versailles Peace Conference. He was appalled at the vindictive nature of the peace settlement, and he was against the heavy 'reparation' payments imposed on Germany. He subsequently published The Economic Consequences of the Peace *in 1919, which denounced the Treaty of Versailles. He argued that Germany could never pay what the victors were demanding. He criticized President Wilson of the US and President Clemenceau of France, as well as Prime Minister Lloyd George of Great Britain. The publication brought him much fame and notoriety. He would prove to be right some two decades later as Germany waged war once again in Europe, partly as an escape from its depressed economic situation.*

Keynes revolutionized economics with his now classic book, The General Theory of Employment, Interest and Money, *which was published in 1936. Because of this* _book, Keynes is arguably the most influential of all economists ever; to such an extent that many aspects of economic theory bear his name: 'Keynesian Economics'. Although the term is widely used in the field, it principally covers the following tenets:[1]_

- _Aggregate demand is influenced by a host of economic decisions, both public and private._
- _The greatest short-run impact on changes in aggregate demand is on real output and employment, not on prices._
- _Prices of goods, services and labour respond slowly to changes in supply and demand, and consequently result in shortages and surpluses._
- _Unemployment is both too high on average and too variable. Also, certain periods of recession or depression are economic maladies, not efficient market responses to unattractive opportunities._
- _Stabilization policies can help dampen the amplitude of the business cycle._
- _Greater priority is given to tackling unemployment over inflation._

The debt of nations

The world has become addicted to debt. A 2003 Economic Outlook Report by the Organization for Economic Co-operation and Development (OECD) revealed that member countries are running up public debt at tremendous and unsustainable rates.

On average, in the first decade of the new century, rich government budget deficits are running at around 4% of GDP. This debt habit has been infectious, even among those nations that used to live by different rules; as recently as 2000, rich country budgets were mostly balanced. This huge increase in deficit financing of government expenditures has so added to the veritable mountain of debt that by 2003 year-end this heap of IOUs amounted to almost the same size as the total output of the OECD countries – the club of rich nations. The reduction of governments' revenues is largely due to the global economic slow-down (excluding China) subsequent to the bursting of the Internet bubble and the September 11, 2001 terrorist attacks. Yet these governments continue to spend beyond their means, year after year. Their inability to balance budgets is irresponsible behaviour that will have long-term economic consequences. Each additional dollar borrowed (deficit) is added to the ever-increasing mountain of debt being accumulated by these countries.

Even formerly prudent Asian governments, including that of Japan, have also caught on to the idea of spending borrowed money and they too are now running into the red by an estimated 3% of GDP per annum – a significant deterioration given that Asian government budgets were largely balanced in the early 1990s. Indeed, this fact was touted as one of the virtues of the so-called 'Tiger' economies of Hong Kong, Singapore, South Korea and Taiwan.

But it is Japan which is today the main culprit in terms of government extravagance. Japan's government spending is in a league of its own. Japan's budget deficit for central and local governments was around ¥40 trillion or 8% of GDP for 2004, exceeding even that of the US in relative but not yet in absolute terms. This of course adds to Japan's already massive debt mountain, which stands at 150% or so of GDP. Simply put, everyone in Japan would have to stop spending altogether and work for free for a year and a half to pay it off! And yet there is no sign of a slowdown in the accumulation of liabilities, nor will there be as long as the Rich World continues to practice the voodoo economics of deficit funding on a scale even Keynes could not have imagined.

The OECD predicts that by 2008 its member countries will be sitting on central government debts totalling 86% of their combined GDP, and that excludes other very significant debt troubles. This is particularly the case in Europe where the future pension burden for baby boomers (people born in the post World War II years) is large. As this demographic bulge enters retirement age (the older baby boomers are already there), there will be a further exacerbation of this already gloomy situation.

But where does this Rich World's borrowed money come from? Who is financing these countries? Between 1990 and 2000, central government debt in OECD countries virtually doubled to $12.86 trillion from $7.18 trillion. By 2005, this figure is estimated to be well over the $16 trillion mark (Figure 2.1). Approximately half of this debt is attributed to the US government alone. Over 80% of the OECD governments' borrowing is typically in the form of marketable instruments such as government bonds and treasury bills.[2] Most of this is held by financial institutions, mutual funds, pension funds and, in the case of the United States, foreign governments and institutions.

The trend towards rapidly expanding central government debt is undeniable and the level of rich nations' government borrowing is, in almost all cases, at or approaching record levels. This does not pose a large problem as long as

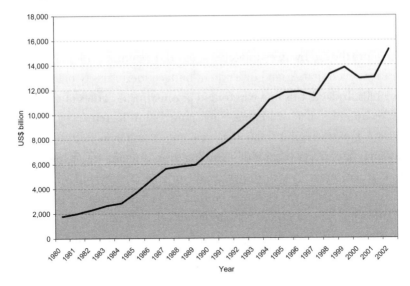

Figure 2.1   Central government debt for OECD member states
Source: OECD.

interest rates remain low, since the interest payable on this debt mountain is relatively trivial. However, should interest rates rise (which they have started to do), the interest burden will become increasingly difficult to support. Under such circumstances it is likely that governments will crowd out other borrowers in financial markets. Governments can always borrow ahead of commercial borrowers or individual borrowers as they control money supply and interest rates, at least in most countries. This means that if a government ends up with an increasingly large interest bill for its hefty and growing debt, it simply borrows at ever increasing rates of interest. Consequently, other borrowers end up under pressure as they will have to offer an even higher interest rate due to their added risk as borrowers. This scenario is one that will make the coming depression in major economies even worse.

Deflation and inflation and the dangers they represent ...

Why is it that the prospect of falling prices (i.e. deflation) is a major concern to central bankers and others in today's world? And why is it that they are much keener to promote modest inflation in their respective economies than to allow deflationary tendencies to take hold?

The answer is simple: falling prices are symptoms of weakening confidence among consumers, investors and companies in major industrialized nations – and signify recessionary tendencies in their economies. This may not appear evident early on in the 21st century. Credit creation in the United States and the mercantilist ambitions and inclinations of China (i.e. acceptance that trade is more important than getting paid in real goods for the output of its factories) have led to the Faustian pact that we have mentioned before. This has allowed growth in many world economies to continue – the temporary high of credit that we are all about to come down from.

Our contention, however, is that basic 'economics' is about to reassert itself. Inflation is *not* going to be a substantial problem, despite low interest rates, despite the credit boom and despite rising commodity prices.

Inflation is not dead, and certainly once the world economy has *deflated*, it will reassert itself, but for now – hard as it may be to believe – *deflation* is the problem that we are to be confronted by. Deflation may well be prove to be the economic hallmark of the 21st century.

A short review of the importance of price movements in economies will demonstrate our perspective of events in the global economy. A simple but effective way of analysing the state of economic activity is to think of it as an equation:

$$\text{MONEY} \times \text{CONFIDENCE} = \text{GROWTH}$$

Money, in all of its various forms, cash, credit or whatever, is the lubricant which allows economies to function. Money is a system of trade which has evolved over many centuries. Furthermore, money is useful because it represents a single standard by which the worth of goods and services can be measured. Without money, we would work in a barter-type world where, for instance, farmers would trade food for haircuts in town. Such a barter-type market would be highly inefficient and it would be difficult for governments to collect taxes, on which they rely to pay for public services.

As money has evolved, its forms and uses have become more sophisticated. Increasingly, cash is a relatively small part of what is known as the *money supply* in sophisticated economies. People and corporations largely keep their money in banks, which then re-lend this money to individuals, corporations and governments to create *credit*. Such credit fuels economic activity and it provides consumers with the means to buy cars, houses and other goods. It also permits corporations to borrow to invest in plants and machinery or working capital.

A big difference between the industrialized nations of today's world and those of the Great Depression of the 1930s is that the money supply of most nations at that time was linked to gold. This so-called 'Gold Standard' meant that the supply of currency and credit in an economy had to be backed – at least theoretically – by *gold reserves*, which acted as a severe limiting factor on a government's ability to print money. Today, governments are not constrained in this way and can act swiftly to use monetary policy (i.e. the creation of new money) to attempt to stimulate economic growth. The problem however, is that there are two elements to our equation – not just money, but also confidence. Printing money and expanding the forms and extent of credit in an economy will have no or only a minimal effect if *confidence* is weak. After all, any school-child knows $1000 \times 0 = 0$, so an unlimited amount of money multiplied by zero confidence still adds up to zero!

And so, today, we are confronted with a key problem of our new age – *confidence* and how it can be maintained, massaged and nurtured.

If governments release large quantities of net new credit and print large amounts of money, without consumers and corporations doing their economic 'duty' and spending it, or alternatively unless governments engage in massive public spending works, then an increase in money supply will have negligible effects. This is precisely what happened in Japan over the past decade or so.

Just because we haven't experienced deflation doesn't mean that we aren't going to. Deflation is not a new phenomenon: in Great Britain, prices fell by 44% from 1920 to 1933, and this despite a devaluation of the pound sterling in 1931. Japan's recent deflation, where prices fell by around 3% between 1998 and 2002, is extremely minor in comparison. In the 19th century, deflation occurred regularly in periods of declining economic activity. The UK price level of 100 in 1800 had fallen to 49 by mid 1850. Inflation then reappeared and by 1864 the price index had recovered to 92. Then a slow and gradual decline set in with prices flattening out at 49 in 1901. Prices rose sharply during World War I as money was printed to pay for the war effort, but by the mid 1930s prices were back to turn-of-the-century levels. In one period, 1844–1850, prices in Germany fell a dramatic 43%.

Deflation was exaggerated in the 19th century because of the shortage of gold (i.e. money supply could not be rapidly expanded as currency was typically backed by gold reserves, which were constrained by supplies of the physical metal).

At the same time and almost throughout the 19th century the supply of goods became abundant. This was partly due to new methods of shipping them as well as to a huge increase in industrial capacity. This last point – a large increase in industrial capacity – is one that also applies today: the world suffers from abundance in the supply of production goods – in large part fuelled by the growth of Chinese industries. This has already led to a substantial fall in prices of manufactured goods. The abundance of factory produced goods is leading to a decline in what economists call *pricing leverage* – the ability of companies to maintain pricing and profits.

Currently the US is suffering, as indeed are all major industrialized nations, from a 'core deflation' in manufactured goods prices – a fall averageing about 2% per annum. The only offset to this is the continued 'core inflation' in service prices (e.g. banking, tourism, etc.) and of course in commodity prices, such as oil and gas.

The US economy as the workhorse of the world, or at least the biggest eater of hay in the planet's stables, is unlikely to enjoy a continuation of economic recovery for much longer. There may be headline figures indicating strong growth from time to time but these will be aberrant and short lived.

As we have pointed out, the jagged effects of excessive credit creation will continue to have some impact on the US economy for a while, but they disguise the fundamental imbalances that will require large-scale readjustment over the next few years. This is because the traditional components of a strong cyclical upwards move have peaked – consumer expenditure and residential construction expenditures are already at near record highs, fuelled by all-time high levels of mortgage debt. The only way for these is down – and the piper needs to be paid for too many years of excess private sector debt-based consumption.

The level of acceleration required to move the US and the rest of the world out of a deflationary trap is just not there. The 'rev counter' of the US economy is already straining and the oil in its engine is dangerously hot. The threat of deflation – in reality, a far more serious threat to society than inflation – is now upon us.

Free trade imperilled

For over fifty years, the major nations of the industrialized world have worked hard to break down barriers to trade between each other. The powers that be of the major countries have more or less understood that the freedom of movement of goods and services leads to generally increased prosperity for all concerned. Organizations such as the European Union, with its genesis in the Treaty of Rome signed in 1957, the North American Free Trade Association (NAFTA) and, of course, the World Trade Organization (WTO) and its predecessor the General Agreement on Tariffs and Trade (GATT) have aided this process.

GATT, the precursor to all of these pro-trade organizations, was formed in 1948. It had the objective of lowering financial barriers to trade, commonly known as customs tariffs.

Today around 150 countries, including China, belong to the WTO, successor to GATT.

The WTO is the supervisory body for international trade. Its decisions are absolute and supposedly every member must abide by its rulings. Its guiding principles are:

- extending trade concessions equally to all WTO members;
- making trade rules more predictable; and
- aiming for 'freer' global trade.

Rounds of talks take place at which tariffs and barriers issues are discussed and alterations made. There have been nine such rounds since 1948.

Trade now accounts for 25% of the whole world's output, up from just 8% in 1950. Over that period, trade has risen in real terms by more than 15 times! Trade is a hugely important part of the world economy. Unfortunately, in matters of trade, rational economics do not always prevail over political expediency. For instance, the Great Depression of the late 1920s and early 1930s was exacerbated by the use of protectionist barriers as countries sought to protect their own struggling industries from the effects of international competition. This had the inevitable consequence of reducing combined world output, making the resulting depression even more pronounced.

Today, the major threat to trade is once again the slowing of growth and, indeed, in the cases of some nations, outright recession. China's fast track industrialization, the emergence of Eastern European economies as sources of low cost labour, and the continuing expansion of several of the so-called Asian Tigers, all pose real threats to mature, struggling economies.

Indeed, the faint rumblings of trade wars can now be heard – and the US has taken limited action using the formidable arsenal of trade weapons. Starting with beef, then bananas, and more recently steel and semiconductors, the world's largest importer tends to use a provision of the 1974 Trade Act. This is known as 'Super 301' which allows the investigation not just of individual products but of the trading practices of an entire country. The inevitable result of US action – with its ability to impose huge financial penalties on supposed miscreants – is to engender retaliatory action.

The extent of the US trade deficit (over $1.5 billion *per day*) is such that further efforts by almost any US administration to limit imports in sensitive areas (i.e. where foreign competitors threaten US jobs) are likely.

It came as no surprise therefore when the WTO ordered the US to reverse its 18-month-old policy of imposing a 32% tariff on imported steel. The WTO has accused the US of imposing the sanctions to unfairly protect the fragmented and inefficient US steel industry and to preserve jobs. The US has now at least partially reversed this ban but only for reasons of political expediency – complaints by car manufacturers outweighed the vote potential of steelworkers! Otherwise, as with many other issues promoted by the international community, such as the Iraq War and the Kyoto Protocol on climate change, the United States will not pay a blind bit of notice.

The US imposition of tariffs on steel is an example of how creeping protectionism is becoming sadly evident in the world's biggest economy. The US also slapped tariffs on imports of Chinese TV sets as a direct response to huge increases in imports of TVs from China and Malaysia from 2001 to 2003, which grew from 210,000 sets to 2.65 million sets – a 13 fold increase!

Other industries are also being targeted in an effort to preserve and protect the domestic sector – textiles and shrimp have also been punished with anti-dumping tariffs. Petitions from just about every US manufacturing industry have now been lodged against the incursion of Chinese goods – furniture, textiles, steel, wire hangers, TVs, radios, etc. China clearly does not want a trade war with the US – it is not in its interests – but other Asian countries also affected by these rulings are quite capable of retaliation.

This gradualist and pettifogging behaviour is a bit like a playground scrap – starting with small slaps and leading to full-on fighting.

Don't underestimate protectionist behaviour – it could certainly lead to a gradual unravelling of the process which has resulted in the single most important factor in the prosperity of many parts of the world: trade.

Protectionism will have a disproportionately hard effect on developing economies, where trade is vital to growth, leading to worsening anti-Western sentiment and possibly social unrest.

Even the celebrated Warren Buffett, the world's most successful investor, has now taken up his protectionist cudgels (see p. 76).

In mid 2004 the WTO ruled that the EU, Japan, Canada and Brazil may impose trade sanctions against the United States. This is because the US has yet to repeal its 'Byrd Amendment' which was declared illegal by the WTO in 2002. The Byrd Amendment takes the cash raised from anti-dumping duties on foreign firms and gives it to home companies that are considered to have suffered as a result. The ruling is worth hundreds of millions of dollars.

In October 2004, another trade dispute erupted, this time concerning the aviation industry. The US filed a case with the WTO over government subsidies, and Airbus immediately filed a counter-case.

Ever since Airbus overtook Boeing as the largest manufacturer of civilian aircraft in 2003, Boeing has been crying foul at the 'illegal' government subsidies Airbus receives. Likewise, Airbus claims that Boeing receives 'illegal' government subsidies. This is clearly a case of a stalemate that can end in no one-sided outcome – both companies are equally innocent or guilty, yet the filing with the WTO by the US (first) indicates the level of frustration from the one time market leader.

In a statement following the US WTO filing, the EU Trade Commissioner Pascal Lamy remarked that the US complaint was 'obviously an attempt to divert attention from Boeing's self-inflicted decline.'

The first shots in a trade war have been fired. The coming seismic shifts in the world economy will be in part created by the revival of protectionism, as well as blindingly stupid reversals in global trade flows.

Global excess capacity

The problem with the rapid economic expansion across the world in the 1990s is that there is now an oversupply of most products. Manufacturers around the world, but particularly in Asia, have built too many factories and have overinvested in them. This overinvestment has been in response to the widely held view that world economic growth would remain at high levels well into the foreseeable future.

Not so. According to OECD data, real global GDP growth fell from an annual rate of 4.9% during the Golden Economic Age of 1950–73, to 3% for 1973–1998, and has continued to decline subsequently.

Basic economics teaches us that the market equilibrium occurs when demand equals supply. If there is excess demand, then prices increase; if there is excess supply, then prices decrease until there is an increase in demand. The baffling situation we are facing today is that supply has not slowly adjusted to demand.

If we consider excess capacity as a long-term phenomenon, then perhaps we can start to understand why there is such a mismatch between supply and demand. In supply–demand matters, there is also a Darwinian element – large firms that are committed to their industry sector effectively have little choice but to continue to invest and compete in order to survive, even if the sector is mature or in decline. Airlines, for instance, continue to invest, even though rational economics show the whole industry to be a value-destroying one. There is nothing like the hope-springs-eternal mentality of investors who continue in their willingness to put good money after bad.

In recent years in most major world economies, we have seen healthily low levels of inflation, low unemployment and high growth. Unfortunately, that halcyon period is over and we foresee deflation and rising unemployment, factors that stifle growth.

So, why are we moving from a structurally inflationary global economy to a structurally deflationary one? One of the principal answers to this question is that we are currently going through an era of overproduction, as we have already mentioned. Particularly in Western countries, supply now far exceeds demand. Manufacturers are therefore forced to reduce their prices to increase the volume of sales, but at the same time this reduces the manufacturers' profits. In the longer term, this impacts employees working for these companies in the form of wage cuts and unemployment, which then reduces the purchasing power of these employees when they go out to shop as consumers, and so the vicious circle continues until we find a new equilibrium.

So where is the new equilibrium? In other words, how can we stabilize or even increase demand for goods and services? First of all, let's identify the buyers. There are three types of buyers in the world:

1 the retail buyer;
2 the corporation (private sector); and
3 the government (public sector).

When buyers (1) and (2) run out of steam, it remains up to governments to stimulate economic growth through the creation of demand that (1) and (2) no longer represent. But governments in rich nations are already running large deficits, i.e. spending money they don't have – and their aggregate debt has risen to extraordinary levels. So there's nowhere to go. As the Rich World economy winds down further, pressured by rises in oil prices and other negative factors, tax revenues will continue to drop. This will make it increasingly difficult for governments to find the money to spend in order to stimulate their respective economies.

One option would normally be to issue more debt in the form of government bonds, but what if there is insufficient demand for them? Governments would then have to increase the real (i.e. post tax, post inflation) yield on these bonds to make them sufficiently attractive to market participants. Then the question would arise as to how governments would service (i.e. pay the interest on) this increased debt. Would investors switch out of corporate bonds for these higher yield government bonds? What would happen to the corporate debt market? The economy of the West is highly interconnected – it's just a matter of time before apparently robust financial structures start to crumble.

The deflationary cycle we have entered will prove to be much longer than most economists are predicting. Perhaps a whole decade of dropping prices, falling incomes and shrinking or static economic activity is in prospect.

The pension burden

When we eventually decide to stop working and retire, we obviously cease to receive a salary, which for many of us also means we no longer have a secure source of income. Consequently we must rely on one of four channels (or a combination of the four) to provide us with an alternative income. These income streams can come from (a) the state; (b) corporations (pension); (c) individual/family savings/pension; and (d) our children or friends.

The vast majority of Europeans rely on the state for their pensions, and this is proving to be a huge burden on their governments for two simple reasons: Europeans are living longer and they are also having fewer babies.

In the past 50 years life expectancy in Europe has on average increased by almost ten years. During that same period, the birth rate has fallen from 2.7 to 1.5 children per woman, which is insufficient to maintain the size of the population (we need at least 2.1). The consequence of living longer is that the state has to write pension cheques for many more years for many more individuals than it did in the past.

A declining population leads to less people in the workforce, which means less income (in the form of taxes and state pension contributions) for the government. Both of these trends are likely to continue for the next 50 years, so the problem will only worsen unless governments act fast.

State pensions are currently costing European countries as much as 15% of their GDP annually.[3] Fortunately for the UK and the US, this number is only around 5% of GDP as these countries have transferred much of the pension burden to corporations (the employer) and the individual (ISA in the UK, 401(k) in the US). For the US and most of Europe, the current worker/pension ratio has fallen to about three workers for each pensioner.[4]

This means that three people in the workplace today are making contributions to service the state pension of one retiree. In 30 years, this ratio will worsen: for Europe it will fall to one and a half (Figure 2.2); for the US it will fall to two. This can only mean one of two things: either workers will have to contribute more (double in the case of Europe), or pensioners will have to receive a lesser amount than they are currently receiving. European governments have made several half-hearted attempts to tackle this problem but they have failed as a result of strong union opposition – and are thus caught in a stalemate.

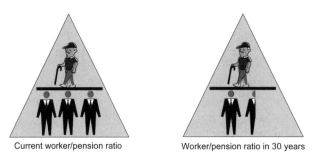

Current worker/pension ratio   Worker/pension ratio in 30 years

Figure 2.2 An ageing population means a fall in the worker–pension ratio

The social security system in the US is also in need of reform. Established in 1935, in a time when the worker/pension ratio was 16 (currently three, as mentioned earlier, falling to two over the next few decades), it poses a serious liability to the state. According to an announcement made in January 2005 by US Treasury Secretary John Snow, social security needs $10.4 trillion to prevent it from ultimately running out of cash. This is a vast sum of money, greater than the entire US national debt. No wonder President Bush, in his second term, has made social security reform a top priority. In his own words he intends to 'transform social security'. Whether or not he can do it remains to be seen.

However, he has certainly been softening up his fellow citizens with 'factoids' designed to show that the system is bankrupt and 'flat out broke'.

Forty-seven million Americans are currently recipients of social security – just under a fifth of the entire population. These people receive on average US$14,000 per annum, and of the 47 million, 33 million are older people, 7 million are the dependents of those already dead, and 7 million are disabled or their dependents.

This amounts in total to about US$500 billion a year, about the total amount spent on the combined Medicaid and Medicare.

Social security is currently funded by a 6.2% contribution from their incomes by employees up to a ceiling of US$90,000 in income per annum; additionally employers contribute a matching amount of 6.2%.

What is happening is that the gap between contributions and outgoings is narrowing rapidly and that by 2018, due to demographic factors, the system will pay out more than it takes in. Whether this is as much of a crisis as Bush likes to suggest is in a sense neither here nor there.

What is important is that it is very likely that in the current presidential term the whole system will be changed – and to the detriment of recipients. This means that anyone who is depending on the US social security system for their retirement should think again. Demographic, financial, budgetary and ideological pressures will put an end to that.

Ultimately, there are only three possibilities for the reform of state pensions: (1) increase the mandatory contributions (possibly in the form of tax hikes); (2) reduce the pension benefits; or (3) a combination of the two.

Changing a nation's demographics could help avert the future crisis associated with the dependency ratio (number of elderly as a percentage of the remaining adult population). There are a couple of possible solutions being considered by some governments: the first is to encourage young workers from poorer countries to emigrate to the rich, ageing countries. This, to some extent, has already been happening in the US where waves of immigrants have moved from Mexico, South America and other parts of the world. This has partly helped to keep America younger than old Europe, where the situation is too dire to realistically be able to alter the dependency ratio in the coming years. For example, Germany would have to average 3.6 million immigrants per year for the next 50 years to prevent the dependency ratio from rising!

The second method that could avert a pension crisis is to increase a country's birth rate. While some European countries are offering more attractive benefits for women to have more children, the longer term effects of such measures remain to be seen.

Martine Durand, deputy director for labour and social affairs of the Organization for Economic Cooperation and Development (OECD), describes it succinctly:[5]

> 'You can increase contributions, reduce pensions, or work longer, given the demographic developments in these pay-as-you-go systems. Increasing contributions is counter-productive in high-tax countries, reducing pensions is also politically unpopular. That just leaves raising retirement ages.'

So it seems highly likely that within the next ten years or so, retirement ages will be increasing to around 68–70 for men and 63–65 for women. After all, there's no such thing as a free lunch, and living longer has a price! In fact the authors consider it *imperative* that the old retirement rules are swept away – they hail from the time of Bismarck. People now live decades longer. Indeed, at the beginning of their lives, people spend much more time in education, so why not, towards the end of their lives, spend more time at work? In fact, work – or at least a productive interest – is *good* for you. Tending the tomatoes and wearing the slippers in God's waiting room is *not*!

Even rich nations that are less reliant on state pensions, such as the US and the UK, do not have an easy road ahead either: corporate pensions are also in a sorry state. It is estimated that US companies have an aggregate pension deficit of about $400 billion, so they will need to make significant contributions over the years to fill this hole, and that money comes straight from the company's profits. In the UK the estimated pension deficit is £160 billion. For example, British Airways' pension fund deficit has grown from £276 million at the end of the 2001–02 financial year to £1.1 billion in 2004.

The case of Enron is no doubt every employee's nightmare scenario. The company's 'book-cooking' activities meant that staff who thought they were putting away a portion of their salary every month towards their pension, usually by buying company stock, ended up losing everything as the true scale of the accounting fraud unravelled and the stock price collapsed.

Warren Buffett, the Sage of Omaha, is bearish! Take heed

Warren Buffett, the most successful investor of the post-war period, turned bearish on US stocks and on the US dollar in autumn 2003. He is the second richest person in the world (after Bill Gates) and he believes that the US economy is being mortgaged for current consumption, setting the scene for a massive collapse in the US dollar and a period of major readjustment in US capital markets. This is entirely consistent with our views, but his is a purely economic one and does not take into account all the other negatives – including the political ones – that we outline in this book.

Buffett said in October 2003, 'Our country (the US) is behaving like an extraordinarily rich family that possesses an immense farm. In order to consume 4% more than we produce – that's the trade deficit – we have, day by day, been both selling pieces of the farm and increasing the mortgage on what we still own.' (Incidentally, the trade deficit has risen to over 6% of GDP since he made that statement.)

Here is a man who avoided the Internet bubble and warned of its consequences – and here is a man who now holds substantial piles of cash ($24 billion at last count), an increasing part of which is non-US dollar denominated. You have been warned!

Not only has he been predicting the imminent collapse of the US dollar (and in this we – humbly – given his and our relative wealth, agree with him) but he is also urging the United States to go protectionist. Yes, really, even a man as savvy as him is following the siren call of Dark Age economics – and because of his influence it underlines in bright red ink the danger to the world of such calls – because, increasingly, they are being heeded. Warren Buffett has taken note of the United States' $500 billion dollar annual trade deficit and wants the administration to do something about it. What he wants is a form of old-fashioned protectionism. He wants import certificates to be issued to all US exporters in a dollar amount equal to their exports. Importers would then have to buy these certificates to be able to sell into the United States market. The process would only allow imports if they matched exports – so *voilà* – a balancing of the US's external position and no more trade deficit.

This, of course, is a tariff to trade because imports would cost more – it's as simple as that. In addition, such a plan would breach just about every trade treaty that the US is a signatory to – including the WTO. Other countries would naturally retaliate and a 1930s type of retaliatory trade war would take place with dire results.

Although Warren Buffett's plan is unlikely to be implemented – after all, how could the US suddenly replace the huge volume of goods it buys from overseas? – his idea is one of many such protectionist schemes being mooted by influential people at the heart of the US establishment.

Dick Gephardt, a leading member of Congress, wants to institute an international minimum wage. This would serve to 'level the playing field' between high wage (i.e. *inefficient*) nations and low wage countries – while bolstering the incomes of Third World labour forces – according to his theory. Of course, such a scheme would be almost impossible to enforce and would be rejected by most of the countries – China in particular – which it is specifically aimed at.

But the implication of his proposal is clear: the US needs to force others to comply with its desire to lower the trade gap. And this even at the expense of creating what are in essence protectionist barriers!

People like Gephardt and Buffett do not consider that actually the US has benefited from its trading relationship with China. In fact, low-cost Chinese imports have helped to keep inflation down in the US (the 'Wal-Mart effect'), as prices for many goods have been driven down by relentless competition from Chinese manufacturers.

Furthermore, as the US exports much less to China than it imports from China, it is paying for real tangible things with bits of paper that it can and will devalue, i.e. it is paying in its own government debt and in its own currency.

Increasingly that option will be closed off to the United States and it will simply have to import less from countries such as China, as they demand payment in something other than US debt and currency. That process would be a natural one, as the US dollar devalues. However, it may not happen if the US adopts an aggressively protectionist policy and forces the pace of what it sees as 'reform', i.e. the attempt to distort trade markets by hare-brained protectionist schemes resulting in economic disaster for the whole world.

Financial instruments of mass destruction

Although we are not supporters of Mr Buffett's protectionist suggestions, the area in which we most agree with him lies with the developing financial risk associated with *derivative instruments*: these are financial instruments designed to shift risk from one party to another.

Mr Buffett has accused these instruments, which proliferate in the financial world, of being potential weapons of mass financial destruction – and he has a good point.

The use of these derivatives has exploded along with so-called '*black box*' technologies for measuring and containing risk. From time to time, derivatives

– which are mostly contracts between banks, institutions and governments for the sale of levels of interest rates, currencies, credit risk – hit the headlines when they go wrong.

Orange County, the rich suburb of Los Angeles, went bankrupt in the early 1990s when its gamble in the derivatives markets went horribly wrong. Procter & Gamble, the big household goods company, lost a bundle on derivatives, as did Gibson Greetings. This is a company that is in the business of making greetings cards and certainly wasn't supposed to be involved in sophisticated financial markets!

Derivatives have a long history, but only today do they have huge implications for global financial markets. Japanese rice traders sold their crops 'forward' as early as the 17th century to protect against bad harvests, and in all sorts of commodity markets, so-called 'futures' markets have existed for centuries.

Derivative contracts generally consist of what are known as *futures and forwards*. These genres of financial crack cocaine are essentially *options* (i.e. the right but not the obligation to buy) or *futures* (the obligation to buy) assets. Almost any asset that is widely traded today is now covered by such contracts. There are also *swaps*, which enable participants to 'swap' streams of interest, payments or whatever in different currencies or a range of other options.

If this sounds complicated, that's because it is; and it is just this complexity and the un-transparent nature of the market for these derivatives which gives Mr Buffett nightmares.

Derivatives have enormous utility – it is possible now, for instance, for farmers to trade in weather futures, mitigating the effect of lousy weather on their crops. The corollary of all this utility, however, is that the market is so large and so unregulated that it is impossible in many cases to quantify the level of risk involved.

The particular area of concern for us, as the authors of this book, is in so-called *credit derivatives*. These credit derivatives are contracts that pay out if a certain company, or indeed country, goes bust.

The point of these is to allow holders of bonds issued by companies or countries to 'hedge' their bets by taking out what is effectively 'insurance' against that worst case scenario – credit default. This is all marvellous – but there still remains the little problem of what is called 'counterparty' risk, i.e. what happens if the people who make the commitment to pay out can't pay themselves.

This counterparty risk is not as unlikely as it would first appear. If, for instance, a big blue chip company like General Motors was to default on its debts, the circumstances in which it would do so would also be exceptionally adverse for everyone else. Top of the list of victims would be the banks and other financial institutions, which issued credit derivatives relating to General Motors' debt in the first place. If one domino falls, perhaps all the others will as well. This wouldn't really matter if it wasn't for the fact that the derivatives market is so large and so unregulated.

In December 2000 the Bank of International Settlements calculated that the gross market value of global over-the-counter (OTC), i.e. unregulated, derivatives contracts was a tad over $3 trillion dollars. By June 2003 it had risen to over $8 trillion – or three-quarters the size of the whole US economy. No wonder seriously bright investors are worried about the negative potential contained within the arcane and currently profitable derivatives markets!

United States' economic situation

It is self-evident that the major industrialized nations have been living on borrowed time and borrowed money for too long. Consumption has become the key driving force for the global economy in place of investment. Nowhere is this more the case than in the world's largest economy – the United States. The champion consumers of all time live here, with their bulging Wal-Mart bags constantly being ferried home. Fly over the port of Los Angeles and you'll see literally dozens of container vessels waiting to be unloaded, most of them full of Asian-made goods destined for American consumers. This untenable consumption boom has gone on for too long, raising the big question: when will the party end and the hangover begin?

The consumption boom of recent years has in large part been the result of artificially high levels of credit. Monetary policy has been vigorously expansive and lending institutions have been less rigorous in applying credit checks. In addition, imports of goods into the United States and Europe from developing Asian nations, particularly China, have been priced to reflect the very low relative labour rates. The deluge of imported goods has coincided with a rapid and massive increase in levels of debt in all strata of society: governmental, corporate and individual. Yet, there has been a great deal of talk about an apparent economic recovery these past couple of years, but the economic indicators remain at odds with this: low savings rates, the record levels of home construction and the dizzying price/earnings ratios in the stock market all seem to indicate the end of an economic cycle, not the start of a new one.

So what can the US do to put a stop to this irresponsible consumer behaviour? There are only two effective options at hand and these are (1) raise interest rates or (2) raise taxes. The consequence? Rising inflation – at least temporarily. Elsewhere in this book we argue that there will be a temporary period of *inflation* in major Western economies, but that ultimately there will be an acceleration of the deflationary tendencies which characterize this period in economic history. This temporary inflation will eat away at America's international purchasing power and real earnings. It will also have a knock-on effect on Europe – a region that will find it increasingly difficult to compete with a heavily devalued dollar – sending the EU into deep recession with unemployment spiralling to levels that could threaten civil stability. Alarmist perhaps but with unemployment in several major European nations already at near double digit levels, it is a strong possibility.

Meanwhile, in the United States, the Federal Reserve is walking the proverbial tightrope between avoiding deflation and preventing the credit bubble from bursting too quickly. It's a perilous situation partly of its own making.

The Fed ... the world's most powerful bank and the world's biggest pusher of its drug of choice – credit

The Fed – the Federal Reserve Bank – is the central bank of the world's most powerful nation, the United States. Established in 1913 by Congress, the Fed's role was and is to provide the US with a safer, more stable and flexible monetary system. Today and tomorrow it's more likely to be unsafe, unstable and out of control.

Before the bank's foundation, the United States had suffered from periodic systemic failures in its banking system. These resulted in bank closures, economic recessions and mass bankruptcies of individuals and corporations.

A particularly severe recession in 1907 led to the eventual foundation of the Fed; a move backed by the then President, Woodrow Wilson. The Fed is ruled by a board of governors and operates twelve regional reserve banks in cities around the US. The major policy-making body of the Fed is the Federal Open Markets Committee (FOMC). It is composed of the Presidents of the five Federal Reserve Banks from the regions in rotation – except that the President of the Federal Reserve of New York is always included. In addition, all the members of the board of governors of the Fed belong to the FOMC.

The Fed's duties in the US are roughly as follows (at least in principle):

1   To maintain the stability of the financial system and to contain major threats to that system.
2   To provide services to the US and foreign governments and to financial institutions.
3   To supervise and regulate banking institutions.
4   To conduct monetary policy, by influencing money and credit conditions in the economy in pursuit of full employment and stable prices.

In order to pursue these goals, the Fed uses three major tools:

(a) Open market operations
This is the buying and selling by the Fed of US government securities in the open market to manipulate the level of reserves in the banking system. To increase the flow of money and credit in the economy the Fed buys government securities. For the reverse effect the Fed sells them. This is the Fed's major tool in influencing short-term interest rates, specifically the Federal Funds rates, and to influence credit levels in the economy.

(b) Discount rate
When commercial banks and other approved deposit taking institutions borrow from a Federal Reserve Bank, they pay the Discount Interest Rate. In fact, this is largely a symbolic rate since the Fed discourages banks from borrowing to meet reserve requirements. Normal borrowing from the Fed is at the market determined Federal Funds rate.

(c) Reserve requirement
The Fed can and does change the percentage of deposits that institutions must set aside as reserves (e.g. for bad debts). Lowering banking reserve requirements injects credit into the economy; increasing reserve requirement reduces potential credit expansion.

The Fed is an independent central bank. It is not subject to the authority of the Executive Branch, including the President. It is subject to overview by US Congress. The Chairman of the Federal Reserve, currently Alan Greenspan, has great influence over the conduct of the US economy … as we are currently about to find out …

The only realistic outcome to this fundamental imbalance in the US economy appears to be deep recession. The bubbles in stock markets, property and credit have built up over 20 years and the recovery from their bursting will take some considerable time. Unfortunately, there is no magic pill, no instant cure for the ills of the US economy. The fallout from American stagnation and decline will be considerable for all other nations in the Rich World. There's no *schadenfreude* for the non-Americans among us to be gleaned here – we're all going to be worse off as much of the global economy is closely tied to that of the US.

US debt – spending other people's money

The recent expansion of credit in the United States represents one of the greatest threats to world economic and political stability. Consumer debt, mortgages, municipal, state, federal and corporate debt have been ballooning over the past few years. Total US debt (public and private) stands at over $37 *trillion* – an unfathomable amount of money. That's over three times the nation's GDP ($10.9 trillion in 2003).

About $10 trillion of the debt has been accumulated by households. Yes, consumers are guilty of contributing to this debt mountain which has, to a large extent, been used to finance the consumption of goods and services. This means that there can be no expectation of a return on that money, i.e. it has been used on consumption rather than to finance future-looking, productive capital investments.

The debt accumulation has been accelerated and accentuated by the Fed which has been running the dollar printing presses at maximum capacity. The Fed's practices have instilled a nonchalant attitude to debt. Its actions in bringing the discount rate (the prime borrowing rate) down from 6% to 1% on 12 separate occasions in a 12-month period between 2002 and 2004 contributed heavily to this *laissez faire* approach to borrowing and lending.

By aggressively buying government bonds and bills at the same time as lowering rates, the Fed allowed banks to expand their loan books by putting cash into the banking system. This compounded the already awful debt problem which threatens to engulf the US economy. The process of credit creation has trickled down throughout the financial system by the prevalent use of such techniques as securitization, which is the packageing of consumer credit, car and other loans, and selling them on to insurance companies, pension funds and other financial institutions. By doing so, big banks have transferred much of their riskier lending to other institutions, such as mutual funds and pension funds. The risk is still there, however – it's just that the new owners of it are a little less savvy.

For a while, all was fine in the blooming garden of America. The credit expansion resulted in the US being the principal locomotive of world growth – since 1995, almost 60% of total growth in the world economy has come from America, nearly twice the share that the country represents in total world economic output. As a result, the world economy has become excessively reliant on the US and, in particular, on its consumers.

In summary, therefore, the US economy has only been expanding in the early part of the 21st century because of the indulgence of foreigners who have been prepared to finance US spending, and due to the rampant increase in its overall indebtedness. Real incomes in the US have barely grown but debt has spiralled into a multi-headed monster. Stephen Roach of Morgan Stanley has termed the Fed a 'serial bubble blower', i.e. it has continued to fuel an economic expansion that is damageing, debt-based and ultimately destructive through the creation of excessive credit.

As we mentioned above, since 1995 total domestic demand in the US has been rising at twice the rate of the rest of the Rich World, nearly 4% per annum in real terms. This has been made possible by a dramatic expansion in credit, initially related to the huge stock market booms of the late 1990s and latterly due to the refinancing of home mortgages as the result of rising house prices and lower interest rates.

While this credit expansion took place against a backdrop of declining interest rates (now partially reversed), investors have been chasing any investment in bonds or similar instruments to get hold of 'yield' (i.e. current income). As banks have been able to offload more and more of their risky loans to yield-hungry investment institutions, this has freed up capital for them to make even more loans. Lending standards, i.e. quality control on the type of borrower, have fallen as this has occurred. So, while the stock market risks have become all too apparent to US investors, particularly those who lost money as a result of the bursting of the technology stock bubble, a new danger has emerged in credit quality. In other words, lenders have been too relaxed in assessing the repayment potential of new debt created in the financial markets.

As unemployment rises in the imminent recession ahead, so-called default delinquency rates will climb, as people quite simply will not be able to repay their car loans or credit card debt, especially if they don't have jobs! In the housing market, a steady increase in US mortgage delinquencies is already becoming evident.

It may come as no surprise that in addition to the dangerous and unsustainable levels of debt, savings in the US remain at near zero. The build up of debt has been substantially financed by foreign capital. For example, over 40% of all US Treasury bills and bonds are held by foreigners.

In the past, foreigners were attracted to the US economy by a strong dollar, favourable interest rates and a robust economy. Why would a weak dollar, low(ish) interest rates and an uncertain economy attract new foreigners to buy more US Treasury bills? And this is the problem. While the US cannot in a broad sense be compared to Latin America, it does have some characteristics in common with, say, pre-devaluation Argentina. This country had rising and unsustainable trade and budget deficits, a fairly sluggish economy without much job-creation, and massive debts. This is not an attractive long-term proposition for foreign investors.

Already over 100% of average US incomes (yes, really) are going to service debt. In other words, incomes are going towards paying interest and capital on consumer and mortgage debt. The post-tech bubble consumption boom has been financed by the so-called re-fi (refinancing) market, where huge amounts of consumer and mortgage debt are being refinanced on the back of higher house prices. This 'release of equity' has been done mostly to free up cash for immediate consumption. As the US savings rate is at an all-time low, the country has to borrow from overseas to continue its wild spending binge. This is evidenced by the size of the current account deficit, which runs at 5% or so of GDP, and is leading to a marked change in America's external debt situation.

As recently as 1980, the US was the world's biggest creditor nation; in other words, it owned more external assets on a net basis than anyone else. But read this next line carefully: today, the United States is the world's biggest debtor.

To add to the fiasco in the making, another new member – the US government – has also joined the US consumer spending party. In 2000, the US enjoyed a federal budget surplus of 2% of GDP. This has swung, worryingly, to a massive deficit of 5% of GDP and it looks like this deficit may increase even further. Both of these big deficits – trade and federal – are only made possible by the indulgence of foreigners, particularly Asian central banks. These central banks (i.e. governments) have been using their expanding foreign exchange reserves to buy US Treasuries and other assets, and have, in effect, allowed consumption to continue. This has been fine for the US while the cost of servicing this ever-rising debt remains relatively small (when interest rates are low).

At a net cost of a few billion dollars a year, the current cost of this debt is low – peanuts in the context of the US economy. But as interest rates rise, as they will have to in order for the US to attract necessary foreign capital, the cost of servicing this debt will rise dramatically. Debt will thus become an increasing factor in America's coming crisis.

The most likely mechanism by which the necessary adjustment will take place to reduce America's dependence on debt is through a large devaluation of the dollar. However, this devaluation-in-the-making is made difficult by the continued explicit and implicit intervention of the Asian central banks. This they do in an attempt to keep the value of their own currencies low, particularly so in the case of Japan, where its central bank has been very active in intervention. Total Asian central bank reserves amount to over $1.5 trillion, or over half of all world reserves and most Asian central banks hold almost all of their reserves in US dollars.

Although a decline in the US dollar has already commenced, a much bigger one is in store and Asian bank intervention will only be able to stem the tide for so long. In our opinion, a further 50% reduction (or more from the lows seen at the end of 2004) in the value of the US currency is in prospect. This will have severe knock-on effects in the world economy, leading to major recessions in all large economies as the US consumption machine grinds to a halt. As these economies slow down, exports from the mercantilist countries of the East will also slow, causing them (dependent as they are on trade for growth) severe economic problems of their own.

The sooner the adjustment of the value of the US dollar takes place, the better for the world economy. It is, however, more likely that the adjustment will be deferred and be more gradual, which could in itself cause severe problems, especially if calls for protectionism in the US become even more strident.

Bear in mind that one in six manufacturing jobs, or 3 million in total, have been lost in the US in just the past three years. A gradualist approach, where US manufacturing continues to be hollowed out and where China's trade surplus remains large, will certainly lead to calls for protectionism, especially against China. Many US workers regard China as the bogeyman. The fixing of the Chinese currency, the yuan, to the US dollar at an exchange rate of 8.28 since 1994 is now causing great concern. It is a fact that China's huge trade surpluses with the US are probably the result, in part, of an undervalued currency. Estimates of this undervaluation range from 10 to 50%. It is true, however, that only with America does China have such a huge trade surplus; overall its trade is more or less in balance – but it is US agitation for a higher yuan that will likely prove potent.

So, backtracking, in the US, the consumption boom of the late 1990s encouraged the rise of the stock market – as share prices rose, people felt wealthier and consumed more. Once the stock market bubble burst, the refinancing of houses and federal tax breaks took the place of shares in keeping consumption going. The big risk now is what happens if people lose their jobs, interest rates keep rising and property prices fall sharply? Any or all of which are very likely. Home refinancing will prove to have been just another big bubble; its bursting will have important consequences for the US. The changes in the financial circumstances of the US have no parallel in modern history. Put bluntly, the US is moving to the gates of the poor house at a prodigious rate.

In 1980 the US had international assets equivalent to about 10% of GDP. Today that figure is a negative 30%. By 2010 that figure could rise to as high as negative 65%, believes David Hale, a well-known and respected US economist. In other words, the US external investment deficit will be well over half the level of its total annual output. The only other time such a huge reversal in external assets has taken place was at the time of the two world wars when Great Britain had to sell off its substantial overseas assets to finance its role in the conflicts. For some time after World War II, Great Britain was in hock to the US and suffered a net external debt position. But that was due to world wars; the US situation is due to profligacy and the pursuit of what can only be described as banana republic economics.

Of course, the United States is not the only debtor nation in the world; many emerging countries are debtors as they need to borrow to finance future growth. Even some large developed nations, such as Australia, are persistent debtors. New Zealand is the biggest relative debtor nation in the world, with external net debt at over 90% of its GDP. But it is the rate of change and the scale of the US situation which is so disturbing. At the moment, the debt servicing cost (the money the US has to pay to the foreign holders of its debts and other assets) is relatively small. But this will grow hugely in future years and will add to the current account woes that are fast catching up with the world's biggest consumer.

US national debt (Federal government debt)

> 'I place economy among the first and most important of republican virtues, and public debt as the greatest of the dangers to be feared.'

> *Thomas Jefferson*

The US government has picked up the spending habit of the US consumer. As we mentioned earlier, in 2000, the US enjoyed a federal budget surplus of 2% of GDP. Just a few years later and that surplus has turned into a massive 5% deficit (see Figures 2.3–2.9).

Although many US administrations and Congresses start off with good intentions – and in some cases legislated requirements to balance the budget – in recent years the US national debt has grown exponentially. This is a dangerous situation which one day will have to be resolved. It is also expensive: the bigger the debt, the more interest the US government has to pay to the debt holders.

Some time in December 2003, US national debt crossed the $7 *trillion* mark (Figure 2.3), that's $7,000,000,000,000 – yes 12 zeros! With four more years in the White House secured for George Bush, we can expect to see a continuation of the irresponsible federal spending that took place during his first term

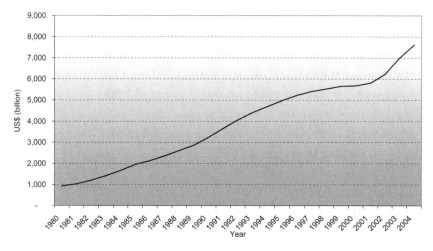

Figure 2.3 US total national debt
Source: US Department of the Treasury, Bureau of the Public Debt.

Balancing budgets 101

in office. Based on current deficit data, by the time George Bush hands the White House keys to his successor, the national debt will be around $10 trillion. For the year 2004, the US government spent over $300 billion on interest payments to the holders of the US national debt. Rising interest rates will mean that servicing this ballooning debt could easily double within this decade. This is a tremendous waste of money, which could have been used to better the nation's healthcare, schooling, pensions, not to mention to pay off some of the national debt itself. Instead, it will be paid to creditors, almost half of whom are foreigners.

There is a website you can visit that displays the latest figure for the

The US national debt is the total amount of money owed by the US Federal government. The debt is a direct result of the government spending more money than it raises through taxes and other sources of income.

Every year at the time of the budget, the government decides how much money it is going to spend; there are a multitude of things the US government allocates this spending to, from defence to education to foreign aid.

If the government spends the same amount of money that it receives over that budget year, the result is referred to as a **balanced budget***. If the government spends more than it earns, it is referred to as a* **budget deficit***. If it spends less than it earns it is known as a* **budget surplus***. If the government runs a budget deficit year after year, the aggregate of these deficits amount to the* **national debt***.*

US national debt: http://www.brillig.com/debt_clock. It clocks up faster than any super-car rev counter and continues to do so every waking and sleeping moment of every day. To put this seriously huge figure into perspective, it would require every man, woman and child living in America to pay around $24,000 each in order for the government to be able to extinguish this debt. That is equivalent to about nine months output for the whole US economy. By the time you read this book, the national debt will be well past the $7 trillion mark, probably on the way to the $10 trillion level by the time President Bush completes his second term.

If you would like to help America repay its debt, the US Treasury has thoughtfully established an account called 'Gifts for Reduction of the Public Debt' – honestly, we are not kidding. But remember, that's a cheque for $24,000 from every man, woman and child in America if the debt is to be repaid in full – and hurry as this amount will already have increased a lot more by the time this book is in the shops!

From September 2004 to the end of that year, the average national debt has been increasing on average by $2.17 billion per day and as interest rates rise further in the US, as we expect them to do, this figure will also have to rise.

So let's repeat this bit – because it is important:

- In 1980, the US had international assets totalling some 8% of its GDP.
- By the end of 2003, this had become a deficit equal to 30% of its GDP.
- If this economic policy were to continue, the US would find itself with an external investment deficit of around 60% of GDP by 2010.

Never before has a country played the role of a superpower while at the same time being the most indebted nation in the world.

Even the last empire to straddle the world with its pot of red paint – that of Great Britain – had external assets totalling 140% of GDP, prior to entering World War I.

In May 2003, President Bush quietly signed a bill that increased the amount the federal government is allowed to borrow from $6.4 trillion to $7.4 trillion. But this upper limit was also effortlessly breached. So, in November 2004 the Senate authorized an increase of the debt to $8.18 trillion (what choice did they really have?). For certain there will be other bills that pass after this book goes to press with ever increasing dollar borrowing limits. This is on a par with asking your credit card issuer to keep raising your credit limit so that you can go on one more shopping spree (fortunately for them the US government pays a lower interest rate than the ridiculous rates credit card companies charge individuals).

So who is foolish enough to lend this money to the profligate US government, we all might reasonably wonder?

Well, first, the United States has been borrowing from itself: the Federal Reserve (chaired by the legendary, veteran, inscrutable, etc. Alan Greenspan) has lent about half the total amount – effectively by printing money to spend (Figure 2.4). How much longer can the printing presses of the Fed keep up with government spending?

The next biggest group of lenders are foreign investors, of whom the Japanese and Chinese make up the largest portion. Just over 35% of the total US public debt is held by foreigners. Japan's repeated interventions in the foreign currency markets have resulted in a massive influx of dollars into its coffers – a large part of which have been invested in US government debt.

Investors in US government debt typically buy government bonds, which are essentially IOUs that pay a level of interest that is calculated based on

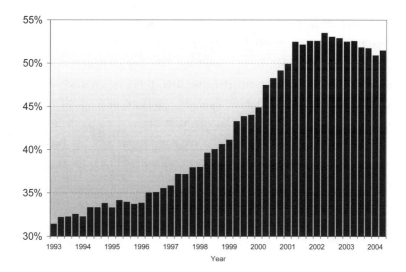

Figure 2.4 Percentage of US total public debt owned by the Fed and government
Source: Financial Management Service, United States Department of the Treasury.

interest rates and perceived risk to the loan. Since the US government is not considered to be a risky bet for lenders (yet), interest rates are keyed to the bond market's view of inflation for various periods. Thus, shorter term bonds tend to carry lower levels of interest because it is more obvious to investors what is going to happen to inflation over a shorter period. Longer dated bonds, i.e. those that will be repaid over several or perhaps many years, tend to carry higher rates of interest because it is not obvious what the rate of inflation will be in 10, 20 or even 30 years. The rate of inflation is important to bond investors because the value of the money they receive when the bond is redeemed (on the date when it has to be paid back) will be affected by the amount that prices have risen during the period they have held the bond. Investors try to look for real returns, which means that the rate of interest paid on the bond should be in excess of the rate of inflation, or the investors would effectively be making a loss on money they lend.

One more thing worth mentioning about the national debt: despite the vast quantity of debt shown in Figure 2.4, this is *only* the US government's debt, and it does not include private sector debt (which we discuss later on).

US government and trade deficit – a country living beyond its means

The United States is the world's largest single economy by far. However, it is also the world's largest borrower and the world's largest consumer of imports. These imports are by no means being matched by its exports.

Just to clarify what we mean by deficits; there are two types of deficit: there is the budget deficit, which is the amount of money the government spends beyond what it earns for a given year, and then there is the trade deficit – the amount of money by which the total value of imports exceeds that of exports for a one-year period. It just so happens that both of these deficits (known, rather charmingly, as the twin deficits) are running at around $600 billion a year each at the moment, which can get confusing. They are very different things, however. For example, a government can run a budget deficit for a given year, but at the same time have a trade surplus (i.e. the value of exports exceed the value of imports).

Figures 2.5 and 2.6 illustrate the US deficits, the first showing the budget spending deficit and the second showing the trade balance.

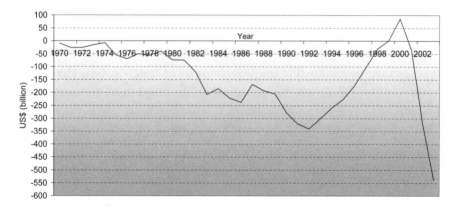

Figure 2.5 US government budget spending
Source: Congressional Budget Office.

The US is only able to sustain huge budget deficits and enormous trade deficits because of foreign capital inflows. These capital inflows are the result of the US dollar's status as the global reserve currency. Every time America spends more than it earns (which it has been doing to the tune of $1.5 to $2 billion dollars *per day*) foreigners end up with surpluses of US dollars. These are then largely channelled back into US government securities, either by institutions or

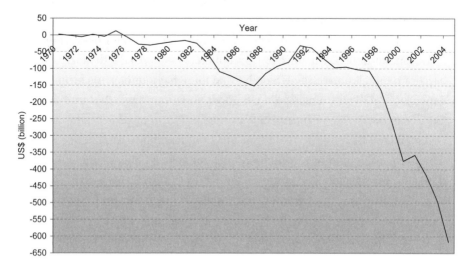

Figure 2.6 The US trade balance
Source: Bureau of Economic Analysis.

central banks. Foreigners continue to do this in the quaint belief that the US dollar will retain value and remain the world's dominant currency. However, there is a substantial possibility that this will change. For instance, Ken Henry, the Secretary of the Treasury in Australia, said in May 2003 that US deficits are:

> 'a substantial risk for international financial stability. If the US is going to remain in substantial deficit for some time and if the net savers of the world are going to continue to fund the US current account deficit, then an economic adjustment of major proportions will have to take place.'

Roughly speaking, for every dollar of goods or services that the US exports, it imports one and a half dollars' worth. The trade deficit in the US amounts to $5 per man, woman and child per day. In 2004, China's trade surplus with the US alone reached $150 billion, which was one reason why China's foreign exchange reserves soared to $610 billion by the end of 2004. The US runs a trade deficit with every major trading bloc on earth, with the biggest deficits, in descending order, occurring with China, the European Union and Japan. This debt has to be financed, ultimately further burdening the US deficits. In November 2004, the US trade deficit crossed the $60 billion mark for the first time. Annualized, that's a trade deficit of $720 billion or 6.5% of GDP – all unhealthy figures for the US economy.

Eventually, the US trade deficit, which represents about one-twentieth of all output in the US, will have to be rectified. This may take the form of such a major depreciation of the US dollar that foreign goods become prohibitively expensive to US consumers, and US goods correspondingly become more attractive to overseas consumers, or may take the form of protectionist barriers being erected by a hostile US administration, leading to a reduction of consumption, or it could be a combination of the two. Neither of these scenarios is positive for the global economy, especially as the US forms such a large part of it. Countries such as Japan and Germany will be reluctant to see too steep a reduction in the value of the US dollar as it will affect their own export industries. China is doing everything it can, despite enormous pressure to the contrary from the US, to keep its currency at its fixed and undervalued level so as to stimulate exports and build up its foreign exchange reserves even further.

Foreign exchange reserves in Asia are now about two-thirds of the global total and by the end of 2004 had crossed the $2 trillion mark.

The US is increasingly at the mercy of China, whose continued support of US assets is vital for the stability of the US economy. If China sells US assets aggressively, the consequences will be dire. It is a sorry situation with no obvious solution.

Private sector debt

It is not surprising that the extremely loose (some would even say reckless) monetary policy of the US has resulted in turning the entire private sector into spendaholics. They are spending like there is no tomorrow but unfortunately there is, and with it comes the debt collector. The private sector is made up of anything non-governmental (the public sector) and can essentially be broken down into three parts: the business sector, the household sector and the financial sector. The combined private sector debt in the US is believed to be around $30 trillion, i.e. it is the total US debt ($37 trillion) minus the public (or national) debt ($7 trillion).

Business sector debt, also known as corporate debt, is the amount that corporations borrow, largely through issuing corporate bonds or through loans arranged with banks or other financial institutions (Figure 2.7). Over the past

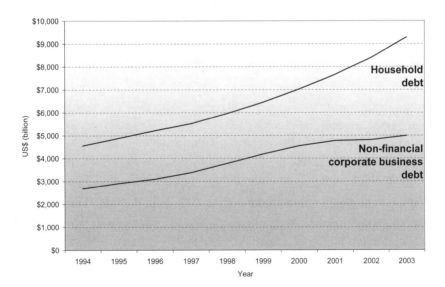

Figure 2.7 Private sector debt in the US
Source: Board of Governors of the Federal Reserve System.

decade, corporate debt has increased by 86%.[6] Household or consumer debt comprises debts accumulated by all of us as individuals. This includes debts such as mortgages, car loans, student loans and credit cards. Over the past decade, household debt has increase by 104%.[7] Let's ask an obvious question before we go on further: doesn't debt at some point need to be repaid?

How or when will the private sector creditors be repaid? No really good answers here we're afraid. Some experts are of the opinion that high levels of debt can simply be eroded through inflation. This may partially address the outstanding debt problem, but it will make it much more difficult to borrow new money as foreigners will no longer find the US dollar attractive if its value is plummeting against all other major currencies.

US business sector debt

Given the picture we have painted so far regarding the US economy, it may come to no surprise to our readers that US business sector debt stands at record levels. Non-financial corporate business debt was around the $7 trillion mark by the end of 2004, i.e. the US corporate sector is roughly as indebted as the US public sector.

The financial sector plays a vital role in economies. Yet in the US, banks are on shaky ground due to their overdependence on consumer debt, in particular mortgages. Mortgage-related assets now make up 28% of American commercial banks' assets.[8] A significant correction in US property prices would spell disaster for many of these banks. With the Fed under pressure to keep raising interest rates, many highly leveraged homeowners may find it difficult to meet those monthly payments.

Swiping up consumer debt

Levels of consumer debt in the West, particularly in the US and the UK, are at insane levels. Unfortunately, the US economy is highly dependent on its consumers, who make up around 70% of GDP. In fact, during the third quarter of 2004, consumer spending accounted for 89% of real GDP! With personal savings at record low levels, this raises further concerns about an economy whose foundation is built on unsustainable debt (Figure 2.8).

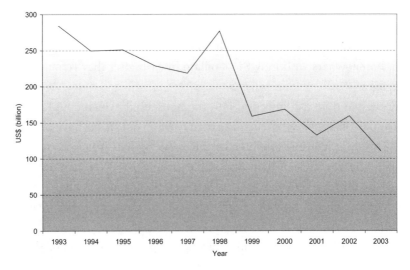

Figure 2.8 Personal savings in the US are in serious decline
Source: Federal Reserve Flow of Funds Accounts of the United States, September 16, 2004.

In Japan, they have the opposite problem: savings rates are high but consumer spending is low, but the past few years have more than shown how American consumers have no problem spending borrowed money. There is no doubt that the US economy will fall on hard times when consumers have exhausted their access to cash and can no longer prolong the spending spree. There are signs that this has already started to happen.

The ease of use of a credit card to buy things, especially on impulse, means that many of us inevitably spend more than if we were paying cash. As a result, a large number of consumers spend more than they earn and maintain a revolving balance on their cards. In fact, 42% of Americans are making just minimum payments or no payments on their credit card balances[9] – again this spells trouble as interest rates rise and the minimum payment amounts increase.

Consumers have also been unlocking cash from their homes under the so-called re-fi market (refinancing market), which is when individuals with mortgages refinance them, either by extending or changing the terms of the mortgage to take advantage of lower interest rates and rising house prices. This re-fi market has been responsible for much of the growth in consumer spending in the US in the past few years and represents a dangerous liability to the US economy. The re-fi market has been huge over the past few years – in 2003, homeowners withdrew $138 billion in cash after they refinanced their mortgages.

Yet despite this cash injection into the household (which could have been used to pay off other debts such as credit cards), Americans have been acting irresponsibly. According to US Federal Reserve figures, American households are spending over 13% of their disposable income to service their debts, which in turn are running at over 100% of their disposable income. Figure 2.9 shows that debt servicing is at record highs – in fact you can see the last peak spiked at around 12.25%, just before the crash of 1987.

Generations and lifetimes will be needed to pay off this level of debt, particularly so in the case of the credit card debt. Despite the Federal Reserve having bank lending rates at near record lows, the interest rates on credit card balances are at usurious levels, typically 18–20%.

The US government has been fanning the flames by encourageing consumers to keep spending, and spend they have – first they enjoyed their tax rebate cheques, then they were encouraged to refinance their homes (taking advantage of low interest rates) for spending cash (although mortgage refinancing

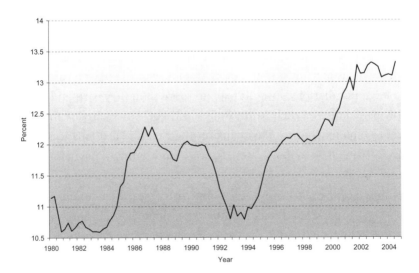

Figure 2.9   The percentage of disposable income used to service debt in the US
Source: US Federal Reserve (seasonally adjusted).

is down some 80% from its peak). It would appear that consumers have exhausted their options for getting their hands on more spending cash.

Even corporations can partly be held responsible for the consumer debt problem; they have been offering consumers very aggressive financing terms on cars and consumer goods – often luring customers in with 0% interest and no money down, which in a deflationary environment means it will be increasingly more difficult to make the monthly repayments!

In fact, it was the introduction of consumer credit and hire-purchase terms that contributed to the 1929 crash and the subsequent Great Depression. An impartial observer would not be able to avoid the uncanny similarities between then and now.

Why are we paying so much attention to the US consumer? Quite simply, in addition to accounting for 70% of the American economy, the US consumer accounts for 21% of the world economy.

In order to put the brakes on the mounting debt, one of two things needs to happen: either interest rates go up or unemployment goes up, or both. This spells trouble for the indebted and indeed the economies of countries that rely on exporting to the US. Even if interest rates remain low, a deflationary environment with uncertainty and rising unemployment will make it increasingly more difficult to service these debts.

Let us leave you with this harrowing statistic: every 19 seconds, someone in the US files for personal bankruptcy.[10]

Sizing it up: super-sized, super-weight consumption machine …

A recent trip to Las Vegas in the United States – world capital of kitsch and public excess – proved an eye-opener to the authors.

Almost everyone on the planet knows that Las Vegas stands for Hedonism with a capital H. It is a city graced by *massive* replicas of 'cities', landmarks and themes from around the world. It has more hotel rooms than any other city on the planet, and most of them are full most of the time. It plays host to over 30 million visitors a year, and its main source of income is gambling, which – along with just about everything else imaginable – is available 24 hours a day, every day of the year.

Vegas is an eighth wonder of the world, a temple to American imperialism and to consumption on a scale unmatched in history. It epitomizes America in many ways, but also evidences the factors that will lead to the United States' eventual relative decline.

An overheard conversation in a fitness centre illustrates a microcosm of just that: three guys from different parts of the United States, never having met before, settled into a discussion about the four things that mattered most to them:

First, as with any society, they talked about their favourite sports teams and how they were doing – not well, as it happened. Second, a discussion about some new SUV (Sports Utility Vehicle – a big super-sized gas-guzzler), now the bestselling type in the United States, and which was their preferred model. Third, how their businesses were doing – well, but with a preoccupation about the level of debt they were carrying. The least leveraged of these three strangers thought of himself as being virtually debt-free because all he had was his 'mortgage and Visa card'. Fourth, one of them explained that he was a private eye, and started talking about the lawyers, clients and other types he dealt with – lots to do with divorce but also a lot to do with debt recovery and the *'deadbeats'* who didn't pay.

This encounter was instructive because it illustrates how consumption is like an addiction. Even though many Americans and other residents of rich nations have more than they need – they still want more. It also illustrates the curious view that it is all right to have a mortgage and a credit card balance because that isn't really debt! A notion that works well when you can meet your monthly payment obligations because you have a job, interest rates are low and house prices are rising. Not such a great idea when unemployment starts to rise further – which it will – and when interest rates rise and credit defaults grow, putting downward pressure on house prices.

Fast food nation

The addiction to fast food is one of the most noticeable features of the past twenty years of rampant consumerism resulting in the increase in size of the average American. Everywhere you go in the United States, you are encouraged to 'super size' – to upgrade to larger portions;

coffee, French fries, soft drinks, etc. For a while the darling of the stock market was Krispy Kreme doughnuts … never bought in quantities of less than half a dozen.

The film Super Size Me *revealed the extent of America's addiction to sugar, burgers and cholesterol-laden foods. One in three American adults is clinically obese (someone whose body fat makes up more than 30% of his body weight); one in four American children is overweight, one in seven is obese – a figure that has doubled in the past twenty years.*

The proliferation of fast food chains, the benign acceptance of being too large for one's size, the decline of sporting pursuits in favour of video games and computers and the overuse of cars are all factors that have contributed to the weight epidemic.

A little known but important contributor to this weight problem in the United States is the intervention of the Federal government: farmers have been encouraged by the government to produce corn, a staple of animal feeds, in order to produce cheap and effectively subsidized food. Since animal feed has become cheap as a result of this thirty-year-old policy, meat prices have fallen by 30 per cent over the same period, encourageing rampant consumption.

Corn is also used to produce fructose corn syrup, widely used particularly in sodas or colas – a leading source of 'empty calories' in the American diet. This has become a weapon of ASS CONSTRUCTION – high fructose corn syrup is not only a huge source of calories, used extensively as a cheap sweetener, but it also has a potentially dangerous chemical effect.

Although other carbohydrates (including sugars) can make you fat over time, high fructose corn syrup makes you fat far more easily. It turns into fat more easily than any other carbohydrate and overrides the mechanism that controls the appetite.

A recent book by Greg Crister, Fat Land – How Americans Became the Fattest People in the World, *talks about how calories have become cheap. Money that was previously spent on raw materials to make food products is now spent on marketing – leading to ever increased consumption.*

In 1970 each American ate about half a pound (0.20 kg) of high fructose corn syrup per annum. By 1997 this figure had risen to 62 lb (28 kg) per person per annum. That represents an additional 228 calories per person per day – and no doubt the figures have increased since then. So in 37 years, the obesity rate among US citizens doubled … and much of the blame goes to the well-intentioned government subsidies to farmers to produce more corn.

China the global player

'Let China sleep, for when she wakes, she will shake the world.'

Napoleon Bonaparte

China is the most populous nation in the world. In addition to that, its economy has been growing faster than that of any other nation over the past decade. China's economy continues to grow annually at near double digit GDP percentage growth. The current consensus is that China will average an annual growth rate of around 8–9% which means that by the year 2020, China's economy will have grown to $10 trillion in today's dollars, making it the size of the current US economy. Our apologies for what may appear to be a series of dry-as-dust statistics – but these are important. Please look at them because they are reshaping the world that we all live in.

China's *trade* has grown exponentially in the past twenty years. From 1993 to 2002, China's exports of goods rose at a compounded rate of 17.3% per annum. By the end of 2004, China's foreign trade topped $1 trillion for the first time. China's biggest trading partners are the EU and Japan, with the US in third place. China's export growth continues at a phenomenal pace and China is set to overtake the US as the world's biggest exporter by the year 2010. Already it is the world's fourth largest exporter after the US, Germany and Japan. China's imports place it sixth in world rankings – but it is about to overtake Japan, Britain and France.

China has a very trade-dependent economy. Although it has lowered barriers to trade by other countries considerably, and continues to do so, it still maintains effective non-monetary barriers which inhibit imports and help to maintain a trade surplus, especially with the United States. But – and this is a big but – China is still turning a blind eye to piracy (a big trade barrier to countries with exports of high intellectual content, such as the US) and it maintains a low currency policy which is vigorously defended. Waffle from China's leaders about buying more US agricultural products and high profile raids on factories producing pirated goods disguise a concerted effort to ignore the less positive aspects of the WTO rules by which China is supposed to play. One key way that China flouts free trade conventions is by effectively subsidizing domestic industries that would otherwise find it hard to compete with foreign competition.

This is consistent with the view of the authors: China is on a mission – to supplant the US as the dominant force in Asia and as a world superpower.

Unique advantage

Make no mistake, China is well on its way to being the world's largest economy.

The reality is that the United States only has a population of 300 million, barely 5% of the world's total, compared to the developing world's population of 5 billion or so – in other words, over 80% of the world's inhabitants. China's population alone accounts for about a quarter of that number, totalling 1.3 billion.

The reason why China will catch up with the West at such a breakneck pace is largely because of:

- its limitless pool of extraordinarily cheap labour; and
- its ability to acquire technology cheaply, which has been dramatically accelerated recently with increased globalization and the advent of the Internet.

The proliferation of the Internet is analogous with Johan Gutenberg's invention of the printing press in the 15th century. It provided a medium for ideas to spread rapidly, allowing processes, knowledge and products to cross oceans and continents. Whereas in former times it often took decades for the superior technological capability of, for example, the British Empire, to be dispersed around the world, today that time frame is shortened by an order of magnitude.

A recent example of this shortened catch-up cycle is South Korea. After the Korean War in the 1950s, South Korea was one of the poorest countries in the world. Yet, today the nation is on the cusp of moving into the ranks of the world's rich nations.

It should be remembered that in the 1600s China was the world's largest economy and it is only in recent centuries, due to mismanagement, civil wars and invasion by others that China has slipped into relative poverty. However, since 1978 when Deng Xiaoping introduced 'The Four Modernizations,' China's economy has grown at a faster rate than any other in history. In this context, it is interesting to note that only in 1993 did China's share of world trade reach its former peak of 1939 – in other words, China has been here before, but this time there is no false start.

Any visitor to Shanghai or Beijing today cannot but be impressed by the enormous glittering skyscrapers that adorn the newly modernized skylines of these huge cities. Likewise, China's rapid accession to near dominance in the production of certain consumer markets is proof that it has the capability of becoming a major player in nearly every field in which it enters.

One anecdotal piece about the new China is the way in which real estate has, for the first time in a century, become the must-have for the rapidly growing ranks of the Chinese affluent. Grand titles are given to new property developments in Beijing and Shanghai, China's most important cities. *The Economist* has reported on 'Château Regalia' described in the brochure as 'an extravaganza for the nobility' – so much for communism! There, a 'Duke' five-bedroom house with swimming pool goes for about $1.5 million! Over-the-top and, frankly, vulgar developments are now so common in the big cities that there is currently a glut of such 'luxury' accommodation.

The Four Modernizations of China[11] – 1978 – the beginning of the modern era for the middle kingdom

After Mao's death in 1976, Deng Xiaoping eventually emerged as the paramount leader in 1978.

Deng launched economic reforms referred to as 'The Four Modernizations' in industry, agriculture, science and defence. These reforms also later became known as 'The Second Revolution' because of the loosening of restrictions in many aspects of Chinese society. Class struggle was no longer the focus as it had been under Mao. Deng set about implementing his reforms in waves. The reforms were implemented at the Third Plenum of the Eleventh National Party Congress in December 1978. The Third Plenum is considered a major turning point in modern Chinese political history.

The essence of the reforms involved the dismantling of collective farming techniques implemented under Mao and encourageing private enterprise.

The first wave of reforms began in 1979 and the new programmes were introduced incrementally. 1979 was also the year that marked the formal exchange of diplomatic recognition between the People's Republic of China and the United States.

China took a pragmatic approach and began to look overseas in search of resources and ideas that could be implemented in China. The changes that occurred as a result of the reforms naturally came up against resistance and created tensions, particularly with those who stood to lose their power and influence. Top party leaders kept a close eye on the reform programmes and discussed them with one another on a regular basis.

In this way policies that originated at the authoritative party level were tested and evaluated in practice and then debated to see whether they required amending or abandoning. Reopening China's doors to the outside world brought in hard cash and valuable technical expertise from the West.

The second wave began in 1984 with the reforming of the urban industrial and commercial economy. The urban programme also developed some aspects of rural industry. These programmes presented considerable challenges for the political system.

The third wave began in 1986 by establishing a base of support in the countryside, where issues and institutions were more clearly defined before moving on to the more diverse and politically complex urban areas. As the reform programme encountered obstacles, party leaders would emphasize the need to extend reform to political structures in order to make the political institutions and processes more supportive of the modernization programme.

The reforms continue today as China works towards lowering its trade barriers and relaxing its protectionist ways following accession to the WTO. But of course, national self-interest predominates and China prefers to ignore rules that are less favourable to it and its economy!

China's economy – still growing fast

China's GDP growth for over two decades has averaged around 10% annually. Between 1995 and 2002, this accounted for 25% of global GDP growth, measured at purchasing power parity, leaving the US in second place with 21%.[12] Some analysts even believe that this GDP growth is understated. A very appealing symmetry appears here – China grows by selling products to the United States and the United States grows because of China's 'savings', i.e. the bits of paper it gets from the US in exchange for its goods go to finance US spending.

The trade concerns with China are certainly valid as the US is the largest importer of Chinese goods. Its trade deficit with China reached $162 billion in 2004 – that's over a quarter of the total US trade deficit, so it is not a trivial number in the context of geopolitics. But that is not to say that China does not import goods – quite the opposite actually – China's demand for foreign goods has been soaring, particularly the desire for Japanese goods (which reached a new record of $74 billion in 2004), and of course for commodities. So despite its massive trade surplus with the US, China sometimes runs a net trade deficit. Already it has built up trade deficits with some of its South East Asian neighbours, such as Malaysia, Thailand and Indonesia. For the year 2004, however, China ran a net trade surplus of $32 billion, with $593.4 billion in exports.

China is showing no signs of slowing down in the long term. The consensus is that this high single digit GDP growth is sustainable for quite some time. Certainly, China's economy may be overheating in the short-term and over-investment appears to be taking root. Investment money is still pouring in, and there is an element of 'China mania' among investors. A slowdown in the United States – indeed a full-on recession which we expect imminently – will impact China's immediate growth prospects. But this downturn, unlike that for the United States, will be of limited duration. China's aspiration to be the world's largest economy – and indeed its dominant political force – is now fully entrenched and its success in this regard is highly likely.

Manufacturing for the world

The principal South East Asian countries lost their competitive edge about ten years ago. The 1990s thus became a decade of transition, in which the world's manufacturing hub relocated from South East Asia (countries such as Malaysia, Singapore and the Philippines) to southern China. Here, labour and land were abundant and cheap. Throughout the 1990s the level of output and sophistication of goods manufactured in China grew at a phenomenal rate; this to the point where China is by far the most attractive location for manufacturing most of the world's consumer goods.

Today China produces the following percentage of the world total output of:[13]

- Cameras: over 50%
- Air conditioners: 30%
- TV sets: 30%
- Washing machines: 25%
- Refrigerators: 20%

So is this unprecedented shift in economic power from one part of the world to another a good thing?

There's no doubt that consumers are the principal beneficiaries of all of this. The US is the largest consumer of these types of product – and thus enjoys competitive pricing that China's ultra-low cost base affords. Everything from Christmas decorations to clothes appear to be so irresistibly cheap that US consumers can't help but fill up their shopping trolleys with them.

The US Labour Department figures show that US shoppers are paying significantly less than they were just a few years ago for their Chinese exports. For example, the average price of TV sets has dropped by 9% annually since 1998; sports equipment by 3% and tools by 1%. Imports of these categories from China rose by more than 13%.

So far, this all sounds like good news for the consumer – lower prices mean more savings. Unfortunately, what most American consumers have only now started to realize is that they are slowly contributing to the closure of their domestic manufacturing facilities, and increasing the prospect of unemployment for themselves and their neighbours. China's vast pool of cheap labour is a major reason for its success. Wages are a fraction of those in the US, averageing about 40 US cents an hour for a factory worker.[14]

Table 2.1 shows indicative hourly wages for a factory worker in some of the big manufacturing countries. As you can see, China's factory wages are orders of magnitude cheaper than their rival manufacturing nations – it's just impossible to compete at those levels!

Table 2.1 Comparative factory wages

Country	Hourly factory wage	Comparative index
United States	$17*	100
Japan	$16.50**	97
Germany	€12*** ($15.60)†	92
United Kingdom	€10*** ($13.00)†	76
China	$0.40	2

* US Department of Labour, Bureau of Labour Statistics
** *Wall Street Journal*, Peter Wonacott, 14 March 2002
*** European Industrial Relations Observatory Online
† Using an exchange rate of €1 = $1.30

At the moment, China has the world market cornered on most household items, but what will it mean for the industrialized nations when China moves into the hi-tech sectors? This has already started to happen with companies like Huawei (telecoms equipment) and Lenovo (personal computers). In addition, the Chinese government continues to promote and encourage the high-tech industry and has invested heavily in scientific research. Even skilled labour is cheap in China: IT engineers cost foreign firms about $15,000 a year each – a good wage given that the national average annual wage is about $1000.

China's overwhelming cost and labour force advantages are not only a threat to the developed Western economies and the more advanced Asian nations, but they are also putting pressure on such countries as Mexico, previously a favourite of US direct investors. In Mexico, the average manufacturing wage is around $1.50 per hour, compared to 40 cents in China. In other words Mexican low cost, predominantly unskilled labour costs six times more than its equivalent in China.

It is not surprising that Mexico's role as a developing nation manufacturer is diminishing. The so-called maquiladora sector in Mexico, which produces one-third of the country's export earnings, is shrinking. These maquiladoras were regarded as low cost assembly points for US manufacturers but are increasingly being undercut by Chinese factories, despite the increased costs of bringing goods from China to the US versus from Mexico to the US. To counter this trend, Mexico has engaged in the old game of protectionism – it has placed anti-dumping levies on Chinese electronic products entering the country in an effort to protect its own industry. This is a blatant, but not unique example of a developing nation which should be right at the forefront of trade liberaliza-tion, acting to try to defend its own uncompetitive industries. Other shrinking sectors in Mexico include shoes, clothing, car parts and tyres. In some cases whole industries are moving lock, stock and barrel to China – with large-scale job losses. So the China phenomenon is not just confined to the hollowing out of developed nation manufacturing – it is destroying large swathes of previously promising industries in other developing nations.

It is also true that China is moving up the value chain in manufacturing – examples of this are only too clear. In June 2003 the International Finance Corporation (IFC), a private sector investment unit of the World Bank, an-nounced that production values of electronics in China are expected to reach

$80 billion by 2005, surpassing those of Western Europe, where output in that sector is forecast to grow to only $73 billion.

For China, progressing towards more sophisticated IT is a logical step in its development. In the longer term this means increasing its market share in some of the more high end and lucrative IT products. Western hi-tech giants are assisting the job migration process and increasingly viewing China as a research lab. For example, Motorola has invested over $3 billion in China, including 19 research and development (R&D) centres and 1600 R&D engineers out of a workforce of 12,000. Many of these jobs were potentially American ones and have been lost to the Far East.

However, there is an upside to this trend: as China moves up the value-added end of the trade spectrum, it will require an increasingly large amount of capital equipment designed to produce technology-related goods. China is using in effect its dominant position in many low value industries to pay for its industrial upgrade to higher end value goods. The means to make such goods generally comes from Western nations and from Japan. So as time goes by, China will buy increasing amounts of hi-tech capital equipment – the machinery that goes into factories and into research labs – and this will tend to reduce the trade deficit between, for instance, China and the United States.

This hi-tech effect disguises the much more important factor of unrivalled competitiveness in manufacturing across the board for the foreseeable future. Other developing countries cannot compete; Western nations and Japan cannot compete – even if, as we expect to happen, there is some realignment of the US dollar against the yuan. China's competitiveness will remain to such an extent that the trend of relocating developed nations' manufacturing facilities to China will continue. This will result in a long period of hardship for the rich nations' manufacturing sector as their labour force adapts to new domestic labour needs. Particularly hard hit in terms of manufacturing (now and in the future) are Japan, Germany and the US. Even poor countries such as Mexico will suffer, as no nation will be able to compete with China's competitiveness in production.

To further assist China in its dominance of the global manufacturing market, the country was admitted to the WTO in late 2001 after 15 years of negotiations. This was a very significant milestone in the global manufacturing economy. China's admission to the WTO will accelerate the development of its industrialization and irreversibly change the shape of the global business landscape. For the West, that spells two things: prolonged deflation from over-supply of products and the death of manufacturing.

China claims that it 'diligently' honours the commitments it has made to the WTO and that only the US makes claims that it does not. Certainly, the US Trade Representative Office criticizes the way that China operates and has accused China of 'deflecting attention from its inadequate implementation of required systemic changes by managing trade in such a way as to temporarily increase affected imports from vocal trading partners such as the United States.'

At purchasing power parity (PPP – a measure which indicates the real spending power of an economy in terms of goods and services and not just in nominal currencies) China's economy was second in size only to the United States, followed by Japan and India. Although in nominal dollar terms China's GDP was only $1.4 trillion versus the United States' $10.9 trillion (2003 figures from the World Bank), the PPP figures provide us with an indication of the real comparative standards of living. In other words, China is not nearly as poor or backward as the usually quoted raw numbers might indicate! As the successful Chinese grow affluent, they will drive the domestic economy further, making it less reliant on trade. At the same time, the vast pool of cheap labour (700–800 million) from the rural areas will continue to head for the big towns where the factory jobs are and where they can earn comparatively better wages.

Batteries in China – made by battery women

Al and Jim's magnificent adventure in China…
To better appreciate China as a global manufacturing machine first hand, Al and Jim decided to take a closer look and arranged to visit a couple of factories there. Here is our tale of one visit to a factory located in Shenzhen, just across the border from Hong Kong, in Guangdong Province.

The plant belonged to GP Batteries, China's largest manufacturer of batteries and supplier to many of the world's leading battery brands. Overall, GP produces batteries in about 20 locations in China with a workforce of about 10,000.

The particular battery factory that we visited one grey morning – and many mornings are grey here because of air pollution – produces around 300,000 rechargeable batteries per day of varying sizes and types.

*This plant – fairly advanced by Chinese standards – was not what we imagined a battery factory to be. For a start, it was evident that the principal input into what is a simple and repetitive production process was **labour** and not capital. This should have probably been self-evident to us, since China's main comparative advantage is its huge labour supply. Nonetheless, it was a shock to see long lines of women (99% of the workforce appeared to be women in their 20s) – assemble batteries in large part by hand. The factory is on several floors, all of which seem to be identical.*

For those readers not familiar with the intricacies of battery production, here's a rough and mercifully brief overview.

Batteries, at least the rechargeable type, are simple things. They are essentially steel tubes sealed at one end, which are stuffed with paper rolls designed to conduct electricity. An alkaline solution is gradually introduced into the tube before it is sealed at the other end, and then put into a rack linked to a charger, which activates the battery. Don't try to make one at home though! It doesn't look like a particularly dangerous profession, except that the alkaline solution is corrosive so presumably could have some long-term health effect. The reason not to try home-made battery production though is of course the simple one – even with retail margins, taxes and shipping costs – there's no way that anyone in the West can compete. And what's more, there's plenty of competition in China itself.

Each batch of batteries is ordered by the company's marketing department and can vary significantly in type and quantity, depending on the end clients' specifications.

Some batteries are made under the GP Batteries brand itself for retail sale, some are shrink-wrapped together in packs that later go into items such as cordless phones, remote controlled toy cars and portable CD players. The company relies on the flexibility of its labour force to 'tool up' for each batch, using machinery only for processes that are common to all batches – and even then the machinery seemed to be fairly antiquated or at least low-ish tech. To be fair though, GP Batteries did inform us that the factory we were going to be visiting was not one of their more sophisticated production facilities.

The factory employs around 1500 workers, almost all of whom are young women who have relocated from other parts of China, many from northerly poverty-stricken provinces. They work five days a week – or six or seven if overtime is required. Production runs for 24 hours a day, split into three eight-hour shifts. The workers are provided with accommodation and three meals a day – on site of course – allowing them to save almost their entire wage *(income tax at that level of earnings is very low). The starting wages are around 500 yuan ($60) per* **month***, that's around 38 US cents an hour. The monthly wage goes up to 1000 yuan per month for more experienced workers. Three weeks' vacation is permitted for each worker, with two weeks typically taken over the Chinese New Year period, when most workers return to their home towns to see their families.*

A worker normally remains at the factory for a few years to save money. And literally that means staying at the factory, since the dorm is right next door to the plant. Once the woman's personal savings target has been reached she usually returns to her home town to settle down and marry – unless she has been lucky enough to meet Mr Right at the battery factory. Of course, those sorts of sparks don't fly very often, since there aren't too many men of any kind in the production process.

Our charming guides on the tour – apart from admitting that the jobs on offer were 'boring' – said that the average battery factory run by competitors was even more labour intensive than in their plant. GP had decided to focus on battery types in which it could be dominant – generally by focusing on niche, but fundamentally declining markets – like the market for 9 volt batteries.

Intense competition is typical of an industry in which Chinese manufacturers compete – they tend to be lower end technology industries with high labour content in the production process and have little regard for intellectual property rights. This means that as soon as Mr Wong is up and running with his factory making ABC widgets, Mr Lee is making them too next door, meaning that margins for both of them tend to be wafer thin. GP is a case in point: it makes about a 3–4% return on capital employed in its business – a reflection of the intensely competitive nature of production in China. In fact, dear reader, if any of you want anything assembled, there are thousands of plants in China that will produce just about anything. In effect, their business is production and the product, raw materials and ideas are provided by someone else.

Several weeks later, Al went to see another factory in China – Fook Tin Group Holdings, an electronic products manufacturer specializing in weighing devices such as electronic bathroom and kitchen scales. Although Fook Tin's production is located in Shenzhen, China, its headquarters are in Hong Kong.

In 2003, Fook Tin received a number of Hong Kong awards including the Productivity Grand Award, the Environmental Performance Grand Award and the Quality Certificate of Merit. Fook Tin has also attained ISO 9001 and ISO 14001 status (worldwide recognized standards for quality and environmental management respectively). This demonstrates that just because China has cheap and abundant labour, it does not mean that the quality of the production and the products themselves are in any way substandard. Furthermore, Fook Tin strives to adopt the latest environmental standards, recycling where possible, optimizing energy consumption and reducing chemical by-products. Due to a higher level of automation, Fook Tin employs 150 workers in a factory that is approximately 55,000 square metres (500,000 square feet). Fook Tin's facility is vertically integrated to a large extent, i.e. it designs its own products, manufactures almost all of its components at the factory from raw materials (thermoplastics, rolled steel, cartons, etc.), assembles them to make the product, tests them and packs them for the container truck pick-up. It even produces its own die-casts for its product lines on site.

Given the somewhat erratic nature of the local power supply, Fook Tin has even installed its own generator which can provide sufficient power to keep the entire facility running.

Maybe next time you see a 'Made in China' stamp on something you purchased (which will be very soon no doubt), you can better appreciate the 1.3 billion labour pool working behind the scenes to produce goods for the entire world!

*The next step for China Inc. of course is to move away from just being a production sweatshop to **owning** intellectual properties associated with some of the goods they produce. They aspire to **own** brands and to achieve for themselves some of the juicy margins enjoyed by Western middlemen associated with bringing China's goods to Western markets.*

In fact, Fook Tin is well on the way in this regard. For example, it was the first company in the world to design and produce electronic bathroom scales that measure a person's body fat (this is done by passing a small electric current through the body and measuring its resistance with electrodes located on the top surface of the scales). It was also the world's first company to produce bathroom scales made of glass. Fook Tin already owns some of the leading brand names in scales in Europe (Terraillon in France and Hanson in the UK) and sells to 500 clients in 80 countries under many other brand names.

China and the currency debate

China has come under increasing pressure, from the United States in particular, to revalue its currency – the yuan – against the US dollar. China's response to this pressure has been that it is an 'internal matter' and that no other country has the right to interfere. Its official view regarding the yuan is that it will not be liberalized until the distant future and that there is no formal timetable for when this will occur. China maintains tight control over the value of the yuan by only allowing it to be exchanged for goods and services in the external sector. Exchanges for financial or real estate investments abroad are generally not allowed. The result is that for more than a decade China has been able to keep its currency pegged to the US dollar at a rate of 8.28 yuan with little deviation.

However, on 21 July 2005, China announced that it was abandoning the 11 year old peg to the US dollar of the yuan and adopting a more flexible peg linked to a basket of currencies. At the same time, it also declared that the yuan's exchange rate to the US dollar will be changed to 8.11 (a 2.1% increase).

So did China cave in to external pressure? Not at all. This move was little more than a token gesture to appease US politicians. The yuan is still widely seen as highly undervalued by many in the US and in Europe. This has led to what some perceive as an 'unfair' trade advantage for China because the 'weakness' of the currency allows Chinese goods to be correspondingly cheap in export markets.

Any further moves in the yuan will likely be small in the shorter term. It suits China's purposes very well to have a weak yuan. Government policy allows exports to continue to grow at a spectacular pace, leading to continued strong overall GDP growth and to the build-up of foreign exchange reserves (over $700 billion by mid 2005), which China, with its mercantilist approach to economics, regards as a sign of national virility. Indeed, it has been argued that the yuan's apparent weakness is one that is dollar-specific – and, in a way, that is true. China runs a trade deficit of some magnitude with other Asian nations, notably Japan and Korea, from whom it imports large amounts of capital equipment.

Since US trade is only about 10% of overall US GNP and China's proportion of that is only about one-tenth, it would take a massive upward revaluation of the yuan to have any effect on the US current account deficit. Such a revaluation is unlikely to occur any time soon and even if it did, it would at best have a palliative effect on the chronic US trade imbalance. Deficits of $2 billion a day, equivalent to about 6% of the total output of the US economy every year, represent much more than inappropriate currency levels. Moves in mid 2005 to revalue the yuan will prove to be too little and have a small effect on the scale of the US/China trade imbalances.

China's token gesture buys it more time. After all, it suits China to make its currency a little more expensive to slow its own overheating economy. It also suits it politically, to alleviate trade pressure from the US.

Japan – a long deflation and decline

In the late 1980s and early 1990s, news-stands and bookshop shelves groaned under the weight of publications celebrating Japan's economic success. The 'Japanese Way' of business became an icon, something every other economy should follow. Japan's economic management was a role model for economies around the world and people flocked to Tokyo to learn about this miraculous system.

Since then, of course, it has been a slow and slippery slope for Japan, which is now widely regarded as a basket case – a victim of a rigid, outmoded economic system and the modern world's first casualty of deflation. Today, images of Japan are more than likely to be of the type seen in the movie *Lost in Translation*, depicting Japan as a quirky, somewhat irrelevant place full of oddball behaviour. The icon of the modern business age is once again the US Corporation, striding atop all others, the colossus of the global economy. Minor matters, like the swathes of scandals which have enveloped the US corporate scene, the weighty burden of debt which the US corporate sector carries and the impinging competitive threat from overseas, are brushed aside.

American, not Japanese companies are considered to be the best in the world. Of course, there is a middle ground which best explains the truth. Japan's corporate sector is beginning to embrace the more positive aspects of free markets, and American companies are not as good as many think. Japan remains the world's second largest economy, with huge foreign exchange reserves and substantial overseas investments. It is also a leader in worker productivity in the manufacturing sector and for the first time in over a decade its economy is showing some signs of growth.

The US, on the other hand, has substantial macroeconomic and structural problems which we discuss in detail. It is not, however, the country described by Michael Moore and his ilk, who would have readers believe that the US is a country with a rich plutocracy and a huge underclass of trailer park living, welfare dependent, medically uninsured no-hopers. But what has happened to Japan in the past fifteen years – from oh-so-confident, swaggering economic miracle to deflation ridden, uncertain tortoise – is a possibility for the United States. Although most commentators believe that the US can avoid the pitfalls of the Japanese experience, the parallels are in fact ominous. Japan's prices have been falling (deflation) because consumers have preferred saving to spending and this is continuing despite recent revivals in economic growth in the country. This preference for saving leads to brutal price competition for the diminished business that there is left. In turn, this is made worse by the failure of the Japanese to promptly tackle serious problems in their banking system, largely the result of wildly optimistic and uncontrolled lending in the 'boom' years of the 1980s. This was particularly rampant in the real estate sector. It is truly amazing to think that at one stage the value of the land around the Imperial Palace in Tokyo was calculated to be worth more than the real estate value of the whole of the State of California!

Of course, this bubble had to burst, with the effect that land prices in Japan have fallen by as much as 65% since 1990,[15] which was also the year in which the stock market peaked (on 29 December 1989, the Nikkei 225 Index closed at 38,916). Since then, the stock market has been in almost continuous decline (see Figure 2.10).

As the bubble deflated, people began to worry about losing their jobs and in turn started saving even more aggressively. Companies also stopped spending so heavily on capital investment, faced as they were with huge debts and

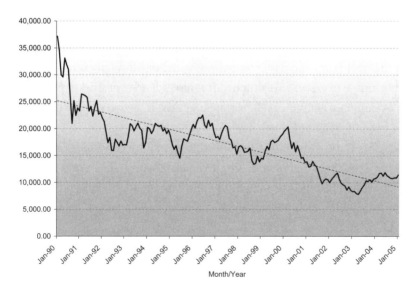

Figure 2.10 The decline of the Nikkei Index since 1990
Source: Yahoo! Finance.

overcapacity. They too were in effect 'saving' by trying to reduce debts. On the other hand, the Japanese government printed more and more money and spent massively on public works projects, including roads to nowhere, rarely used bridges and increased military expenditure. This has fundamentally not worked, and despite enormous government debt, interest rates are set at close to zero. Households have been desperately trying to find a safe haven for their extremely large savings, which they continue to accumulate. People either fear losing their jobs or recognize that, as Japan's population ages, there will be less and less workers to take care of an ever increasing number of dependants.

The situation in Japan remains dire, and notwithstanding huge inflationary efforts by the Japanese authorities, little progress is being made. It is interesting to note that despite recent growth in the Japanese economy – the first for nearly a decade – deflation still persists. This is because the growth has in large part come from the export sector and not from consumption. Furthermore, the great industries that propelled Japan from ruin after World War II, and enabled it to become the world's second largest economy, are under severe threat from low cost labour countries. Textiles, steel, cars, electronics and chemicals are among the industries now under threat.

Japan had been an isolated and feudal society for nearly three centuries until the so-called 'black ships' of US Commodore Matthew Perry arrived in 1853. Its great success since being opened up has led ultimately to where it is now – the world's largest creditor nation, i.e. it is owed more money than any other nation on earth.

Its purchases of US financial and other assets in particular are in large part responsible for plugging America's colossal trade deficit. Its investment in capital and factories in South East Asia and China have been vital to that region's growth. However, all of that is under threat because of Japan's inability to change its 'old' ways. Entrepreneurship in Japan remains constrained by the power of the big industrial conglomerates and by an education system that tends to discourage individual thought – although there is some evidence that this 'learning by rote' is changing.

While the US, as the world's largest economy, does not suffer from a lack of entrepreneurship and flexibility, there are some close parallels in key areas between it and Japan:

1 The US went through a huge 'bubble' in the Internet/technology era of the late 1990s, which has resulted in massive overcapacity and substantial corporate debts.

2 The US government is highly indebted, as is Japan's, putting limits on its ability to counter recessionary trends with further fiscal expansion.

3 Confidence in the US economy is gradually waning as consumers become more nervous. This will lead to an increase in savings, which are currently at a pitiful level in the US – and a commensurate decline in consumption. This represents the beginnings of the deflationary spiral that has proved so difficult for Japan to break out of.

4 The US also has an ageing population (although to a lesser extent than Japan) and no obvious way to support a deteriorating ratio of workers to dependants.

5 US banks and other financial institutions will have increasingly strained balance sheets as the US economy worsens.

It is interesting to observe that the economic 'recovery' which began in 2003 in the US has essentially been a jobless one – very few new jobs are being created because companies are still scared to invest – and of course there is also the 'off-shoring' phenomenon.

Off-shoring is where low value added jobs – such as call centre positions – are moved overseas to benefit from lower wage costs (in countries such as India), as well as improved global communications. There's nothing wrong in this, but as US manufacturing jobs go, where are all the service sector positions going to come from if many of them are being successfully 'off-shored' too?

None of these factors bode well for the medium-term outlook in the world's largest economy. Business magazines which today tout the benefits of the 'American Way' of doing business may be as wrong about that as they were about Japan in the late 1980s! Indeed, falls in the relative value of the US dollar has meant that if the UK and Sweden are included, the euro economies are in total about the same size as that of the United States. But Europe has its own problems, as we will see below.

Eurosclerosis – the trouble with the old world

Origins of the European Union

Before getting to the bottom line of these problems, i.e. why the rigidities of the single currency are causing and will continue to cause considerable trouble for Europe, it is best to provide a brief description of how and why the European Union evolved and how the single currency came into play.

The European Union developed out of an organization named the European Coal and Steel Community (ECSC) that was set up in 1952 by France, Germany, Belgium, Italy, Luxembourg and the Netherlands. This was designed to reduce tariffs on coal and steel products as well as to more closely integrate the formerly warring parties. In 1957 the ECSC evolved into the European Economic Community (EEC) and this became a true free-trade zone, including concessions to manufacturers and producers of agricultural products.

The EEC, subsequently renamed the European Union (EU), was joined by the UK, Denmark and Ireland in 1973 and by Greece in 1981. Portugal and Spain became members in 1986 and Austria, Finland and Sweden in 1995. A further ten countries, mostly from emerging Eastern Europe, joined the Union in May 2004. These were Poland, the Czech Republic, Slovakia, Hungary, Slovenia, Malta, Latvia, Lithuania, Estonia, and Cyprus. Bulgaria and Romania may join in 2007, as may Croatia. Turkey has also applied but no date is in prospect.

In 1987 the Single European Act moved the EU to a closer harmonization not just in terms of trade but also in respect of the freedom of movement of labour, services and capital. The EU thus has free trade in goods and services between its member states and a common external tariff and quota system for trading with the rest of the world.

The EU is governed by the European Commission, which administers its affairs and also establishes policy guidelines and initiatives. These proposals are put to the European Parliament, which may then amend them and pass them back for ratification by the Council of Ministers. The latter group makes the major decisions in the EU. It consists of one member from each state. The member is chosen according to the type of decision to be taken. For instance, if the decision to be taken is a financial one, then usually the Finance Minister or equivalent will represent his or her country. For the Commission, the representation of countries is population weighted – two members for each large country and one for each of the smaller ones.

The euro – the single currency now the source of some considerable strain in the Union – evolved out of the European Currency Unit (ECU). The ECU was used as a form of international money by several members of the EU prior to the introduction of the euro in an early non-retail form in 1999. The ECU was a weighted average of several European currencies, including the Deutschmark and the French Franc. Although the euro was introduced in shadow form in 1999 it wasn't until June 2002 that it became the currency used in all transactions in 12 members of the EU. These were Austria, Belgium, Finland, France, Germany, Greece, Luxembourg, Ireland, Italy, the Netherlands, Portugal and Spain.

Initially launched at a rate of $1= €1.18, the currency has swung wildly since its inception. It reached a low of around 83 cents to the dollar in 2000 but since then, in line with the dollar's gradual depreciation, has recovered to levels higher than its launch price and is now becoming an alternative reserve currency of choice. This rise of the euro has had more to do with the US dollar's structural weakness than with any inherent strength in euro-land: indeed, the stronger the euro, the more difficult it is for the Eurozone to export its way out of stagnation.

The euro's launch in November 1998 was accompanied by a so-called Stability Pact, which called for penalties for any member of the Eurozone running fiscal deficits of more than 3% per annum. These levels were pegged in the Maastricht Treaty, which formed the basis of the single currency and was designed to bring all the Eurozone members into economic line.

By 2003 the whole Eurozone had breached the 3% limit, in effect making a mockery of the pact. In the cases of France and Germany, the deficits were much higher. This failure to comply with what in effect were their own diktats reflects the deep-rooted problems in their economies, which cause deficits to mount rapidly in times of recession.

Despite attempts at structural reform, for instance pensions in France and shop opening hours in Germany, both these economies remain outmoded and ill-suited to the financial straitjacket that is the Stability Pact. The result is that the Eurozone growth for 2004 was only 2%, and the forecast for 2005 is more of the same – the sluggish economies of Germany, France and Italy are weighing down the average Eurozone percentage growth.

The addition of ten countries which joined the EU in May 2004 has rendered consensus decision-making even more difficult and unlikely. The ten new members of the club came with some considerable baggage, particularly Poland, which is the largest by far of the ten in terms of population.

Poland's agriculture is considered to be far behind the standards required for the EU, and its healthcare services are lamentable. All ten of the new entrants went into the negotiations to join the EU some years ago in high spirits and with optimism that a Spanish-style or Irish-style economic miracle would be wrought on them. This would be one where EU subsidies and access to EU markets would allow them to raise their living standards, still far below the EU average, quickly and with little pain. They were wrong to be so optimistic.

The larger nations of the EU, and in particular Germany and France, are no longer so generous in their inclinations. Additionally, with the exception of Ireland, all the members of the 'club' have introduced entry and work restrictions on the citizens from the new entrant countries. Attempts to change the way that the EU votes take place, where decisions will require less consensus, have stalled. It is a fairly obvious conclusion: expand a small cosy club from 15 to 25 members – especially when the new members have on average about one-quarter of the incomes per head of the existing membership – and you are bound to end up with friction and a sluggish decision-making process.

The problems of the members of the Eurozone are multiple, but the most important one that relates to the full adoption of the single currency in June 2002 is as follows: the great bond market rallies of 2002 and early 2003 are being deflated by the two major Eurozone economies. Certainly, the growth rate of the new entrants has been and will continue to be much faster than the Eurozone average. The same applies to the relative growth rates of the other hopefuls queuing up to join the European Union – including Croatia, Bulgaria, Albania, Bosnia, Macedonia, Serbia, and of course Turkey. But these fast relative growth rates have more to do with the low bases from which these countries come than from the generosity of the existing club members. Indeed, the Economist Intelligence Unit has calculated that even if new and prospective members double the compound growth rates of the existing membership, they will take up to 50 years to catch up with their richer cousins. In the case of Romania it could take 80 years!

The larger nations of the EU, and in particular Germany and France, are no longer as generous in their tendency to hand over large sums of money to the new entrants as they have been in the past. In addition, attempts at changing the voting system, where decisions would require less consensus, have failed. So, little clubs within the club are being formed. Rules are being flouted and bitchiness over who gets what from the European Union budget is reaching new levels. The original concept of 'creating a level playing field' for the countries of Europe to enable mutual prosperity and to put a halt to the perennial disputes that have wracked the continent for so long is a theory that's proving difficult to put into practice.

Meanwhile, the Eurozone, the area formed by countries which have adopted the euro currency, is in deep trouble. This trouble extends to other European nations also, but not to the same extent. Members of the European Union outside the Eurozone, most important of which is the United Kingdom, have their own difficulties but have not been as constrained by the strictures of a 'one size fits all' monetary policy. The European Central Bank has indeed been labelled as a 'central bank in need of a country' and that isn't a bad description. The problems of the members of the Eurozone are multiple, but the most important is the one that relates to the full adoption of the single currency in June 2002 – where the same rules and constraints are imposed on a spectrum of countries.

France and Germany suffer from what might be best described as 'Japanitis', i.e. they are both stuck with economic models which have outlived their usefulness in a different economic world. These models, broadly expressed as socially inclusive capitalism, have left both countries with slow growing/stagnant economies, massive pension liabilities, awkward demographics (see section on ageing population) and unresponsive labour markets, not to mention large central government indebtedness and perennial deficit problems. Not a pretty picture and a situation for which an easy fix does not exist, especially as the euro currency is the one taking the brunt of the fallout from the US dollar's inevitable further depreciation. This has highly negative consequences for the Eurozone's growth potential.

The European economic 'model' is essentially an interventionist one – leading to high social charges, labour rates and, ultimately, unemployment.

Control-freakery is at the core of the EU – a drive against 'unfair competition' is, in practice, an embodiment of the 'tall poppy' syndrome – chop down any poppies that don't match the height of others. Anywhere with lower wages, lower taxes, or longer hours of employment is 'unfair' and needs to be brought into line. Britain's unique success among the large economies of Europe has been due to a general resistance to the constraints of this 'regulation by jealousy', but intervention is beginning to consume even the UK. Its fate too could be one of low growth and of the 'twitching curtains' of its inquisitive neighbours – hell-bent on making sure that nobody succeeds if they don't!!

The constraints that the Stability Pact have imposed on the Eurozone countries are onerous and leading to severe imbalances. Germany and France are the principal victims of this problem, and they are of course also the main architects and champions of the single currency. Both countries went into the brave new world of a single currency with high hopes. But both were already saddled with huge and expensive welfare states as well as infamously rigid labour markets. This meant that as their economies weakened in the face of prolonged recession, they were hit by a rising welfare burden as more and more people went out of work, which was the result of companies going bust because of their inability to rapidly reduce workforces in the first place!

The German example is perhaps a good one for students of what went wrong in euro-land. Since we are British authors (and of a certain age,) we remember very well the glory days of what was West Germany in the 1970s and 1980s. In our youth, West Germany operated the most successful post-war economy. It grew consistently and was the pinnacle of technical prowess. The autobahns were filled with shiny new cars, German machinery hummed around the world and German workers in their blue and orange dungarees ate bratwursts and drank steins, laden with good beer, safe in the knowledge that theirs was a real *wirtschaftswunder* (an economic miracle). Inflation was near zero, the Deutschmark was one of the world's strongest currencies, and the Bundesbank (West Germanys Central Bank) was highly regarded. Then it all went horribly wrong … and badly so.

Today, Gerhard Schroeder, the German Chancellor, is charged with imposing reform on a country burdened by sclerotic labour and retail practices. The state's pension liabilities are potentially enormous and the welfare state has grown too big for the diminishing numbers of economic providers. To top it all, the country has had to absorb the huge burden of assimilating the Eastern part after the Berlin wall crumbled in 1989. Schroeder's plan, Agenda 2010, is aimed at deregulating labour markets and at reducing the welfare burden – both factors which have contributed to Germany's recent stagnation, no growth for three years and barely 1% a year for the past decade.

Germany has become a nation literally enmeshed in red tape: this tape is a bit like furled up wire for stereos or PCs – it is difficult and frustrating to unravel and simply trying to pull it apart makes it worse! The good news is that even the Germans are fed up with this red tape and are trying to do something about it. The bad news is that it is going to be a long time before they accomplish the simplification of their form-filling and rubber-stamping society. It is amazing to note that in 2003 output per worker in the United Kingdom surpassed that of Germany for the first time in 50 years! Britain's GDP per capita is much higher today than that of Germany – and it's all down to economic policy.

Germany's federal system of government also makes matters more complicated: several layers of government often end up effectively competing with each other. The states or 'Lander' are often at odds with the wishes of the Bundestag (national Parliament), with the state's interests being represented by the upper chamber, the Bundesrat. Even the word used to describe the joint decision-making process *Politikverflechtungsfalle* is indicative of the cumbersome nature of German government.

The sixteen 'Lander' are involved in an almost continual cycle of elections. Control of the Bundesrat often makes decision making even more difficult. The 'Basic Law' of Germany also makes things hard in that it requires a uniformity of living standards throughout the country and thereby forces complex revenue sharing between rich and poor 'Lander'. A commission is currently engaged in trying to untangle some of this mess, but in the view of most commentators it has little chance of major concrete success, simply because there are so many and competing vested interests at work. Just writing about this complex morass of governmental layers gives us a headache, so we apologize if we did the same to you, dear reader.

At a micro level, this bureaucratic ensnaring of entrepreneurship is just as bad. It takes, for instance, 45 days to register a new business in Germany, compared to 18 days in Britain and only 4 days in the United States. No wonder productivity growth in the Eurozone, with Germany at its head, has only been a mere 1% or so a year over the past 25 years.

While Britain has undoubtedly suffered from decades of inadequate infrastructure investment (contrast its railways and hospitals, for instance, to those of Germany and France), its relatively open economy, prised open by Margaret Thatcher in the 1980s, has led to strong relative economic performance. British incomes are now ahead of those of every major European nation and British unemployment levels are less than half of the European Union average.

Germany's tentative steps towards reform may be too late, just as Japan's relatively feeble effort to reform its bureaucratic and rigid economy in the 1990s was insufficient. In addition, Germany, above all other European nations, has had to shoulder the burden of the integration of poorer nations into the European Union. Countries such as Spain, Portugal and Ireland have benefited mightily from 'transfers', which have in large part emanated from Germany.

As we mentioned earlier, in May 2004 a further ten nations joined the EU. While the benefits of membership for these countries are not as obvious as they were for the wave of poorer entrants in the 1980s and 1990s, they will probably put a further yet less visible burden on Germany. This is because wage costs in these countries are much lower than in Germany, which remains the most industrialized of the major European nations and thus the most vulnerable to 'wage competition' from places such as Poland and the Czech Republic. The German rate of unemployment, which was stuck at around 10% for some time, has started to creep up further as a result of job relocations to cheaper countries. In the first quarter of 2004, Germany's unemployment rate had reached 12.6% (of the working age population). This is the highest in Europe and the highest in Germany since the 1930s.

Germany and France are not alone in their sclerotic states. Italy, for instance, is struggling with pensions that already absorb over one-eighth of national income. And that is before the ageing of the population and its dire effects seriously kick in. Italians retire at ridiculously young ages; it is possible to retire on a full pension today at 57! Indeed, some 62% of Italian adults retire by the age of 55.

Proposals in Italy to increase the minimum age for retirement to a reasonable 65 for men and 60 for women have been met with serious resistance.

Reform of the pension system is a major impediment to growth in Italy, which suffers from a grave demographic problem.

Another example of this deteriorating dependency ratio is to be found in Germany: the elderly there are costing the country 15% of its GDP – and that's around a third of all government spending.[16]

Indeed, all of these major countries of the Eurozone have extremely adverse demographic profiles. By the year 2050 Germany's population is expected to drop by 4% and its trend rate of economic growth to 1.5% per annum – the lowest in Europe. By 2050 Germany will have only 79 million people, down from 82 million currently. As its population drops, so will the ratio of workers to dependants. Similarly, the average age in France, Italy and Spain (the other large members of the Eurozone) is also rising.

Economic growth is a function of two factors: labour and productivity. While productivity may rise in the EU, it cannot compensate for the paucity of workers. When 50% of Finns, as an example, retire by the age of 55 but live on average for well over 20 years more – something has to give.

By contrast, China is generally unburdened with pension liabilities – they just don't pay them as it is not a legal requirement for an employer; 80% of workers in China have no formal pension and must rely on their own savings. This is another factor helping Chinese firms to compete!

*part*THREE

Geopolitics

US foreign policy

Shortly after the September 11 2001 attacks, the US declared war on 'terrorism' – a suitably ambiguous declaration for a threat from a new type of enemy. The first overseas military operation following this declaration was in Afghanistan. After a relatively short period of combat, the US declared victory, having successfully ousted the incumbent oppressive Taliban regime. Unfortunately, despite exhaustive efforts, public enemy number one, Osama bin Laden, proved too elusive to capture. Undeterred by this, a new 'project' to disarm Iraq's Saddam Hussein became the focus of US foreign policy. Initially, this created some confusion for the American people until the Bush administration assured Americans that this man posed a serious threat to their safety and proceeded to build a case around this point. Sadly, the hunt for weapons of mass destruction (WMD) in Iraq (a key point in George W. Bush's argument) has been unsuccessful. In January 2005, US intelligence officials finally admitted that they had given up searching for WMD in Iraq, making it one of the largest intelligence blunders of all time.

Today, the America's war on terrorism is suffering from a 'branding' issue: is America really fighting a global war on terrorism? No, it is fighting a war against al-Qaeda (and Iraq – but that wasn't al-Qaeda motivated, as we will discuss later). The US has no interest in fighting terrorist groups such as the Tamil Tigers in Sri Lanka, the IRA in Ireland, the Basque separatists in Spain/Southern France and the Chechens in Chechnya, to name but a few. Therefore it needs to send a clearer message to the American people and to its allies across the world what its war is about. Failure to do so will deepen the already widening rift between the US, the EU and the Muslim world, as even many Americans cannot clearly distinguish between the war on terrorism and a war on Islam, leaving the United States' Muslim population confused and caught in the crossfire.

Yet, despite repeated denials that the war on terrorism is not a war between Christians and Muslims, President Bush is very much a Christian and reads the Bible daily. Many of his senior staff are Christians and the people of the United States (over three-quarters of whom are Christian) have voted for Mr Bush twice, supporting the Christian values that he upholds when making decisions as president. At the outset of the war on terrorism, President Bush actually used the word 'crusade' in one of his speeches – a word with very religious connotations used by Christians to recapture the 'Holy Land' from the Muslims by means of a 'Holy War'. It would seem therefore that, under the Bush administration, the US has blurred the line between Church and State.

The only non-Muslim nation under the watchful eye of America is North Korea. Under the Axis of Evil, North Korea is accompanied by Iran and Iraq. Both North Korea and Iran claim to have nuclear programmes, and the US is treading carefully as it engages in dialogue with each of them. The success in peacefully disarming Libya from WMD has inspired the US to try this approach with the remaining two evil axis nations. Unfortunately, the signs are not looking good so far.

With hundreds of thousands of troops still on the ground and billions of dollars spent in the 'post-war' efforts in Afghanistan and Iraq, the last thing the US needs is another war. It is therefore not surprising that both North Korea and Iran are resistant and suspicious of discussing nuclear weapons with the US.

Amir Mohebian, an Iranian politician and adviser to Iran's supreme leader Ayatollah Ali Khamenei,[1] summed up rather succinctly the perceived double standards concerning nuclear weapons back in March 2003.

> 'The Americans say, in order to preserve the peace for my children, I should have nuclear weapons – and you shouldn't have them.'

Pax Americana

The effectively unilateral war in Iraq against Saddam Hussein and his regime followed as a result of the failure of United Nations' weapons inspectors to locate Iraq's WMD. This event will also be viewed in the future as a significant milestone in how the course was set for the global economy in the 21st century.

From an economic point of view, the war itself was less significant than the rifts that were created between the United Nations, Europe (including Russia) and the United States. Even though the US budget for keeping the peace in Iraq and Afghanistan are now having a perceptible negative effect on US government finances, it is these rifts that will have longer term consequences on the global economy.

The Bush administration's decision to go to war on Iraq without the approval of the UN was a defining moment for the world body. It demonstrated to the world that the US considers the UN a nuisance to be ignored if it cannot be manipulated.

The French threat to veto the UN resolution to go to war resulted in the US government effectively acting unilaterally under a token coalition force that included Britain and Spain. The French were heavily criticized for their proposed veto by the US government as, historically, the United States has come to France's aid in times of need. (Actually, the French did come to America's rescue during the War of Independence from British rule, but that was kept out of the news media when French-bashing became *de rigueur*.)

However, the French were in fact playing bigger picture politics – they were trying to discourage the US government from future actions that might pose a more direct threat to their own national security. They were also taking the bullet for the other members of the Security Council who had reservations about wageing war on Iraq, such as Germany and Russia, but were caught in a diplomatic triangle and didn't want to upset their relations with the US. It appears that this power play was what the UN Security Council standoff over Iraq was all about and not so much about toppling Saddam Hussein from power.

The US government and many Americans resented the French for being obstructive, and anti-French sentiment ran high for a while: some Americans boycotted French products such as luxury goods and wines and American tourist numbers to France were significantly down in 2003. In Washington DC, three restaurants in Congressional buildings renamed French fries 'freedom' fries and French toast became 'freedom' toast. The irony in all this of course is that the US is constantly espousing the virtues of democracy under which its people live, but when France chose to exercise its democratic right to disagree with the idea of invading Iraq, the US government began to, rather undemocratically, embark on a spree of French-bashing.

In the end, of course, the US government's new pre-emptive stance meant that it didn't bother to go through the UN Security Council to invade Iraq. The following excerpt is taken from a speech President George W. Bush gave in June 2002 at West Point, a United States military academy:

> 'Our security will require transforming the military you will lead – a military that must be ready to strike at a moment's notice in any dark corner of the world. And our security will require all Americans to be forward-looking and resolute, to be ready for pre-emptive action when necessary to defend our liberty and to defend our lives.'

It is the reference to pre-emptive action that caused quite a stir among many observers. This doctrine was repeated in several subsequent speeches in 2002 and 2003. Such a strategic global view means that the US government believes it can strike against any nation, government, group or individual based on its administration's perception of a threat to its liberty. Many observers of world politics are naturally worried that this renders the UN, the EU and NATO irrelevant.

So the question has to be asked: has US foreign policy gone too far? Is the Pax Americana, the benevolent policing of the world of the past forty years been replaced by 'Brutus Americanus', the swaggering playground bully? Critics have described this strategy as arrogant and dangerous, while the Bush administration sees it as an overdue assertion of the United States's mission of global leadership.

There are of course analysts who argue that it merely makes explicit what the US has already been practising for years, and that the Pax Americana has been a misnomer for a more aggressive foreign policy. Whatever the reality, it is certainly the case that under the new Bush doctrine, the pre-emptive war on Iraq was justified. This stands in contrast to an earlier view of US policy expounded in the 1950s by the then administration:

> 'Our free society, confronted by a threat to its basic values, naturally will take such action, including the use of military force, as may be required to protect those values … [Military measures should not be] as excessive or misdirected as to make us enemies of the people …'

Truman administration, 1950.

The Bush administration has a very black and white view of what is right and what is wrong, a worry in a world that in reality is made up of many shades of grey. It expects its allies to see things the same way, or at least give the impression that they do. Meanwhile, the rest of the world looks on in bewilderment at the unprecedented flexing of US muscle across the world.

Nations such as France, Germany and Russia are joining forces in an effort to balance the might of the world's unchallenged superpower. Also joining this emerging alliance is China. This alliance is likely to grow in strength, its objective being to contain US unilateralism. It is an alliance of convenience at the moment for the Chinese who, while by no means anxious to upset the US, remain in 'developing mode' and regard a brake on US imperialism as being beneficial.

A lesson the world is starting to learn, which was not immediately evident at the time of the collapse of the USSR and the subsequent end of the Cold War, is that an uncontested world superpower tends to stimulate conflict in the world, not peace. For relatively recent cases of this, see the sections on the World War I and World War II. These are excellent examples of unchallenged forces eventually being challenged by a countervailing power.

During the Cold War two superpowers had been in a sort of military equilibrium which served to ward off a large scale war. In addition, between them they had managed to contain smaller conflicts within their respective spheres of influence, for instance, the Arab–Israeli wars, the Chechen rebellions and the various uprisings in Soviet client states – such as in Hungary and the then Czechoslovakia.

Given the current global political landscape, the next few years will undoubtedly see increasing efforts by the US government to manipulate geopolitics to serve its own interests. At the same time, this will lead to the formation and consolidation of an anti-US coalition of the less mighty nations. This will also be accompanied by the spread of anti-US sentiment in civil societies across the world, including the West.

The US-led Coalition of Deception

It is incredible to think that there have been no high profile dismissals as a result of the Bush administration's justifications for going to war with Iraq. All the finger pointing has gone to the source of the information, the Central Intelligence Agency (CIA). But did the CIA truly believe that Iraq possessed WMD, or was there an invisible persuasive force that suggested to them that this was the case and asked them to 'find' evidence to support this argument? The truth may never be made public.

It is worth mentioning that in the past it has not been uncommon practice for the CIA to attempt to adapt facts to fit the US foreign policies of the time, Iraq being the most recent and most controversial example. Former CIA director Stansfield Turner has already openly accused the Bush administration of 'overstretching the facts' about Iraqi WMD in making its case for invading that country.[2] In Britain, Prime Minister Tony Blair's reputation has also been severely damaged by the inquiry probing into certain circumstances of Britain's participation in the Iraq conflict.

'We made it clear to the dictator of Iraq that he must disarm,' Bush said in a speech in June 2003 at Northern Virginia Community College in Annandale. 'He chose not to do so, so we disarmed him … He is no longer a threat to the free world.'

Bush was right in that Saddam Hussein is no longer a threat to the free world. The question posed by many – including ourselves – is, was he ever a threat to the free world? There can be no doubt about the threat he posed to the Iraqi people, but a threat to the free world is another case of 'overstretching'.

The US is bogged down in Iraq – the body bags are being flown in daily from Baghdad to American airfields and there seems to be no end in sight to the occupation mayhem. There is a seemingly never-ending supply of suicide bombers and militants prepared to act against the US occupation.

The fundamental point of warfare is that you can choose when to start a war but you cannot control its end or its outcome. Insidious guerrilla warfare waged by fighters in the shadows is extremely hard to overcome. In addition, as President Bush and presidents before him at the time of the Vietnam conflict discovered, the battle for public opinion is easy to lose. Although at the time the Bush administration was adamant in preaching to the American public that the second Iraq war was not going to be another Vietnam, the daily news reports in the media indicate just the opposite.

With every passing day, more coalition troops are dying and the Iraqi people are feeling more resentful towards their liberators who have overstayed their welcome and are reluctant to grant them the real – not just token – democracy that was promised.

The Bush administration is caught in an incredibly delicate situation. If the US exits too soon, Iraq will undoubtedly descend into an even worse state of violent chaos. The consequences would clearly be grave, not to mention the harm that will be done to US credibility in global affairs (many of course would argue that this has already happened anyway). Staying too long, on the other hand, continues to cost American lives, money and votes!

Even the neo-conservatives, who have been in the ascendancy in US foreign affairs over recent years, are realizing that they have bitten off more than they can chew. As a result, the US is increasingly seeking the involvement of other nations to share in the burden of maintaining Iraqi security and stability. This is a bit like trying to get people on to your team when you are losing and there isn't much to play for except humiliation. Rational nations ask themselves why they should go in and help clear up other people's messes.

It is difficult to say where US foreign policy would be today had a less right-wing president been sitting in the White House when the September 11 terrorist attacks took place. But it is safe to say that the war on terrorism has become the overarching feature and justification of US foreign policy – and a *casus belli*[3] that possibly has dangerous implications for the whole world. Some critics argue that US policy could not be better designed to promote terrorism.

The war in Afghanistan has had the unintended effect of destabilizing Pakistan and Saudi Arabia. In several Muslim countries across the world Osama bin Laden is viewed by fundamentalists as a courageous leader who has the audacity to stand up to the American 'bully'. The war on terrorism has further polarized the world between the West and Islam and has created a 'schizophrenic' category of moderate Muslims who live in the West and can see both sides of the coin. Osama bin Laden is still at large, and Afghanistan remains a highly unstable, divided nation. The spectre of Osama, however, is a useful bogeyman for a US foreign policy increasingly strident in its efforts to protect what it sees as its global interests.

Superpower contenders

After the collapse of the Soviet Union, the United States was left uncontested as a world superpower. Although, this did not have an immediate impact on the geopolitical landscape, the terrorist attacks of September 11, 2001 resulted in a change in tack in US foreign policy. Under the Bush administration, the US adopted a controversial foreign policy that has antagonized many of its own citizens. In addition, it has strained ties between its traditional allies, particularly those in Europe, and it has made a few new enemies along the way.

Despite how the US government is perceived domestically and overseas, American military might remains unchallenged and will likely remain so for the next decade. However, the period of economic hardship that awaits the US economy may shorten this time frame.

Which country will emerge as a second superpower to balance US hegemony and eventually replace the US as the world superpower for the 21st century? Although we state clearly throughout our book that we believe this nation to be China, we have written this section to explain to you why and how we came to this conclusion, versus the other two likely contenders. Acknowledging that China is in its ascendancy to being the world's second superpower will be vital to investors and business managers as it will help them determine where to invest and to identify opportunities related to this long-term trend.

Some commentators argue that the next superpower to emerge will be India or Russia, but we believe that these nations have too many internal issues that will hinder economic growth for many years to come. That is not to say that there are no investment opportunities in India or Russia, but from a macro perspective, China easily emerges as the winner, both economically and militarily. We provide an overview of each of these three countries below and discuss some of the trends and factors that are likely to influence how each nation will develop as we head for the second decade of this century.

China

Fast facts
With 1.3 billion people, China is the world's most populous nation. It is roughly the size of the United States and covers an area of 9.6 million square kilometres. A large percentage of the population is atheist – religion was banned during

the Cultural Revolution (1966 to 1976). The People's Republic of China was formed on 1 October 1949. Although many dialects are spoken throughout its provinces, Mandarin (or Putonghua) is the official language, which is based on the Beijing dialect. China is administratively divided into 23 provinces, 5 autonomous regions, 4 centrally administrative municipalities and 2 special administrative regions (Hong Kong and Macau).

Increasing power and influence
With the world currently under the influence of one superpower, an additional superpower would possibly bring the 'yin–yang balance' back. It is looking more than likely that this balancing superpower will be China – how convenient, since that is where the yin yang term comes from.

Although China's growth rate has fallen somewhat since the start of the global economic slowdown, its annual GDP growth is still forecast to be in the 8–10% range. If this growth rate is sustained then China's GDP will surpass that of the US within a generation.

There are a lot of commentators who point the finger of blame for almost all of the world's ills on the Big Looming Asian Menace (acronym BLAM – we invented it first). If inflation and commodity prices are rising, it must be China's fault; if there is deflation in the price of manufactured products, blame it on China!

Certainly, China – as readers will get a flavour of from our detailed examination below – is no angel when it comes to trade, human rights, the environment, etc. but it is no worse than many other countries. China is attempting to grow its way out of poverty and there can be no finer aspiration than that.

What worries many is the scale of China's emergence as a world economic power, supplanting long-standing members in the charts of world output with consummate ease. The emergence of China will not by any means be smooth sailing; in particular, growing tensions between the United States and China will have important implications for investment and for world security.

Already, China's global influence is increasing and this will be reflected at the United Nations where, as a Permanent Member of the Security Council, it will better represent its own increasingly separate views and sentiments, diluting the current US bias.

With sustained economic growth will come China's increased military and technological strength – and the strength perhaps to resist international (particularly US) pressure to reduce the margin of its competitive advantage in trade. The Chinese are modernizing their armed forces at a rapid – but as yet little commented on – rate.

Military strength development

Within 10 years, it is possible that China will have a nuclear and military capability comparable to that of the US and may pose a credible threat to the current balance of power in the world.

In addition, China's large population will be able to sustain a bigger military capability which will be unrivalled anywhere else in the world in terms of sheer numbers – even though these have been reduced in recent years to create a more professional and flexible corps.

In June 2003, China announced that it would reduce the size of the People's Liberation Army (PLA) by 500,000 over the next five years.[4] In September 2003, a further announcement of cuts was made,[5] indicating that 200,000 troops will be trimmed from the ranks, reducing the size of the PLA to 2.3 million by 2005. This still leaves China with the world's largest army, but the shift is clearly away from the historical philosophy of military superiority through overwhelming numerical superiority. This announcement was made in a speech marking the 50th anniversary of the PLA's National Defence Science and Technology University, Xinhua. In the speech, the Central Military Commission chairman Jiang Zemin announced:

> 'The state of war is being transformed from mechanized warfare to information warfare.'

China's official annual military budget is published to be $30 billion for 2005, but unofficially it is reported to be as high as $60 billion. This is a military budget that is comparable to that of Russia, which also happens to be China's largest foreign supplier of military hardware.[6]

Logically, China's long-term objectives would be to modernize its military capability as it continues to grow economically. Already the sixth largest economy in the world,[7] these twin objectives are likely to be met. It is very likely that the EU will lift the arms ban on China in the very near future (the economic rewards are too great to turn down). When that happens, China will have access to the West's latest weaponry, bringing it closer to its goal of modernizing its military.

Despite the coming global economic slowdown, China will continue to outpace every other major economy and in terms of raw output will more or less catch up with the United States within fifteen years. Of course, its capacity to engage in conflict with the US and its allies will be significantly enhanced well before then.

According to the United States Department of Defence (DOD), China is also developing home-grown military weapons systems, such as destroyers, frigates and submarines. The DOD reports that China has around 350 short-range ballistic missiles, a number growing by about 50 per year. In addition, China is replacing its Inter Continental Ballistic Missiles (ICBMs) with even longer-range versions. All of these missiles have potential nuclear capability. For its air force, China has bought modern and effective Su-30 fighters from Russia and can itself produce the Su-27 aircraft. The Chinese have also developed an airborne early warning aircraft and are looking to acquire the A-50 Mainstay Airborne Warning And Control System (AWACS) aircraft from Russia.

In terms of naval power, China's World War II era landing ships have recently been replaced with around 600 modern landing craft. China has also bought Russian destroyers and a Kilo-class submarine – probably the first of many. Its artillery forces have had gun upgrades fitted to more than 1000 tanks – and counting. China expects to have 1800 new Type 96 tanks deployed by 2005. In addition to the massive increase in hardware capability, China is working on improving its tactics and military strategy for air, sea and land.

With its growing economic and military strength, China will seek to become even more active in geopolitical affairs. Indeed, this trend has become evident over the past few years, an example being the hosting and brokering of the talks between North Korea and the United States in August 2003 over the issue of the former's possession of nuclear weapons.

As China gains experience in international diplomacy, it will start to play a greater role, firstly in regional politics in Asia and subsequently on the world stage. China is thus beginning to gather the support and respect of other nations as a credible peace broker and mediator in world affairs. It is presenting itself as an alternative to the currently hegemonic United States, and is laying the foundations towards becoming the second global superpower.

The world's political landscape is changing and whereas 20 years ago the world's major point of potential conflict was clearly between the USSR and the United States, China is moving into the void left by the disintegration of the Soviet empire. The reasons why China and the United States, Europe and Russia might well engage in future conflict are to do with the acquisition of raw materials, or perhaps mounting disputes over trade. Japanese militarism/imperialism in the 1930s was encouraged by worldwide protectionism and its shortage of raw materials.

A perception by the Chinese that their overwhelming superiority in numbers gives them an ultimate advantage in any war with the United States may lead to armed action. However, in our opinion, it is China's desire to acquire raw materials to fuel its factories and cities that may well prove to be the deciding factor. China is short of some critical economic inputs to fuel its growth machine and in the same way as Nazi Germany and Japan looked to invasions to satisfy their need for raw materials, it is conceivable that China could do the same. This will be one of the greatest geopolitical threats facing the world.

Targets for a future militarist China could well include: the Russian Far East, Indonesia and Australia, all of them rich in natural resources. Indonesia, with its vast oil and gas fields and Australia with its abundance of commodities, particularly minerals, are obvious focal points of a future Chinese land grab.

While it may appear to be somewhat hypothetical today that such invasions or territorial annexations could take place, long-term thinkers would be well-advised to review the lessons of history. The ambitions of Germany and Japan in the last century and the building of empires, from the Roman to the British, involved the acquisition of the raw materials of others.

Political reform – communist capitalism
There are faint signs of reform in China. Being very aware of how the former Soviet Union disintegrated following its embrace of Western democratic values, China is more cautious about accepting change too rapidly, and is taking a much slower and more deliberate path than its former communist rival.

China is also aware that it is perceived by the West as oppressive, totalitarian and abusive of human rights but, to be fair, China has come a long way since the infamous military assault by the Chinese government on pro-democracy demonstrators in Beijing's Tiananmen Square in June 1989.

Sure, there are still unresolved issues such as Taiwan's independence and the persecution of Falun Gong followers (considered an 'evil' cult by the Chinese government) to name a couple, but remember that China thinks long term: 10, 50, 100 years; the West tends to think in fractions of a year – Q1 to Q4.

The state-owned enterprises (SOEs), which last decade were riddled with scandals and corrupt officials, are being cleaned up through restructuring and better corporate governance. There are even signs of voting reform too. Although the Communist Party is still the authoritative party, it has started to encourage candidates to recommend themselves for district congress seats without the party's prior endorsement. Granted, these are seats at the bottom of a multi-layered parliamentary system and offer negligible power to the elected.[8] In May 2003 the city of Shenzhen, which is across the border from Hong Kong, held elections in which candidates were permitted to put up campaign posters – a big no-no in the past.

We are not saying that by next year, China's democratic system will rival any in the West, but we are trying to highlight that political change is slowly happening. China is a big ship carrying 1.3 billion passengers; everything must be done slowly and carefully, and then reviewed before the next step can be taken. China does not want its people to confuse increased democracy with the ability to question the Communist Party's right to rule the country.

Look at what happened in Russia in December 2003, when President Putin ended up arresting billionaire businessman Mikhail Khodorkovsky under the pretext of a tax-evasion charge; the unofficial reason was because Khodorkovsky was providing funding to a political party running against the President. The arrest was in fact a flag waving signal to Russia's other oligarchs (the wealthy businessmen of dubious financial ancestry) – ordering them to back off from any political ambitions they might have. Khodorkovsky, despite all his money, is in the same situation as any reader of this book who fails to read the tea leaves: all the money in the world won't save you if you make the wrong political and physical choices!

China and the United States in a historical context

In 1972 Richard Nixon became the first President of the United States to visit China, which since the Communist takeover in 1949 had been virtually shut to foreign influence. The view of Nixon at the time, and of all US administrations since, is that by establishing friendly communications with the world's most populous nation and engaging it in dialogue, eventually China would embrace 'American' values. What the US and much of the rest of the world has failed to recognize is that China's ultimate goal is to be the dominant Asian power, a policy very much at odds with the goals of the United States. The US indeed has sent combat troops three times to Asia – in World War II, in the Korean War and in the Vietnam War – to prevent the emergence of any power to rival its own dominance of one of the world's most important regions.

Today, China is usurping this long-held policy by stealth and economics – and there is little the US can do about it.

When the British returned Hong Kong to the Chinese in June 1997, it marked an important triumph for China. Hong Kong is a leading gateway to trade in China and elsewhere in Asia. It is a repository of much needed entrepreneurial skills and a vital communications hub. Its seizure by the British in the 19th century was a major snub to Chinese pride and its restoration has righted one of many perceived wrongs. One of the most pressing of these is Taiwan; the move by the Nationalist government of China to the island of what was then called Formosa in 1949 was and remains a major thorn in the sensitive side of the Chinese government. Taiwan has been phenomenally successful, enjoying American military protection and a laissez-faire economic regime that has enabled its income per head to be many multiples of that of the mainland.

Taiwan is furthermore seen as a proxy for US power in direct confrontation with the People's Republic of China, and although Taiwanese capital has invested heavily in China, and indeed many Taiwanese work in China, there is no doubt about China's ambition for the island – to reclaim it.

Indeed, Taiwan does its part to bait both the United States and China – a bit like North Korea. President Chen Shui-bian of Taiwan plays up to the pride of Taiwan's indigenous people in their own country. He recognizes that support for the one-country policy (reunification) has largely evaporated in the island-state. Rather, people in Taiwan are more concerned with the unique viability and prosperity of Taiwan and increasingly regard Beijing as a bully-boy to be countered. This is a process which is regarded as provocative by the mainland, which is estimated to have 50 or so missiles targeted at Taiwan. The clash between Taiwanese nationalism and China's long-standing desire to take back the renegade island is a serious issue in Asian politics. As part of this process, China has been expanding its military capability and its medium-term objective in this respect is to control the South China Sea, the main trade route in the region. One of the purposes of this is to discourage any renaissance in Japanese military capability.

Japan's invasions of China in World War II rankle deeply, and no amount of apologizing or economic aid from Japan seems to put any dent in the historical antagonism that has resulted. Japan is also considered to be a close ally of the US, which is believed to want to encourage a build-up of Japan's 'Self-Defence Forces' to counterbalance the rising military might of China.

China wants to keep Japan subordinate to itself while at the same time increase its influence over the peripheries of Asia – the Indo-Chinese states of Vietnam, Cambodia and Laos, for example, or the Central Asian (formerly Soviet) states. Kazakhstan is particularly important in this respect because of its huge oil and gas resources. Indeed China has become an important investor in the oil industry in Central Asia.

China's long-term goal is generally unexpressed publicly. But take this quote from Lieutenant General Mi Zhenyu, Vice Commandant at the Academy of Military Sciences in Beijing:

> 'As for the United States for a relatively long time it will be absolutely necessary that we quietly nurse our sense of vengeance. We must conceal our abilities and bide our time.'

This statement is consistent with the strategic thinking of a great Chinese philosopher, Sun Tzu, much admired by the Chinese leadership. In his *Art of War* he wrote that to fight and conquer is not supreme excellence, but rather supreme excellence is breaking the enemy's resistance without having to fight. Sun Tzu's encouragement of military planners to feign incapacity and inactivity is one that the Chinese generally follow except for the occasional rush of blood to the head when they test-fire rockets over the Taiwan Strait. China denies any long-term aspirations of dominance, pointing instead to its ambition to improve the economic lot of its citizens. It is true that China does have severe problems amidst all the headline talk of rapid growth: education remains generally poor, rural incomes are barely rising, pollution is a growing problem and the need for infrastructure investment remains critical. But despite these negatives, China's power is growing. China has always regarded itself as being at the centre of the universe … indeed the word China in Chinese – Zhong Guo – means 'Middle Kingdom'.

China was in no position to exercise any sort of power for hundreds of years from the mid 1700s to today, because of a variety of crises that befell it – some of them its own making, others that were caused by outsiders.

China's dissolution in the 18th century into a collection of weak decentralized states, was followed by a period in which its economy was dominated first by the European powers (the 19th century), then the Japanese, culminating in Japan's invasion in the 1930s.

Russia – undergoing an identity crisis

Fast facts

Although Russia has a population of only 144 million, it is by far the world's largest country, even after the break-up of the Soviet Union, covering an area of 17 million square kilometres. In terms of religion, the majority of the population is Russian Orthodox. Russia gained 'independence' from the Soviet Union on 24 August 1991. Since its financial crisis in 1998, Russia has been averageing just over 6% GDP growth annually. Russia's gas reserves account for around one-quarter of the world's total and its oil reserves rank sixth in the world. Following the collapse of the Soviet Union, Chechnya remained under Russia, even though many Chechens have been trying to win independence; but Russia refuses to accept Chechnya as an independent state and in 1995, 10,000 Russian troops marched into Chechnya. Since then, Chechen rebels have struck repeatedly throughout Russia. Examples of such terrorist acts include the Moscow theatre siege in 2002 and the school siege in Beslan in 2004. Russia is adamant that Chechnya will not gain independence.

Post-Soviet Russia

Today, Russia is a curious amalgam of vestiges of the old Soviet system and a reformist economy, one partly based on a crude rendition of capitalism. Quickly following on from the collapse of the Gorbachev 'interim' regime, which served as a sort of bridge between a command-style communist economic regime and what was to follow, there took place an unseemly and rigged redistribution of key state assets.

In 1994, all citizens of the Russian Federation over 18 were issued 'privatization vouchers' which entitled them to participate in auctions of state-owned assets, right from the local bakery to the major oil companies (repositories of much of Russia's mineral reserves).

A scheme known as the 'shares for loans' scheme, a blatant swap of short-term funding to the government at a critical time, in exchange for long-term strategic positions in Russia's key industries, led to a substantial increase in the power of the oligarchs. But these super rich individuals were prospering at a time when Russian people generally were being robbed of their life savings, in large part by devaluation of the rouble. This was compounded by the default of the Russian government on its domestic debt in 1998. Thus, for a period, Russia became the pariah of the world's financial markets. Of course, memories are short in capital markets, and soon Russia began to benefit from the effects of the devaluation and from a rise in the price of oil and gas, its principal exports. Foreign exchange reserves soared. The government allowed the market economy to function, reduced and simplified taxes and encouraged foreign investment.

Jim went to Russia during the 'gold rush'

In 1994 Jim, then working as a fund manager in Hong Kong, decided to go to Russia on an exploratory tour. Making the trip with his business partner Jayne Sutcliffe, his first stop was in Vladivostok.

It is hard to believe now, but just a decade ago there were no direct scheduled flights to the Russian Far East, and Jayne and Jim were holed up in a down-at-heel hotel in Seoul, South Korea, for a few days, waiting for a charter flight to Vladivostok. At last the flight departed and the pleasures of the Russian Far East, i.e. none, became apparent. A motley collection of rusting fishing boats and decaying cranes were offered for the consideration of the adventurous foreign investors, but were politely declined.

In the meantime, various attempts had been made to get into Jim's hotel room by some of the locals, intent on separating Jim from his cash. But tricks learnt from James Bond films, such as putting a chair under the door handle, proved effective in thwarting these efforts!

So Jayne and Jim decided to leave and head for Moscow, with a bag of carefully hidden cash. Down they went to the market where the privatization vouchers, which were freely tradable and worth about $25 each, were being sold by babushkas. These old ladies had assembled bundles of them in the provinces and taken these to Moscow to make a quick turn. Jayne and Jim invested $2 million of their company's money in these bits of paper, then attempted to identify which of the incomprehensible list of Russian names they should apply their vouchers to. With a bit of useful advice, they put in their bids and left Russia.

Six weeks later, Jim was on holiday in Spain when a fax arrived (hard to believe also, email wasn't yet prevalent). The voucher investment had soared to $16 million in value, this despite the fact that the intrepid duo had chosen some real lemons – as well as some spectacular gainers. So a new business was born for Jayne and Jim – investing money in Eastern Europe – a business that exists to this day.

This diversion is used to illustrate a bigger point: while Jayne and Jim were making what for them was amazing money, <u>really</u> huge amounts of wealth were being created for those in Russia who became known as the 'oligarchs'. Smart, streetwise individuals (some in their twenties) took advantage of the economic chaos of the times to accumulate controlling positions in key companies in the economy, mostly centred on oil. This new wealth was reinforced when Boris Yeltsin found himself in electoral trouble in 1996, and needed cash to ensure his victory.

Conversely, and at the same time, the government has gradually increased state control of broadcasting and print media – to the point where in the last Parliamentary (or Duma) elections, no one reading newspapers or watching TV would have believed that an opposition even existed.

Russia's tentative steps towards democracy, which began in 1995, have effectively been put on hold, with the complicity of the population. The people of Russia genuinely appear to favour stability and toughness over democracy and the perceived lawlessness that came with the immediate post-communist years.

The economy has become the major focus: it has begun to boom and a limited middle class has started to emerge, though in many parts of Russia outside Moscow poverty remains rife and conditions appalling. This new prosperity and stability resulted in part from the installation of Vladimir Putin as President of Russia, following the resignation of Boris Yeltsin due to health problems. Putin's control of the Duma will almost certainly give him the opportunity to change the constitution, which on paper limits his ability to run for another term in office; so President Putin is likely to be president for some time to come. This has interesting implications for the Western world: Putin is a pragmatist and his first priority appears to be improving the economy. Certainly this has been happening and Russian bonds are once again known as 'investment grade' (i.e. big institutions can buy them).

Putin's imprisonment and harassment of certain oligarchs is more a reflection of Putin's unwillingness to see rich men use their wealth to gain influence in politics and to challenge his rule – rather than the result of any desire to confiscate assets. Having said that, Russia's oil and gas reserves are precious assets in a world with a growing thirst for energy. Russia's macroeconomic fundamentals look excellent and, while corruption, evasion of taxes and inequality remain rife, the country is now a significantly improved place.

The downsizing of the military in the post-communist years is also positive for the West, and indeed for China. Russia no longer is – as it used to be described –a 'Third World country with nuclear rockets'. Its military bias and its expansionist tendencies are now confined to Chechnya and possibly to maintaining influence in the countries bordering the Caspian Sea, where great oil wealth lies. Its ambitions are no longer imperial and the focus is no longer on beating the US. Russia's priorities lie with its economic self-preservation and on improving the lot of the average Russian. In this it seems to be succeeding.

So, the bottom line is that Russia is no longer a significant factor in world geopolitics. China has supplanted its role as the natural balancing factor to the US as a superpower. If anything, Russia's leanings are more towards allegiances with Western nations than alliances to the East. Russia is much more likely to favour the West in any future conflict with China, and certainly China must covet Russia's huge Siberian natural resources – something to consider in drawing up a map of future flashpoints on the globe.

India – too many issues at home to be a global player
Some commentators have argued that India will emerge as the next global superpower. With its nuclear capability, vast population and high economic

growth, it shows a great deal of potential in becoming a significant global player. Yet, while we agree that India has enjoyed some recent economic success, particularly in software and outsourcing, it has too many political and economic obstacles to overcome before it can truly reach its potential as a global heavyweight. These issues, we believe, will take many years to resolve.

Fast facts

India is the world's second most populous country after China with a population of around 1 billion. It ranks seventh in terms of size, having a land mass of approximately 3.3 million square kilometres. It is also home to the second largest Muslim population in the world after Indonesia, even though they only make up 12% of the country's predominantly Hindu people. India is an ex-British colony, having gained its independence in 1947; hence the English language is widely spoken. India is a nuclear power and borders two other nuclear powers – Pakistan and China – both of whom have histories of conflict with India.

Some progress yes, but still a long way to go …

India joined the World Trade Organization (WTO) in 1995, but has been very slow in lowering its trade barriers to foreign investors and is under increasing international pressure to do so. India's GDP in US dollar terms is around $500 billion – around 40% of China's ($1.23 trillion) – almost half of which comes from agriculture.[9] Since the early 1990s, India's GDP has managed to grow annually by an average of 6%.

In recent years India has enjoyed the global spotlight as an outsourcing hub for the world (also known as off-shoring). Initially it provided competitively priced software application development but increasingly it has taken care of entire business processes on behalf of large global corporations. The services include customer support, help desk, processing of application forms (for banks, insurance companies, etc.) and preparation of tax returns. All processes considered to be non-core by the private or public sector can, in theory, be outsourced, and India is an increasingly popular choice for outsourcing services.

India appears to be the most competitive globally in terms of cost for its skilled, English-speaking labour force. Announcements by large American and European firms of outsourcing to India (such as AT&T, GE, Amex, HSBC and LloydsTSB) are becoming more common and are sparking calls for job protectionism by lobby groups in the affected countries (largely English-speaking Western countries).

The corporations justify their decision by stating that they in turn are under constant pressure to remain globally competitive; a failure to do so would put the entire company's existence at risk, which would jeopardize a much larger workforce worldwide in the longer term. The savings made by corporations could (again in theory) be passed on to the customer. Additionally, the laid-off individuals could re-train and re-enter the workforce as higher value, less commoditized service providers, resulting in the nation being more competitive.

It all sounds very sensible, but it's too early to see whether it works in practice, as some key assumptions remain untested, such as how long it will take for the redundant workers to re-train as value-adding service providers. But clearly, from a business point of view, the difference in annual salary, for example between a call centre agent in the UK (£18,000) and India (£2500), is too compelling to ignore.[10]

In 2002, India's exports grew by almost 20% – the growth rate is indeed impressive. Yet despite this and all the bullish press on India's economic expansion, its exports for that same year accounted for a mere 0.8% of the world total. India remains a country that is punching well below its weight on the global stage. Notwithstanding its efforts to differentiate itself from China, it has to date been unsuccessful in stepping out from under the shadow of its Asian neighbour to the east.

In terms of its global political status, India is not a permanent member of the UN Security Council. It argues that it should be because it is: (a) the world's largest democracy; (b) a rapidly growing economic power; and (c) a contributor to peacekeeping operations. India must no doubt feel extremely frustrated to see that its rival China is a permanent member.

On the home front, corruption is rife and numerous factors continue to hold India back from attaining its true potential. The majority of the rural population live in abject poverty and remain illiterate. Caste tensions and regional and religious conflicts, fuelled by ad hoc terrorist attacks, continue to shake the country's ethos.

Disputed Kashmir– should we be worried?

The dispute involves India and Pakistan, two nations that have continually been at loggerheads over a territory known as Kashmir, which is situated to the north of India and to the east of Pakistan. The dispute goes back to when India was declared an independent state from British rule in 1947. At this time Kashmir was ruled by a British approved maharaja, whom Britain granted the freedom to choose which nation to accede to – either India or Pakistan. But the maharaja could not make up his mind. He was a Hindu ruler (so the tendency would be to join India), yet his people were predominantly Muslim (which would fit better with Muslim Pakistan). So he played both sides of the fence rather than making a clear and indisputable decision. Fast forwarding through 50 years of armed conflicts and heated debates between India and Pakistan, both countries continue to stake a claim to Kashmir. However, many Kashmiris want independence for themselves, but neither India nor Pakistan is prepared to entertain this option (so far at least). Kashmir is currently divided into two halves – Pakistani administered Kashmir and Indian administered Kashmir.

Kashmir has all the hallmarks of an intractable conflict: long-standing claims to the territory by both India and Pakistan; religion-based suspicion and animosity; religion-based persecution/terrorism; and mass population displacement resulting in refugees fleeing trouble spots.

Both countries have nuclear weapons so the worst case scenario for this dispute is a nuclear war. With over 20% of the world's population living in the Indian subcontinent, it could result in the destruction of human lives on an unimaginable scale. Hence this region is never far from the news headlines whenever the tension thermometer rises. Furthermore, although Pakistan is the underdog in this 'stand-off', its elevation to being a 'major non-NATO ally' to the United States in March 2004 will provide it with more advanced military capability. It could lead it to become more cocksure, possibly increasing the likelihood of a regional conflict.

Furthermore, this special status of Pakistan could backfire on the US if the currently unpopular President, General Pervez Musharraf, were overthrown or assassinated (he has had several close calls) in a coup and replaced by an Islamic extremist. If this were to happen, Pakistan would likely be a new base for al-Qaeda, with nuclear weapons at its disposal – a very daunting thought.

Osama bin Laden is already understood to be hiding in the wild north-west frontier region. The West would have little choice but to go to war again.

Terrorism

Today, World War III is well under way: the 'war on terrorism' is the first of a kind in that it is the first such conflict not specifically targeted at a particular country or region. Perhaps the closest analogy to it is McCarthyism, a term first used during the Cold War in the 1950s. McCarthyism was a label that was started by the US government to describe the fear, mistrust and suspicion of all things communist among the American people. Even if one was only suspected of being communist, one became tarnished with the same brush.

An example of the level of paranoia that existed at the time of McCarthyism was the banning of various actors, screenwriters and film directors. Even the great comedian Charlie Chaplin (who had moved from England to Hollywood) was denied entry back into the US after he returned from attending a London premiere for one of his films. Although Chaplin was never a communist, his unconventional views and refusal to denounce communism had the US government so concerned that he was subsequently blacklisted from making Hollywood films and banned from entering the US for a while and as a result moved to Switzerland.

Today, some argue that the level of fear in the US derived from terrorism is comparable to that of communism during the Cold War. In a similar way to the ideological battle of the Cold War, the war on terrorism is a war against a belief or an ideal rather than the more traditional land-grab motivated war. It makes the enemy very difficult to identify as cells of terrorists are dispersed throughout the world – many in Islamic nations but also in Western countries.

As stated previously, the first military operation as part of the war on terrorism began in Afghanistan. It had been determined that the group of militants responsible for the September 11 attacks had belonged to the infamous al-Qaeda network whose headquarters were in Afghanistan. The objective was clear – this threat had to be eliminated and its leader Osama bin Laden captured. This first foray of the war on terrorism then continued with military action against Iraq. This action was preceded by controversial speeches made by President George W. Bush and his advisers in which references were made to an 'axis of evil' comprising Iraq, Iran and North Korea.

Today Iran and North Korea remain in the cross-hairs of the US military and diplomatic machine. We have yet to see any concrete signs of military action against them, and of course the clean-up operation in Afghanistan and Iraq will continue to occupy the largest part of United States military capacity for a long time to come. However, these countries remain rogue states in the minds of the US administration – to be 'dealt with' at a later date.

While the US prevaricates on engagement or otherwise with Iran and North Korea, both are undoubtedly building a nuclear capability, and in each case this capability has the potential to be destabilizing to world order.

Terrorism is a word never far from the news headlines – and it has in some way affected all of our lives. Yet the term 'terrorism' itself has been so overused that its meaning has become uncertain. Although there is no definition which describes terrorism with precision, here is how the US Federal Bureau of Investigation (FBI) delineates it:

> 'Terrorism is the unlawful use of force or violence against persons or property to intimidate or coerce a government, the civilian population, or any segment thereof, in furtherance of political or social objectives.'

It is rather interesting that this definition is applicable to any act of war or aggression, regardless of the perpetrator. The entire definition conveniently rests on the definition of the word unlawful. If a state supports the act, it is lawful aggression, but it may still be deemed unlawful by other states. If the state does not support the act, it is terrorism.

Hence unbiased observers might take note of the adage that one man's terrorist is another man's freedom fighter. Is the terrorist always against the state? That is a tricky question and not always easy to answer.

Let's use an example: throughout the 1980s the US (CIA) spent billions of dollars recruiting and funding the Mujahideen (a Muslim force) in Afghanistan to fight a Holy War ('Jihad') to drive out the Moscow-backed Kabul regime and thereby undermine the Soviet Union's influence over Afghanistan. They recruited extensively from the Muslim world; one of those recruits arrived from Saudi Arabia in 1980 – his name was Osama bin Laden. In 1992 the Mujahideen succeeded in accomplishing their mission, partly because the Soviet Union had disintegrated and Moscow could no longer afford to maintain its grip over the country.

So, were the Mujahideen terrorists? After all, they tried to overthrow the government. And if so, does that make the US a supporter of terrorism? If not, when is it OK to fund a military force to overthrow an incumbent government? Therein lies the dilemma.

Just suppose that the US had not assembled the Mujahideen Muslim fighters in the first place to overthrow the incumbent Afghan regime, a regime which would probably have dissolved shortly after the collapse of the Soviet Union anyway. Under such a scenario, Afghanistan would never have had the radical Muslims in the first place, nor the US-backed weapons and training that they received with them. In a parallel universe, it's just possible that the September 11 terrorist attacks would never have happened.

Al-Qaeda-linked terrorism

Osama bin Laden and his al-Qaeda network of terrorists have gained a terrible infamy following the terrorist attacks on the United States in September 2001.

For the first time, the dreadful crime brought home to Americans the stark reality of mass terrorism. Al-Qaeda's mission today remains the destruction of Western democratic values and Western society as a whole. Islam as practiced by fanatics is more than a religion – it is in their minds the future state – and that's what makes Islamic fundamentalism so dangerous. In fact, it's what makes fundamentalism of any religion dangerous.

Osama bin Laden has become the recognized icon of terrorism in the 21st century. In some ways, it suits Western governments to keep his shadowy appearances and utterances in the forefront of current news, even though there is no certainty that the man himself is still with us. The continued spectre of Osama allows for a conservative agenda to be imparted on a nation – and here we are thinking of the United States – a country once famed for its liberal values. Osama bin Laden has single-handedly reinforced the move of American values to the right.

The war on terrorism has also been used to justify rapid expansion of the military in the United States, as well as to justify intervention by US armed forces in every conceivable part of the globe. Of course, the so-called war on terrorism did not start following the attacks that brought down the Twin Towers in New York; what that event did was to re-energize the United States' focus and resolve to combat terrorism.

In the years prior to September 11 2001, al-Qaeda's terrorists had blown up US interests overseas, such as the American Embassies in Nairobi, Kenya and Dar es Salaam, Tanzania.

In 2000, a dinghy packed with explosives attacked the American ship USS *Cole* in Yemen.

In 1996 a bomb-carrying fuel truck exploded outside the Khobar Towers (a US military housing facility) in Dhahran, Saudi Arabia, killing 19 US Air Force military personnel and wounding 515, including 240 US personnel.

There have been many other horrific terrorist attacks since September 11 2001, most of which have been linked to al-Qaeda. Sadly, there are too many to list but here are some of the more infamous events:

- The fertilizer truck suicide bomber outside the US Consulate in Karachi, Pakistan, in June 2002.
- The nightclub bombing in Bali, Indonesia, in October 2002.
- The bombings of the main shopping district of the mostly Christian city of Zamboanga in the southern Philippines in October 2002.
- The Moscow theatre siege in October 2002.
- The Kenyan hotel bombings in November 2002.
- The US expatriate housing compound in Saudi Arabia in May 2003.
- The bombing in Casablanca, Morocco, in May 2003.
- The bombing of the JW Marriott Hotel in Jakarta, Indonesia, in August 2003.
- The bombings in Istanbul, Turkey, of the HSBC building and the British Consulate in November 2003.
- The train bombings in Madrid, Spain, in March 2004.
- The train and bus bombings in London, England, in July 2005.

Although America's military power will likely remain unrivalled for at least the next ten years, it is in some ways impotent in the face of determined terrorism.

Those with the mentality to kill themselves in the name of religion or some other cause are undeterred by normal punitive sanctions. There are increasing numbers of such potential martyrs around the world and the level of sophistication of their attacks is also increasing.

No matter how much money is spent, it is very hard to fight an unseen, well-funded and highly driven enemy, particularly when that enemy is operating right under our very noses in the West. Airport security lines may get longer, ID cards may be introduced and police raids may occur with greater frequency – but the bright and determined unseen attacker will probably get through.

It is surprising, in fact, that a greater number of terrorist atrocities have not occurred since September 11 2001, but that they will occur in the future, and that their scale and impact will be huge, should not be in doubt.

The US and its allies' war on terrorism is essentially a war to exterminate the al-Qaeda terrorist network around the world. However, the United States on its own – in the pursuit of its unique interests – has used the war on terrorism and on Osama and his gang as a reason to do some tidying up of other problems. These perceived issues affecting US foreign policy are the root cause of this modern equivalent of gunboat diplomacy – step out of line and the Marines will be paying you a visit.

Since 1993, the US has declared these countries to be sponsors of terrorism:

Cuba
Iran*
Iraq*
Libya
North Korea*
Sudan
Syria.

*Declared as part of an axis of evil by President George W. Bush in his State of the Union address on 29 January 2002.

Dismantling and dispersing al-Qaeda – the regenerating organism of hate
Afghanistan was a country that was effectively hijacked by the Taliban and al-Qaeda, which used it as a headquarters for planning and training purposes.

Following the September 11 2001 attacks, the US and its allies realized that other nations had the potential to become alternative Afghanistans – countries with poor governance, ethnic or religious tensions, weak economies, low standards of education, high rates of unemployment and easily penetrable borders. There are lots of these around in the developing world, of course. A combination of these ingredients makes for an ideal terrorist haven. But what was really surprising to the United States and to its allies was just how sophisticated the al-Qaeda network was in their own backyard – operating in tight cells with seeming access to substantial financial and material resources.

The recipe for terrorism

Despite the huge oil wealth of certain countries in the Middle East, it has suffered from a lack of investment and a surplus of corruption and mismanagement for such a long period that the seeds of social unrest are now well and truly planted. Some of the young and disaffected people in many of these countries turn to Islamic fundamentalism in an effort to find meaning and purpose in their lives.

Organizations such as al-Qaeda feed off this disaffection and capitalize on the frustrations of the many Arab supporters of Palestinian independence. The legions of potential suicide bombers who are prepared to follow the al-Qaeda banner will strike repeatedly in coming years, no matter what action Western and other security forces take to prevent them. They and other terrorist organizations benefit from advances in modern technology allowing them to move freely and covertly to cause maximum disruption.

Terrorism in the future

So what does the future hold for terrorism and how will it affect our regular lives?

For now the threat seems to have been diminished through exhaustive intelligence efforts and tight security controls. In the longer term the outcome of the war on terrorism remains to be seen, but here is an alarming quote from the National Intelligence Council's report (December 2000) *Global Trends 2015: A Dialogue About the Future With Non-governmental Experts*, which in hindsight was frighteningly accurate:

'Between now and 2015 terrorist tactics will become increasingly sophisticated and designed to achieve mass casualties. We expect the trend toward greater lethality in terrorist attacks to continue.'

As the world increasingly polarizes into the rich, comfortable part and the poor, larger part, so the seeds of future terrorist activity are planted. Numerous would-be suicide bombers are at the disposal of terrorist organizations. The Israeli–Palestinian conflict provides a large number of these foot soldiers; others come from Saudi Arabia where anti-monarchical sentiment runs high among sections of the population; the US occupation of Iraq is another source of disaffection. And so the list goes on.

The potential of terrorists to use nuclear or biological weapons is one that increases by the day. Without a doubt, investors and readers of this book should be prepared for a much larger terrorist attack than that mounted on September 11 2001. This will have dire consequences for world markets and for global political and economic confidence.

Israel and the Palestinian Territories – intractable problems
The crisis between the Arabs and the Israelis is the consequence of the convoluted territorial engineering that has gone on through the various wars that have characterized Israel's existence since 1948. They have left a huge problem: what to do about the Palestinian people who live in the Palestinian Territories and Israel itself, as well as the many displaced refugees in neighbouring countries such as Jordan and Syria. The many unsuccessful attempts by world leaders to resolve tension and conflict clearly show that there is no easy solution to this problem, and provocation by both sides continuously inflames the situation.

Terrorist organizations such as Hamas and Hezbollah, supposedly representing the interests of the Palestinian people, are the legacy of enormous bitterness towards the Jewish state by many Arabs. On the part of the Israelis, the placing of Jewish (and ultra orthodox) settlements in the middle of the Palestinian Territories further exacerbates the divide between the two peoples. The Israelis suffer because they live under constant threat; their economy suffers from a lack of inward investment and the huge drain in terms of security costs and manpower resources. The Palestinians suffer as a result of the heavy-handed responses to terrorist attacks on Israelis, leaving their territories in turmoil and depriving them of many basic freedoms. To further complicate matters, the people of Israel are themselves divided, as are the Palestinians – the moderates would like to see peace with their neighbours, but the more right wing citizens do not want to compromise with the 'enemy'.

The construction of a wall around Israel's borders has also created another point of contention with the Palestinians as the wall passes through several areas that are considered to be Palestinian land. Whether it succeeds in increasing the security of Israelis remains to be seen.

A recent visit to Israel by Jim confirms our view that economics and politics are closely linked: poverty is an excellent breeding ground for terrorism and its organizations. Whatever the history of the region, there is no doubt that the State of Israel deserves to exist – and that it should do so in peace.

On a micro note, the fact that Jim had just come to Tel Aviv from Beirut – schlepping it via Cyprus because Israelis and Lebanese are not supposed to travel to each other's countries – aroused the suspicions of the Israeli border police! A little light interrogation ensued, even though Jim hardly ranks as any kind of threat to Israel's security. This episode, though minor, illustrates the deep paranoia that exists throughout the Middle East because of this seemingly intractable and deepening problem. The combatants have evolved into seasoned and implacable adversaries – and we see no solution in sight. This is a real pity because Israel has a nearly unrivalled repository of brainpower and energy that makes a potentially compelling case for investment. But sadly, the Israeli economy has stalled: poverty is now evident on the streets of Tel Aviv, and the Palestinian people continue to live under some of the most difficult conditions in the world. In the meantime, over 50 years have passed and thousands of lives have been lost.

Islam

Although most Muslims object to the association of their religion with terrorism, it is a fact that Osama bin Laden uses Islam's name to justify his terrorist acts and he himself is a Muslim. Therefore, it is not easy to isolate al-Qaeda from the Muslim faith, and hence the concern that it is all too easy to interpret the war on terrorism to be a war on Islam, hence Arabs and Muslims have all been affected by the West's war on terrorism in some way.

But why is Osama bin Laden waging war against the West anyway?

Through self-appointment, he and his followers believe that they are under obligation to protect Islam because it is threatened by the West on two counts:

- First, they are under attack from Western military hostilities (such as in Iraq, Palestine and Afghanistan).
- Second, they hate the spread of Western values and immorality that chips away at what (they believe) it means to be a true Muslim. Most Muslims in the world would disagree with these fears, but Islam, like Christianity, is a highly fragmented religion.

As well as having two divided branches (Sunni and Shia), Islam also has many Muslim leaders, preachers, respected intellectuals, etc. but no unifying leader at the top, a 'Chief Muslim Cleric' of sorts, to set the record straight regarding various interpretations of the Islamic scriptures, the Koran. At least the Catholic Church has a Pope to give the final verdict on disputed matters relating to the Catholic faith, but in the case of Islam, this is left only to God, which means that intra-faith debates remain unresolved, at least in this life. Hence, moderates and radicals are free to interpret the Koran in any way that suits their interests. Al-Qaeda could be considered to be an extreme breakaway group of Muslims, comprising several thousand at most, who have decided to interpret the Koran in their own very violent way.

The birth of Islam

In AD 570, Mohammed was born in Mecca into a family belonging to a clan of Quraysh, the ruling tribe of Mecca, a city in north-western Arabia. Mohammed's father died before he was born and his mother died when he was only six years old, so he was raised by his grandfather and later his uncle.

In AD 610 Mohammed (by then aged 40) received from God through the angel Gabriel the revelation of the Holy Koran and the revelation that God had chosen Mohammed as his prophet. Unlike the Bible, the Koran remained in Arabic (until very recently), which from a practical point of view meant that it was only going to be read by literate Arabs and scholars of Arabic. Nevertheless, the simplicity of its doctrine meant that Islam spread rapidly. Islam calls for belief in only one God and it repeatedly instructs human beings to use their powers of intelligence and observation. Within a few decades, the territories under Muslim rule had extended to three continents: Asia, Africa and Europe.

The foundations of Islam are its five pillars:

1   Faith – the belief in only one God, Mohammed being his last prophet.
2   Prayer – performing prayers five times each day.
3   Zakat – the giving of a percentage of one's wealth and assets each year (in excess of what is required) to the poor and less fortunate.
4   Fasting – every year in the month of Ramadan, all Muslims fast from dawn until sundown, abstaining from food, drink, and sexual relations with their spouses.
5   Pilgrimage – the pilgrimage to Mecca (the hajj) is an obligation only for the physically and financially able. Over 2 million people go to Mecca each year.

Islam is based on:

• The belief in only one God, who is all-hearing, all-seeing, all-knowing. His knowledge encompasses all things, open and secret. He knows what has happened, what will happen, and how it will happen. Nothing happens in this world except by God's will. God's will is above the will of all the creatures, hence the commonly heard term 'inshallah', which in Arabic means by the will of God.
• The belief in the existence of the angels, who are honoured creatures. Angels worship only God and obey only His command. Gabriel is the angel who passed down the words of the Koran from God to Mohammad in the form of revelations.
• The belief in prophets and messengers from God including Adam, Noah, Abraham, Ishmael, Isaac, Jacob, Moses and Jesus, Mohammed being the last of the prophets.
• The belief in the Day of Judgement.
• The belief in 'al-Qadar' – divine preordainment.

Muslim population

Today, there are as many as 1.5 billion Muslims in the world – that's up to a quarter of the world's population. It is said to be the world's fastest growing religion, surprisingly, the Middle

East is not where Islam has the highest number of followers – South Asia makes up virtually half of the world's Islamic population.

Table 3.1 Top 10 largest Muslim populations (totalling 930 million)

Country	Muslim Population
Indonesia	206,706,000
Pakistan	146,174,000
India	125,964,000
Bangladesh	114,912,000
Egypt	70,236,000
Turkey	67,973,000
Iran	67,596,000
Nigeria	66,941,000
Algeria	32,490,000
Morocco	31,277,000

Source: CIA, *World Fact Book.*

Rogue states and weapons of mass destruction

Iraq

Lessons from Iraq's earlier invaders

For almost 400 hundred years, the land that is now known as Iraq was ruled by the Ottomans (modern-day Turks). Then, it was occupied by Britain during World War I.

The British were concerned about a hostile German presence in Iraq and the threat this posed to vital communication links to British colonies to the east, particularly India. In addition, the oil supply in Iran (Iraqi oil had not yet been discovered) which was important to the British war effort was imperilled by German occupation. In 1914, British forces from India landed in Iraq and by 1918 the British had gained full control of the territory. Thus began the first Western occupation of Iraq – a fiasco for the British, as it may well turn out to be for the Americans.

Keeping control of Iraq proved difficult and costly, including a bloody revolt against the British in 1920. By this time 500 British soldiers had lost their lives – déjà vu, perhaps? The then British Deputy Civil Commissioner, Gertrude Bell, was very controversial for the period in her viewpoints. For example, she wrote in a letter to a friend in January 1920:[11]

> 'I pray the people at home may be rightly guided and realize that the only chance here is to recognize political ambitions from the first, not to try and squeeze the Arabs into our mould and have our hands forced in a year – who knows – perhaps less.'

Miss Bell proved to be right and by 1921 her superior, Arnold Wilson, stepped down and the British granted Iraq nominal independence under a provisional government and a puppet monarch, King Faisal I, who was from present-day Saudi Arabia.

The names of the players may be different, but the United States is un-nervingly going through the same process that the British went through over 80 years ago. The Americans have started to realize the vintage wisdom of Miss Bell and have scaled back their ambitions as colonists of Iraq, outlining a new political timetable that supposedly concludes with the election of a new government by the end of 2005. Although multi-party elections went ahead in January 2005 to elect a transitional assembly, the future of Iraq remains uncertain.

The guerrilla war that has ensued since the seizure of Baghdad claims the lives of American troops and innocent Iraqis on a daily basis. Any US adminis-tration would want nothing more than to keep combat deaths out of the media and out of people's minds – and of course to demonstrate what a 'success' the Iraq invasion has been. Sadly, the 1,000th American soldier was killed in Sep-tember 2004 and Iraq's future is no more certain for it.

At the end of the day, however, if Joe Six-pack is sitting at home, out of a job because his company has moved its factory to China, he will surely have far more pressing concerns than to assess whether a war fought in a faraway land proved to be a victory. What he will surely ultimately resent, though, is seeing his tax dollars being spent on an occupation and reconstruction of Iraq, rather than on trying to create jobs for the US economy. Iraq is not yet Vietnam – but it could become one.

It's not about the oil (honest!)…

Commentators have suggested that the invasion of Iraq by the United States and the United Kingdom is a prime example of the type of power play for natural resources that will become an increasing feature of global politics.

The invasion could certainly be seen as a way to secure oil reserves by invading Iraq under the pretext of deposing a cruel tyrant. Regardless of whether this was actually the case, it is certainly true that there are many tyrannical dictatorships in the world. However, none of them have vast proven oil reserves like Iraq does. So, while the US can never openly declare oil as *the* reason for the war on the Saddam Hussein regime, any other reason given appears to be far from convincing. For example, so far there has been no evidence of WMD, cited as the key reason for going to war. In addition, there has been no evidence of the former Iraqi government's purported links to al-Qaeda. Probably no WMD will ever emerge and it is now improbable that Osama and Saddam had much in common at all. In fact, Saddam could hardly have been more secular, and enjoyed smoking, drinking and fornicating.

Taking a look at the three countries with the highest oil reserves in the world (Saudi Arabia, Iraq and Iran) the 'geo' picture looks much clearer. Iran and Iraq were both considered to be part of the so-called 'Axis of Evil' until the invasion of Iraq. Saudi Arabia is unofficially referred to as a 'shadow' member of this axis since a large majority of the hijackers that perpetrated the September 11 attacks were Saudi nationals and, of course, Osama bin Laden is from a large, influential Saudi family. It is not surprising then that relations between the United States and Saudi Arabia have been faltering since the war on terrorism began. The Saudis themselves are increasingly concerned about the growing issue of home-grown terrorism.

Together, Saudi Arabia, Iraq and Iran account for almost half of the world's proven oil reserves (46.7% to be precise).[12] If we add in Venezuela, then that percentage increases to well over 50%. Venezuela was an important source of oil for the United States in the past, but oil exports have been severely disrupted and the country has been in a state of chaos under President Hugo Chavez.

Furthermore, President George W. Bush is from an oil town called Midland in Texas and Vice President Dick Cheney is the former chief executive officer of a company called Halliburton (an oil and gas equipment services company). No matter what you believe to be the true motive for the invasion of Iraq, oil must be somewhere behind the logic for military action.

Iraq is not the only country whose people have been oppressed for decades. Zimbabwe, for example, has long been under the dictatorship of President Mugabe, who has tortured, murdered and detained his people as well as managing to ruin the country's economy. Where is the 'coalition of the willing' for the people of Zimbabwe? What about the poor starving people of North Korea under the ruthless rule of Kim Jong Il – don't these people deserve to be liberated too?

Unlike other dictators with delusions of grandeur, Saddam Hussein was a dictator who controlled the world's second largest oil reserves, and with demonstrably aggressive tendencies (i.e. the Kuwait and Iran wars). So, sorry, people of Zimbabwe, North Korea and other nations who suffer under cruel regimes, although we do empathize with your pain and suffering, the succinct but unspoken reply from the US to your cries for help is – no oil, no rescue!

The US is the world's number one oil consumer. So much so that it cannot satisfy its thirst through domestic production alone and has to import over half of its oil (see pp. 25–28 for an in-depth look at oil supply and demand). Ensuring a large and reliable supply of oil is of paramount importance to the US economy. There is also a more subtle yet very significant connection between the US and the oil industry – oil around the world is sold in US dollars. This has in fact been the case since the oil crisis of 1973 when by fiat OPEC quadrupled the price of oil and announced it would only accept US dollars as payment for its output. When the gold standard was abandoned (see sidebar below), the dollar effectively transmuted from being a gold-backed currency to one backed by oil. Thus it has been able to remain an international currency, accounting for around two-thirds of the world's currency reserves. For this and other reasons to do with its superpower status, the US has in the past been able to continue to spend and run up debts and deficits like no other nation, even though technically it is bankrupt – at least to anyone who reads a balance sheet.

People and nations need dollars – even if a country does not trade with the US but needs to buy oil, it has to buy dollars. However, for the first time since the 1970s oil crisis, the petrodollar or the 'oil standard' is being challenged by a more robust suitor – the euro – and should the euro succeed in supplanting the US dollar as the currency of oil denomination, the repercussions will be serious. The US economy will be put under further threat by an acceleration of the dollar's demise. As foreign governments and individuals alike sell dollars and buy euros and other currencies, the supply of dollars in the market will increase. Even the US would be forced to sell dollars and buy euros to purchase its oil imports!

How real is this threat? Well, it is real enough that:

- Iran (the number three oil-rich nation) has switched some of its foreign reserves from dollars to euros.
- In 2000, while Saddam was in power, Iraq switched its foreign reserves to euros and announced it would only sell its oil to the UN (under the oil for food programme) in euros.
- In October 2003, Russian President Vladimir Putin announced in a joint news conference with Germany's Chancellor Gerhard Schroeder that he could switch the price of Russia's oil (the number six oil-rich nation) to euros – 'We do not rule out that it is possible. That would be interesting for our European partners,' he said.[13]
- OPEC has held meetings to discuss the possibility of selling oil in euros.
- In May 2004, the population of the Eurozone grew to 450 million, challenging America's long-standing dominance as the world's largest economy – and, of course, coming up in the fast lane is China.

'Liberating' Iraq and allowing a US-friendly leader to be appointed might ensure that the world's number two oil-rich nation will continue to sell oil in US dollars, thus maintaining some international status for the currency and at least forestalling a cataclysmic collapse of its currency.

It may well be that US administration thinking does not have the sophistication that we are attributing to it – but the dollar's vulnerability must be well known to the economic advisers to the president and to others. We just don't buy the idea that George W. Bush wanted to avenge his father's failure to dislodge Saddam from power after the first Gulf War in the early 1990s – and that it was the *raison d'être* for starting the second Gulf War.

How trusting are the American people?

How can the US ensure an uninterrupted supply of oil imports and hold on to the oil-backed dollar?

The gold standard abandoned

In 1971 President Nixon abandoned the gold standard – a system whereby anyone holding US dollars was entitled to exchange them for gold at a rate of $35 per ounce of gold. As a result of the growing US balance-of-payments deficit, foreign banks ended up accumulating more and more dollars. When finally Britain and other nations asked for some of their accumulated dollars to be converted to gold, they were told that the gold standard was no longer in effect. US dollars in circulation by then had grown in value to around eight times the US government's gold reserves and as a result the US could no longer honour the exchange of dollars for gold. Eventually, the dollar was allowed to float freely on the world market, as it still does today.

Saudi Arabia is continuously on the brink of civil unrest. Iran's hard-line Islamic regime usually finds itself at odds with the US, and Iraq was, until recently, only authorized to sell limited quantities of oil exclusively through the United Nations. The US had a problem. And what is more, it lacked an adequate strategy for the oil-rich Middle Eastern region. In this respect, near unconditional support for Israel does not help matters when trying to strengthen ties with Arab states.

With anti-US sentiment running high in the Middle East, what if Saudi Arabia, Iraq and Iran joined forces and decided to refuse the sale of oil to the United States unless, say, the Americans stopped procrastinating and found a solution to the Israeli–Palestinian problem? What if, at the same time, these countries and possibly OPEC announced that they would only sell oil for euros? This 'worst case' scenario would be too devastating not to warrant a contingency plan in the White House. Remember that the US imports more than half of its oil and oil is crucial to its economy (see pp. 25–28 for more details).

Let's consider a hypothetical scenario where a think-tank in the US government sat down and came to the same conclusion that we outlined in the previous paragraph. The think-tank perhaps identified Iraq as a possible secure and stable supply of oil, so it began to prepare a list of possible justifications for toppling the regime. The list on Iraq may have looked something like this:

1 Has a track record of aggression – the war with Iran and the invasion of Kuwait, followed by the first Gulf War.
2 Has in the past possessed and used chemical and biological weapons and attempted to develop nuclear weapons.
3 Has committed horrendous crimes against humanity on a mass scale – genocide, torture and murder.
4 Has a leader who is hated by his own people, particularly the oppressed Shia Muslims (who make up over 60% of the population) and the Kurds.
5 Is not popular with neighbouring countries, hence is unlikely to win the support of other nations in the event of a conflict.

Yet all of these reasons would not be sufficient to justify the actual waging of a war against a sovereign nation, so they put on their thinking caps (being a think-tank) and realized that the only way to justify an act of aggression would be to create a sense of imminent danger. 'How about using the September 11 attacks to stir emotion and patriotism,' said one member of the think-tank. 'Americans would surely support a war against Iraq if they were told that their lives and those of their children were being threatened. What if we could persuade the public that democracy itself was under threat because this evil man has weapons of mass destruction and would use them against Americans?'

'Oh,' responded the American people, 'we had no idea he was such a threat to us. Why didn't you say so? In that case, let's go over there and kick some proverbial ass.'

How close to the truth is this hypothetical scenario? We may never know.

With every passing day, it is increasingly obvious that there never were any weapons of mass destruction and no imminent threat to the American people. Al-Qaeda remains at large, but they never had anything to do with Iraq anyway. So both reasons used by the Bush administration to rally support for the war – possession of WMD (later revised to WMD programme) and links with al-Qaeda – turned out to be false. It is very unlikely that we will ever really know whether this was (a) due to incorrect intelligence gathering or (b) a ploy to justify going to war (for oil). And quite frankly, whatever the truth really is, option (a) is the only acceptable answer and is the official one given to the public by the US government following a series of investigations. After all, how can answer (b) be the official one without there being mass resignations throughout the highest echelons of government?

North Korea – cornered dog

North Korea, the so-called 'Hermit Kingdom', is a nation which resulted from the division of the Korean Peninsula after the Korean War. North Korea is in some ways a 'Paper Tiger', though in other ways a major threat to world stability.

It is true that the North Korean 'million man army' is probably no more effective than Iraq's million man force, which was so easily defeated by the US-led coalition in early 2003. In addition, North Korean troop deployments along the Demilitarized Zone and coastal areas to fend off possible attacks by South Korea eat up substantial resources. This makes a conventional assault by North Korean forces against South Korea unlikely. South Korea has 700,000 men under permanent arms and 5 million reservists, 30 times the economic output of the North and 3 times the military expenditures of the North. What the South does not have, however, is a desperate regime, with frequent famines and a probable and growing nuclear capability. Certainly, deployment of nuclear weapons by North Korea would invite instant retaliation from the United States, but there is no accounting for the sheer irrationality of the regime in the North. It is not yet certain that North Korea can build an intercontinental ballistic missile but for sure their missiles can already reach South Korea, Japan and China.

Increasingly, sceptics in the Untied States doubt the economic cost-effectiveness of maintaining 37,000 American troops in South Korea. Consequently, Washington plans to reduce this number by a third by the end of 2005. The argument is that South Korea can handle any Northern threat on its own and that China, which helped the North in the Korean War in the 1950s, will no longer support it in a future war. US expenditures in Korea annually run to many billions and it is tempting to halt those and use the money elsewhere. These are valid arguments and are likely to prevail. The problem is that the withdrawal of US forces may encourage the North Koreans to attack, using nuclear weapons.

If North Korea does attack with nuclear weapons, the consequences will be diabolical. Mass destruction in Japan or South Korea, for instance, would cause an international terror not seen for decades. Certainly, such a move would accelerate the move towards depression in the Rich World.

There was a time in the 1990s when South Korea's pursuit of a 'Sunshine Policy' towards the North yielded a great deal in terms of optimism and excitement – though little else. Tearful exchanges took place between families separated by the war – elderly children greeted their ancient parents for the first time in fifty years, for instance, in three-day reunions in Seoul and Pyongyang. A train was mooted to run between the two countries – though even today it is not yet operating as a direct service.

In 2000, over 500 South Korean companies announced plans to invest in the North, and the largest of them was Hyundai. Hyundai, a South Korean 'chaebol' or industrial grouping of companies, had great plans for the North but it all came to a sad end – in a way epitomizing the entire effort to bring the Hermit Kingdom into the real world. The visionary founder of the Hyundai Group – Chang Jug Yang – turned his company into the largest investor north of the border. He started by running tours across the line to Geumgangsan (Diamond), a spectacular range of mountains, and to create a 'Special Economic Zone' (such as exist in China) across the Demilitarized Zone at Kaesong. Hyundai's investments, estimated at $1.5 billion, have been all but lost. In true Korean style a large part of this loss was the result of bribes and 'special payments', which reached all the way up to the then South Korean President, Kim Dae Jung. Some say President Kim effectively 'bought' his Nobel Peace prize, which he was awarded in 2000, having transferred money to his northern counterpart through Hyundai.

In the past North Korea has used its nuclear weapons development programme as a blackmail card to extract food and other aid from the United States. This is still a tactic in use. In early 2004, North Korea invited a private delegation from the US to visit what it said was a stack of bomb-usable plutonium extracted from 8000 fuel rods used in nuclear energy programmes. Members of the delegation were divided as to the exact state of North Korea's nuclear capability. The visit was part of the carefully choreographed use of blackmail tactics ahead of key meetings between the two Koreas, Japan,

Russia, China and the US that in some combination or other occasionally take place.

The harder-line attitude adopted by the Bush administration has lowered North Korea's chances of success in this tactic. Further blackmail efforts may well result in more brinkmanship, which precipitates desperate action. In those circumstances deaths will almost certainly run into many millions. This scenario should not be discounted. For sure, a conventional war is unlikely but an unconventional pre-emptive strike by the North Koreans is a distinct possibility.

North Korean officials have privately said that they now have nuclear weapons and might test them – or even sell them. When faced with such political manoeuvres, South Korea is an appeaser, Japan and the US are firm-liners and an exasperated China is caught in the middle. With no concerted approach it is difficult for them to knock this particular threat on the head once and for all.

Meanwhile North Korea undoubtedly improves and deepens its nuclear capacity, making the eventual solution – if there is one – that much more difficult to achieve. Take note, though, that the Institute for Strategic Studies in London believes that in a few years North Korea could be producing 5–10 nuclear weapons a year, to add to its current stockpile of what they believe to be enough plutonium for between 2–5 nuclear weapons. The Institute also believes that North Korea has probably produced and stockpiled chemical weapons and that it has conducted research and development on biological agents.

North Korea has repeatedly pledged to abandon its WMD programme if the US ends its hostile policies towards the communist state, but this 'offer' is widely derided and unlikely to be taken up. Meanwhile, readers should watch events on the Korean peninsula – not the world's top danger point but certainly a menace – with a weather eye.

North Korea is a weird place – the Kim family dynasty has ruled the garrison state for more than half a century and a personality cult of incredible proportions has been built up around the father and son. The current leader Kim Jong-il has been ascribed the authorship of over 1000 books, and all written while he was at university. Kim Il-sung, his father, though long embalmed, is President for Eternity and statues of him are a lot more numerous than those of Saddam ever were.

He is described – seriously – as the Greatest Genius of Mankind, the Most Famous Man in the World. It cannot be easy for Kim Junior to follow in his footsteps. He appears to lead a life of vulgar luxury amidst the famines regularly endured by his people. But he is shrewd in his dealings with the West, and has clung to power remarkably successfully. His winning card with his people is the incredible brutality with which the US waged war against the North in the 1950s – and this is a brutality that he plays up as likely to occur if the US had its way again.

This is a regime that still – despite starvation, mass privations and a backwards economy – has a strong grip on the government of the country and 'normal' is not a word in its vocabulary.

Iran – the other axis

Iran is one of only two non-Arab countries in the Middle East – the other is Israel. The language spoken in Iran is Persian – also known as Farsi – a language similar to Arabic in the same way as French is similar to English, i.e. they share a common alphabet, some words are recognizable, some are the same, yet they remain two distinct languages. Many Iranians learn Arabic in order to be able to read the Koran in its original form. Iran is situated in a rather lonely position in the world – the Arabs to the west, the former Soviet states to the north and the Indian subcontinent to the south-east.

In ancient times (circa 500 BC) Persia had an empire that extended from Greece to India. In modern times, the country has never been far from the news – the US hostage crises of 1979 that cost President Carter his re-election, the Iranian Embassy siege in London, the Iran–Iraq War, violations of human rights, Axis of Evil member, supporter of terrorism, etc. But prior to the Islamic revolution of 1979, Iran was a moderate country that was aligned with the West. The Shah, however, who was popular with the West, fell out of favour with his people. Tensions mounted and by January 1979, the Shah was deposed and a new Islamic Republic was subsequently declared, headed by Ayatollah Khomeini, who returned from exile in France.

Approximately one year later, its neighbour to the west, Iraq, declared war on Iran. It would prove to be another long, bloody and pointless war for the history books – one that lasted eight years. The Americans, who were against

Iran's new leadership, backed Iraq and provided Saddam Hussein and his regime with military support. Iran received its military supplies from the Soviet Union. Estimates of lives lost vary but it is believed to be in the region of 1 million, the majority of them being Iranian.

Iran is the world's third richest oil state and is an appointed member of President Bush's now infamous Axis of Evil. It is therefore a country that never falls off the radar screens of the US administration. For the past 20 years Iran has been on the US State Department's list of countries that sponsor terrorism – it actively supports a number of organizations considered to be terrorist groups, such as Hezbollah, Hamas and Palestinian Islamic Jihad – all anti-Israel organizations. Former Deputy Secretary of State Richard Armitage told the Senate Foreign Relations Committee in October 2003 that Iran *'continues to be the world's foremost state supporter of terrorism.'*

Nuclear ambitions
During the second half of 2003, the world realized that Iran's nuclear uranium enrichment programme was more advanced than previously thought and that the country was within two years of possessing nuclear weapons. To quote a US official involved in monitoring Tehran's nuclear programme: '*… that is not a prospect any sane person would welcome.'*[14]

Iran initially stood firm by its nuclear development programme and declared that it was an alternative fuel source to its 100 billion barrels or so of proven oil reserves! This further aroused the suspicions of the US, the UN and the International Atomic Energy Agency (IAEA), which went in for a closer look. Iran was left tongue-tied again when the presence of highly enriched uranium was discovered – a type only used to make nuclear weapons. The Iranian excuse this time was that it must have 'inadvertently' been imported in equipment purchased from overseas.

Fortunately, as a result of mounting international pressure, in October 2003 Iran provided assurances to the IAEA that it would provide full disclosure of all its past nuclear activities. The international community welcomed this statement, although many remained sceptical. By November 2003, Iran agreed to suspend all uranium enrichment and reprocessing activities and, by the following month, had signed an Additional Protocol to its Nuclear Non-Proliferation Treaty (NPT) safeguards agreement, granting IAEA inspectors greater authority in verifying the country's nuclear programme.

Indeed, UN inspectors have discovered evidence of Iran's clear intentions to acquire nuclear technology: key components in enrichment equipment have been found in the country, equipment that Tehran failed to declare. Pakistan's now infamous 'father of the atomic bomb' (conveniently pardoned for his many sins), Abdul Qadeer Khan, has had close links with Iran's nuclear programme, as indeed with several others. This man, in return for large amounts of money, has sold bagfuls of secrets to rogue nations – as well as facilitating the direct transfer of key elements used in military-grade uranium production, such as centrifuges.

These centrifuges spin at high speed and are used to separate fissile uranium 235 isotopes that can be used in nuclear bombs. The presence of these centrifuges in Iran is fairly clear evidence, despite vehement denials by Tehran, of Iran's intention to acquire nuclear military technology. Khan – by all accounts a greedy man with 22 properties in Islamabad alone – sold information and designs to, among others, Libya, Iran and North Korea. The damage this man has done – and many suspect it was with the complicity of the Pakistani government – is incalculable. The horse has bolted from the stable and those secrets, particularly those used in the making of the centrifuges, are now presumably widely disseminated.

While Iran appears to be playing along with the UN weapons inspectorate, to the US it may appear guilty of a different interpretation of 'playing along'. Perhaps a further 'cat and mouse' game is being staged, *à la* Baghdad not so long ago – and perhaps another invasion will have to be contemplated, or at the least a pre-emptive strike? The tightening grip of religious hardliners in recent elections in Iran – with many 'liberal' candidates simply disbarred from standing for a series of bogus reasons – is further disturbing news for those who fear the proliferation of 'Islamic' nuclear bombs.

MISSILE TRANSPORTERS

12 PROBABLE GUIDELINE MISSILES

HEAVY EQUIPMENT

5 MISSILE DOLLIES

20 LONG CYLINDRICAL TANKS

MISSILE TRANSPORTERS

OPEN STORAGE

*part*FOUR

Lessons From History

At the outset of this book, we drew attention to the obvious and scary parallels between the current state of the world's economy and the time just before the Great Depression of the 1920s and 1930s. There is an eerie similarity between the two periods, then and now. Both are characterized by the following: excessive debt, overenthusiasm for the immediate outlook for new technologies, and excessive credit creation followed by a tightening policy by major central banks.

This is the most obvious 'lesson from history' that we can draw from our studies – and it is an important one. The speed of the collapse in trade, employment and prosperity which occurred during the Great Depression, which lasted for years, should provide a wake-up call to all those who doubt that we are about to enter a difficult period.

But there are other lessons that we can glean from a study of history too. In a geopolitical sense, we face partly similar conditions to those that prevailed before the outbreak of World War I in 1914, the so-called 'Great War'. We draw attention to the commonalities later in this part of the book.

These similarities between past periods in history and our own present should not be ignored. Complacency is the enemy of the successful investor. It is not necessarily the case that what happened in the past is bound to repeat itself – and certainly the world we live in is a far different one to that of 100 years ago or even 50 years ago. Our world today has positive attributes not apparent just a few decades ago: greater interdependence, lessened tensions between major nations and medical and scientific advances that have the capacity to make the lives of all who inhabit the planet better ones.

There are also negatives that we should take into account when comparing our period with times past: a much higher population that is squeezing the limited resource output of the earth, far greater destructive power available to governments worldwide, and the possibility of this to fall into the hands of terrorist groups. And of course the rise of China, which is a potentially far more destabilizing force than any other in human history.

The lessons of history are not clearly written for us. However, it is important to review the past to get a sense of where our present is going.

We do this first by looking at wars. Just because most of the people alive today in the relatively rich nations of the world have had little personal exposure to wars in their lifetimes, it doesn't mean that wars cannot or will not happen again. The message from this review is to hope for the best but to be prepared for the worst.

Past wars and conflicts

There are possibly more good quotes available on the subject of war than on any other. Just about anyone who thinks seriously about conflict or who has ever taken up arms is against war. So why is war still waged and why does war still remain the principal threat to our lives, liberty and health? Why was it that, in the 20th century, hundreds of millions of people were wiped out through violence initiated by nation states?

In World War I, the British and Commonwealth troops going 'over the top' were famously described as 'lions led by donkeys.' This, of course, was a generally unfair description of the reality, but it does capture the essence of what wars are really all about, i.e. older men, sitting somewhere out of harm's way, directing testosterone-filled younger men to go do their bidding in bloody conflict. All great fun: bands, pretty girls and admiration, at least to begin with. Yet, as we've mentioned elsewhere, wars can easily be started but cannot so easily be stopped. We list below some war-related quotes from individuals who realized the futility of war. They express our thoughts about war better than we possibly could. Sadly, the human race is not yet ready to make armed conflicts a thing of the past any time soon – and that provides a powerful message to us.

'War is too serious a matter to be entrusted to military men.'

Georges Clemenceau

'Older men declare war. But it is the youth who must fight and die!'

Herbert Hoover

'You can no more win a war than you can win an earthquake.'

Jeanette Rankin

'I hate war as only a soldier who has lived it can, only as one who has seen its brutality, its futility, its stupidity.'

General Dwight Eisenhower

So, readers, you get the picture. No one really wins in wars, but it doesn't seem to prevent wars from breaking out. We think it is important to examine a few of the wars in relevant history that have lessons for the modern age.

The American Civil War – breakdown of civil society

Lessons for ideologues today

The American Civil War of 1861–1865 is one of the seminal events of American history. Not only was it the war that led to the abolition of slavery, but it was also the event that gave identity to modern-day America.

The war was caused by conflicting principles which set in motion a series of events – and, at the time, conflict seemed unlikely. The fundamental root of the war was slavery, a trade which thirteen of the states considered to be legal, despite the fact that the US constitution stated clearly that all men were created equal. These southern states relied on slavery to sustain their agricultural plantations; this was especially the case after the invention of the cotton gin by Eli Whitney, allowing America to become the biggest producer of cotton in the world.

Meanwhile, in the northern states, populations grew rapidly due to mass industrialization and were swelled further by new migrants, who by 1850 made up two-thirds of the North's numbers. This allowed these states to elect proportionately more members of Congress than the southern states, due to their greater populations. The South therefore started to feel under-represented in Congress – and threatened.

Opinions in the US of the time were sharply divided over the issue of slavery. While many agreed in principle that slavery had to be abolished, others were indifferent and felt that such a move would be bad for business as it would hurt the cotton and textile industry. Indeed, even in the supposedly 'enlightened' North, only four states permitted freed slaves to vote.

The tense situation between abolitionists and the southerners continued to escalate to the point that, when Abraham Lincoln, a leading abolitionist, was elected president in November 1860, South Carolina seceded from the Union the following month. This led to other states following suit: Mississippi, Florida, Alabama, Georgia, Louisiana and Texas. Federal forts throughout these states were taken over peacefully.

By the time Lincoln took office in January 1861, the rebel states had had plenty of time to strengthen their positions. Lincoln was reluctant to strike the first blow. In the end, it was the southern states that began the hostilities when they shot at a federal supply ship despatched to re-provision Fort Sumter in Charleston Harbour, South Carolina. It was 4.30 am on 12 April 1861 – and the start of the worst period in US history.

Lincoln immediately reacted by requesting the draft of 75,000 troops to serve 90 days against 'combinations too powerful to be suppressed by the ordinary process of judicial proceedings.' At this point, three additional states seceded from the Union: Virginia, Arkansas and Tennessee. On 20 May, North Carolina decided to 'leave' the Union. Although other states voted to secede, North Carolina voted to 'undo' the act that had brought it into the United States in the first place. In August and December of that year, Missouri and Kentucky respectively seceded from the Union.

The states that did not want to be part of the Union any longer became known as the 'Confederate States'. The ensuing war resulted in over a million casualties from both sides (3.6% of the US population at the time) and cost the country $15 billion in the dollars of the time; this was during an era where an unskilled labourer earned a dollar a day.

The war's conclusion established the supreme authority of the Federal government over that of the individual state, abolished slavery and stimulated the industrial growth and prosperity of the United States – but not without terrible cost. Again, a chain reaction of small events led to war, disruption and carnage.

Today, the US is once more a nation deeply divided: there are those who view the path the country has taken following the September 11 attacks as the right one, i.e. the Patriot Act, the pre-emptive strike policy and the wars in Afghanistan and Iraq. Yet there are others who believe that the US has embarked on an arrogant and unsustainable path that has compromised the civil liberties of its citizens, alienated their nation from its allies and the rest of the world and made the planet a more dangerous place than it was before September 11.

The lessons of the Civil War are not directly applicable to the US today, though. Despite the divide that exists between the states that are ideologically liberal (in an American sense) and those that are typically more conservative and influenced by religious beliefs, the potential for internal conflict is minute.

However, a tangential lesson can be learned from the American Civil War. There are strong conflicting pressures in American society today – for instance over the right to life, over the conduct of American foreign policy, over trade etc. The battle over these ideological issues is a more serious one than any that has occurred since the Civil War, and while the potential for any conflict in the US itself is negligible, the outcome of the battle is very important to the rest of the world. It will in some ways determine the relationship of the US with China, with other key nations and with supranational bodies such as the UN. It will determine the US outlook and policy on the environment. It will determine US policy on free trade and on the Third World and it will determine US domestic policy on the alleviation of poverty. And the outlook on all of these isn't looking good.

World War I – lessons for the present day

In Flanders Fields

In Flanders Fields the poppies blow
Between the crosses row on row
That mark our place; and in the sky
The larks still bravely singing fly
Scarce heard amid the guns below.
We are the dead. Short days ago
We lived, felt dawn saw sunset glow.
Loved, and were loved and now we lie
In Flanders Fields.
Take up our quarrel with the foe:
To you from failing hands we throw
The torch; be yours to hold it high.
If ye break faith with us who die
We shall not sleep, though poppies grow
In Flanders Fields.

John McCrae, Punch, *December 8, 1915*

The above is perhaps the most famous of the poems to come out of World War I. A young Canadian doctor, who had just seen one of his best friends blown up by a shell, wrote it. The doctor too was to die of his wounds later in the war – along with millions of others.

The churned up soil of Flanders in Belgium provided ideal growing conditions for the bright red poppy, now an international symbol of loss and destruction. What is most interesting about this poem is that the author believes in the 'cause' and urges the successors to the dead to take up the torch. The 'cause' of World War I at the time, which each side believed to be righteous in their own case, can hardly be remembered today. And that is the point: wars start quickly, for reasons that in most cases are spurious. They cannot, however, be ended the same way and so their length and destructive power is frequently underestimated.

The catalyst to war is often something relatively trivial, such as in the case of World War I. Although the *casus belli* may appear to be stupid with the benefit of hindsight, astute observers can foresee a build-up to war.

Today, it is hard to imagine just how atrocious World War I was. And its eventual continuum, World War II, accounted for the deaths of perhaps 200 million people in total.

In the course of research for this book, Jim visited the flatlands of Belgium, where so much carnage took place for so little reason. Anyone who has visited the great battlefields of World War I, particularly those of Flanders in Belgium and of the Somme in France, is struck by the immense scale of the conflict and saddened by the appalling loss of life.

Small, rebuilt towns exude an air of prosperity, but all around them lie the killing fields of a war that shaped the 20th century. Even now, these battlefields yield up about 500 spent or live shell cases from the period – every day. Farmers regularly come across the badges, water bottles and other equipment of the now nameless men who fought across a narrow distance in hellish conditions.

The most evocative of all the war memorials for that period, the Menin Gate in Ypres, records the names of 56,000 British and Commonwealth troops whose bodies were never recovered. The four Battles of Ypres between 1915 and 1918 saw advances on both sides of no more than three miles. For years the armies fought over a narrow strip of churned up earth. By the end, over a million lives were lost on that one battlefield alone. The futility of the conflict, the awesome destructive effect of modern warfare and the poignancy of loss are all illustrated on the Menin Gate and we recommend any reader sceptical of the scale and tragedy of uncontrolled and uncontrollable warfare to pay a visit to this now bucolic yet sinister former battlefield. Perhaps then there would be less 'rooting' for 'our boys' to go into battle.

Origins of World War I
It is hard to believe that World War I started only one long lifetime ago. The conflict essentially began because at the turn of the 20th century there existed an imbalance of power among the nations of the then fulcrum of the world – Europe.

The British Empire had only recently peaked in strength, and it defended its colonial possessions and trade routes with a navy that was larger than all others combined. The only rival in Europe to Britain was the newly unified Germany, fast becoming its largest economy and with a population of over 60 million, which at the time was 50% higher than that of Britain and twice that of France. As a result of Germany's economic rise and of France's relative underpopulation, the latter had by then fallen to second-power status.

Meanwhile, a military elite, the 'junkers', who remained imbued in a tradition of hierarchical deference and discipline, ruled Germany. At the top of this elite was Kaiser Wilhelm II who reflected and expressed openly the national desire for expansion and the demand for recognition of Germany as a world power.

In conventional arms, Germany had the largest and best-equipped army in the world, with over 700,000 regular troops and millions of reservists. At that time, Britain was not too concerned about this German superiority, since its principal interest was not in European affairs but in the maintenance of its trade routes and empire, which it did with naval power.

However, when Germany started to build a navy to match that of Britain, the British responded in two ways: first, they expanded their own naval power and by 1914 had impressively and decisively won that aspect of the first 'arms race'. Second, they realigned their allegiances in Europe, siding with France, which in turn was allied to Russia. Germany's Kaiser along with the ruling classes were concerned that the nation's economic power was not reflected in its small colonial presence; envy of Britain was compounded and abetted by the fall and dissipation of alternative empires – the Austro-Hungarian and Ottoman ones which by then were shadows of their former selves.

Germany allied itself with the fading Austro-Hungarian Empire, which by that time consisted of a collection of 'submerged' states with widely differing peoples and aspirations. The divisions in that ragtag empire – epitomized by the assassination in Sarajevo on 28 July 1914 of the heir to the Hapsburg Austro-Hungarian throne, Archduke Franz Ferdinand – provided the spark for the ensuing global war.

This single incident triggered one of the greatest conflagrations yet seen by humanity. The assassin was part of a Serbian terrorist group, and as a result Austria demanded that Serbia be more fully subsumed into its empire, so that it could be better controlled. Russia, as Serbia's natural ally, could not tolerate this, which was exactly what many observers had expected. Meanwhile, France, as Russia's ally, took the same view and war between Russia and Germany became inevitable.

What the Germans paid little attention to, however, was whether or not Britain would join in on the side of France and Russia. The German calculation was that Britain would remain neutral as it was a more natural ally of Germany. After all, their entire royal families were closely related and the French had been the historical enemies of both countries.

This calculation was rendered inaccurate when the Germans decided to launch a pre-emptive strike on France by invasion, and by conducting the invasion through neutral Belgium. In the 19th century, Britain and Belgium had entered into a treaty which obliged the British to come to the aid of the Belgians; this it did, with the support of outraged and pumped-up British public opinion.

Thus the perceived and actual imbalances in military and economic power among the European nations, coupled with a desire to gain a first-strike advantage, led to a war resulting in the partial destruction of an entire generation.

For the first time in modern history, all armies in the conflict deployed up-to-date weaponry, whose destructive power far exceeded anything else ever arrayed. For example, modern rifles were by now deadly accurate at long ranges of up to three-quarters of a mile. Field guns could be deployed several miles behind the front lines, and the rapid development of the railways and the telegraph meant that large movements of men and materiel could be accomplished in short periods. Prior to this war, weaponry had been more 'point and hope' in its general capacity; now weapons were accurate and large-scale deployments were rapid. What had not been modernized were many of the tactics employed on the battlefields, hence the 'digging in' that became the muddy, brutal apocalyptic feature of much of the fighting for the years of conflict that followed the initial German advance.

As early as 1899 the Polish writer Ivan Bloch had predicted that battles fought with such new weapons would quickly degenerate into bloody deadlock – and he was right. For four years a war of attrition was fought, punctuated by occasional and generally disastrous frontal assaults. These largely took place on the Western Front with little progress on either side. On the Eastern Front, the Germans had more success and the Russian Revolution led to an armistice – a one-sided truce which humiliated the Russians and freed up resources for Germany to continue the war on the Western Front. The Treaty of Brest-Litovsk in 1917 marked this peace in the East and effectively removed Russia from the conflict.

The entry of the United States into the war in 1917 led to an overwhelming superiority of men and material for the Allies and gave the conflict the dubious cachet of being the first global war in history. As the Americans arrived in larger numbers in the European theatre, the German nation was crumbling under the effects of a sea blockade of all shipping routes by the British Royal Navy as well as under the continual strain of war. Defeat became inevitable. This defeat was famously marked by a cessation of hostilities on the 11th hour of the 11th day of the 11th month – of 1918. The Armistice and the subsequent Treaty of Versailles imposed conditions on the defeated Germany that were punitively onerous. This led to hyperinflation and poverty, and aided the rise of Nazism, leading within just twenty years to the second major war of the 20th century.

World War I resulted in nations with total populations of about 500 million people being engaged in combat. Of these, about 64 million were mobilized into military service and a total of 8 million were killed in the period (or about one-third of all men in each country). France lost nearly 20% of its military combatants. Germany lost about 17% and Britain about 13%. The scale of the tragedy was unparalleled in human history … until, that is, World War II, where Russian losses were so great that it has an effect on its total population even today.

World War I – parallels for our times

- *First, the Great War started because of imbalances in world power* – the countervailing force to British hegemony became a militarist German nation. Today, we have an imbalance in the world with the US as the sole superpower and the obvious countervailing force is China, which will become a major military power in the next decade or so.
- *Also, World War I demonstrated that old alliances and treaties quite often have no efficacy* if the parties to them choose to ignore their meaning. Modern treaty

organizations, such as the United Nations, similarly may have no effect when it counts – look for instance at the US and Britain, which went to war with Iraq in clear defiance of the UN, technically making it an illegal act of aggression.

Only ninety years ago many of Europe's comfortable lives were quickly ruined or eradicated by a series of ill-judged diplomatic and military manoeuvres. It could happen again.

The Vietnam War – history and its foolish repetition

There are countless examples of situations where warfare was not only unnecessary, but counterproductive, Vietnam being one such relatively recent example. This war was fought on questionable ideological grounds where the United States sought to halt the spread of communism in Asia. It was a war with no winners. The US was forced out of Indochina – the mad scramble for the last helicopter out of Saigon forcefully illustrating its final humiliation. Vietnam, unified but broken by retaliatory sanctions and the effects of egalitarian politics, has only just recently joined the modern world.

Unlike other wars, the United States was gradually drawn into the Vietnam conflict over a period lasting a full 15 years. US involvement initially began in 1950 when President Truman provided economic and military aid to the French who were fighting a communist army in Vietnam in order to retain Indochina (present day Vietnam, Laos and Cambodia), which was then a French colony.

Despite US support, by 1954, the French had lost to the Vietnamese Nationalist army at Dien Bien Phu. They were consequently forced to accept the creation of a North Vietnam Communist state, with South Vietnam remaining non-communist and under Western influence. However, the United States, which had in effect bankrolled the French military campaign, refused to accept this outcome and the recently elected President Eisenhower proceeded to take control of South Vietnam from the French. The Americans also established a South Vietnamese government and sent US soldiers to train the local army.

In 1961, this time under President Kennedy, the United States sent 400 Green Beret soldiers to teach the South Vietnamese how to fight against communist guerrillas, by then highly active in South Vietnam. This process escalated as the problem of communist insurgency grew worse. By 1963, the United States had sent over 16,000 'military advisers' to South Vietnam, although the South was still not officially at war with the North until after the assassination of President Kennedy. This defining and fateful moment took place under the presidency of Lyndon Johnson in August 1964 when he passed a 'functional' declaration of war through Congress. By March 1965 President Johnson authorized a bombing campaign over North Vietnam and sent over 3,500 Marines to the South. The US got drawn into a conflict which led to ignominious and comprehensive defeat and retreat after the commitment of 500,000 men.

What initially drew the United States into this war was a deep ingrained fear and hatred of communism; the US government was highly concerned that it would spread like a virus across the world. Communism was perceived as a threat to democracy and American values. Since at the time, the Soviet Union, Eastern Europe, Central Asia and China were all ruled by communist regimes, this was not such a fanciful view.

Although fighting communism was the initial reason for the war, the reasons for its involvement became more ambiguous as the conflict wore on. The communist victory in China in 1950 was a catalyst to the expansion of US involvement. Then there was the issue of pride – no US president wanted to be known for losing a war against communists. Each successive president involved in the Vietnam debacle wanted to be re-elected, so there was the matter of winning votes – and the public didn't want to lose to the communists either. The credibility of the United States government as a reliable ally was also at stake. If it abandoned South Vietnam its reputation would be severely damaged. So pride, nationalism and ideology all conspired to drag the Americans into what was in effect an unwinnable war.

Today's US administration is driven by the ideology of democracy, but instead ends up creating further instability as its mighty muscle sets about righting the perceived wrongs in the world. The situation in Iraq bears a strong resemblance to that of the Vietnam War, with the word 'communism' substituted with 'terrorism' as the rationale for conflict. Who knows how long America will remain involved in this latest worldwide crusade for democracy and how many more enemies it will create along the way?

Already, Iran and North Korea are lined up in the sights of American policy makers. In these cases, any action would be a stretch too far. The United States military is unmatched in technology but is unsuited to waging long periods of quasi-guerrilla warfare. In a period when there is no draft, and no prospect of one, the US armed forces are extremely short of ground forces and could not support further overseas adventurism, notwithstanding the political desire to see wrongs righted in further parts of the globe. Indeed, the US would be better served by using economic force and diplomatic pressure, as well as covert actions to attain its goals.

After all, the collapse of the Soviet Union did not happen as a result of US troops marching into Moscow – the Soviet Empire imploded – its own people had had enough. Imposing new ideals on nations or regions whoever or wherever they may be will create a new line of resistance from patriots who will strive to defend their nations from the perceived foreign aggressors. Longer term, being the world's policeman is placing intolerable strains on the United States' economic and military reach. And right under its nose is the much greater threat of resurgent Chinese nationalism. What does the United States do if a belligerent Chinese government invades Taiwan?

The Cuban Missile Crisis – world on the brink

Today the nuclear threat remains
In May 1962, Nikita Khrushchev, the leader of the Soviet Union, decided to site nuclear weapons in Cuba, which at that time was a Soviet client state. This was ostensibly done in order to counter the developing US lead in strategic nuclear weapons, although it was dressed up as a means of protecting Cuba from another US-sponsored invasion; the most recent of these had been the failed attempt at the Bay of Pigs in 1961.

This decision led to the closest encounter the world has so far had with major nuclear conflict. By October 1962 the US had become aware of the presence of Soviet missile installations under construction in Cuba. A week after this discovery, President Kennedy announced to the nation that the sites had been spotted and warned the Soviet Union of dire consequences if the missiles remained. The US also imposed a naval blockade on Cuba to prevent the arrival of further missiles.

A series of correspondences between Kennedy and Khrushchev then ensued. The Soviet Union first demanded that the US give assurances that it would not invade Cuba and, second, that the Americans would withdraw their nuclear capability in Turkey. This was all to be done in exchange for the removal of the Soviet missiles in Cuba. The US accepted the first condition publicly, but not the second. A tense period followed. The Soviets agreed to the non-invasion guarantee and began to remove their missiles. The US also secretly agreed with the Soviets to remove the missiles from Turkey within six months, but the US made it clear that it would deny such a claim if it was publicized.

However, just prior to the resolution of the crisis, on Saturday October 27 a US reconnaissance plane was shot down over Cuba. At this stage the pressure on Kennedy to launch a pre-emptive strike on the nuclear bases in Cuba had been exceptionally high and in fact President Kennedy agreed to a Cuban attack on the Monday, but fortunately a diplomatic solution was reached just one day before. If he had not resisted the pressure to attack, a full-scale nuclear conflict almost certainly would have begun, and today, forty years on, we would no doubt be living in a very different world.

Today, it seems hard to imagine a crisis of this sort emerging. However, the nuclear capability of China, India and Pakistan or even of North Korea and (perhaps) Iran provides the possible basis of a similar, maybe irresolvable, crisis – and in the not too distant future. In the days prior to the fall of the Berlin Wall, the Soviet Union was sometimes described as 'Upper Volta with rockets' – in other words, a poor country with a nuclear capability. In those days, there was a real threat of a hair-triggered nuclear confrontation – and that was government to government.

Today we run perhaps an even greater risk of nuclear conflict – partly because so many more nations now have a nuclear capability or are actively trying to acquire it, and also because nuclear issues are no longer nation to nation. What happens if a terrorist organization gets its hands on a 'spare' nuclear device? This is a very real possibility. Is it one that you are prepared for?

Cuban Missile Crisis – a different perspective

At the time of the Cuban Missile Crisis, Al's father was living in the Soviet Union (see Chalabi family history). As an engineering student in Leningrad (now St Petersburg), he recalls how there was never a sense of being on the brink of a nuclear war between the superpowers:

'I lived in a hostel with other students. In each room there was a radio that broadcast the state-run station – "this is Moscow speaking".

'During the radio broadcasts, the situation was described very differently from the Western version: the government stated that it was helping and protecting a fellow socialist country, Cuba, from US imperialist adventurism. It had long accused Americans of adventurous behaviour and of escalating situations unnecessarily. The government believed that the US was threatening Cuba and it had come to its aid. The Americans were interfering with Cuba's defence policy.

'It was also made clear to us by the authorities that the Americans had surrounded us with nuclear bases, particularly in Germany and Turkey.

'In the height of the tensions, we were told that high level discussions were under way with the United States to diffuse the situation in the interest of world peace – the authorities claimed that they were ready to defend their position and ensure that peace prevailed.

'At no point were we led to think that the country was on the brink of war. In fact, I didn't find out the severity of the situation until after I left the Soviet Union some four years later in 1966.'

World War II – recent history shapes our modern world.

World War II has (so far) been the most destructive event in human history. Some 55 million people lost their lives and it left a large part of the world burdened with war debts and decades' worth of repairs.

The roots of the tensions in Europe that led to this conflict are directly traceable to the end of World War I when the peace agreement was signed. This agreement became known as the Treaty of Versailles and was signed in June 1919. It was designed expressly to humiliate the Central Powers, and in particular, Germany. Great Britain and France wanted to ensure that Germany would not pose a military threat to any of its neighbours in the future and so the treaty was exceptionally burdensome – with appalling consequences. Magnanimity in victory was an alien concept to the triumphant Allied powers.

Germany lost its monarchy and became a Republic. The treaty that Germany was obliged to sign meant that:

- Germany gave up approximately 10% of its territory and population, some of it going towards the creation of new states: Poland, Czechoslovakia and Lithuania.
- France took back Alsace-Lorraine, an area it had lost to Germany in 1870.
- Belgium and Denmark received German territory.
- The French were permitted to occupy parts of the Saar Basin, a German industrial region, for 15 years.
- Germany gave up all of its colonies in Asia and Africa.
- Germany was made to admit responsibility for the war and had to pay reparations in the amount of $33 billion in instalments, an amount which in current dollars would be equivalent to the entire output of Germany for a year.
- Germany was not permitted to have tanks or aircraft and its army was limited to 100,000 troops.

As a result of this imposed settlement, Germany struggled. Within a few years hyperinflation had set in and the government was forced to print ever larger sums of money to try to offset the effects of the crippling burden of war reparations.

By 1923, the exchange rate had become 4.2 trillion Deutschmarks to one US dollar! Wheelbarrows were used to transport what were in real terms trivial amounts of money. The lower and middle classes were in large part ruined. The country was politically divided and unstable. But despite this, a coalition government was elected and some semblance of normality was temporarily regained. But then another body blow hit Germany: the world was plunged into Depression as a result of the US stock market crash in 1929. This was the final straw – the inflection point where overwhelmingly adverse economic conditions tipped over into political change and Nazism began to rise.

By the time that the Great Depression's effects had worked their way into the German economy, overall production levels in the country had halved. As unemployment continued to rise, the National Socialist (Nazi) party drew increasing support among the disaffected. Its leader – Adolf Hitler – persuaded a large number of his countrymen that the way to economic prosperity and the restoration of full national sovereignty was to reclaim the lands east of Germany and to neutralize France.

He promised to unite Germans under an empire (Reich) that would rise and dominate Europe. He directed much of the blame for Germany's difficulties on the Jews living in Germany and referred to them as 'parasites'. He had a vision for Germany and he set about organizing the German economy for war. He started to develop a powerful army, navy and air force. He also went about trying to nullify the Treaty of Versailles and reclaim the territory Germany had lost as a result of it.

In January 1934, he lulled other European nations into a false sense of security by signing a non-aggression pact with Poland, which the Germans had no intention of honouring. He also went about weakening the border with France – the Rhineland served as a buffer zone under the Versailles Treaty. In 1936 he sent lightly armed troops there and neither France nor Britain made any military moves in retaliation. Germany began to fortify the new border, which became known as the West Wall. Hitler also signed an 'Axis Agreement' with Mussolini, the Fascist leader of Italy who also had his own ambitious plans for dominating southern Europe.

Germany then proceeded with its expansion plans by proclaiming Austria a German state and eventually occupied the country, declaring that Germany had acted in defence of democratic principles and it had come as a liberator not an occupier (sounds uncomfortably familiar!).

Hitler then turned his attention to Czechoslovakia, which stood firm against his threats, knowing that the country had a security guarantee from France and Russia, which effectively meant that Great Britain would also be drawn into the war. Britain's then Prime Minister, Neville Chamberlain, tried to resolve matters peacefully, the War to End All Wars still fresh in everyone's minds. Hitler, however, had every intention of going to war with Britain and France, but he led everyone to believe (including Germany) that he was willing to negotiate.

As the pressure mounted, Chamberlain went to meet with Hitler and tried to pacify French concerns by telling them that Hitler was only after the Sudetenland, not all of Czechoslovakia. However, the crisis deepened as Hitler made more demands over Poland, Hungary and further concessions from Czechoslovakia, which then did fall into German hands without any support from those countries pledged to guarantee its security. Czechoslovakia felt deserted. However, within two weeks of the fall of Czechoslovakia, Britain and France issued a guarantee for Poland. Undeterred by this, on 1 September 1939 Germany invaded Poland. Two days later, having no alternative choice, Great Britain and France declared war on Germany. Two weeks after that, the Soviet Union invaded Poland – the result of a secret non-aggression pact with Germany agreed between the two former enemies – and one which divided up Poland between them.

Thus began the second and greatest global war, one that was to last five years and to engulf all the major nations of the world, including those in the Pacific. This war bore witness to the most obscene and large-scale genocides in history, to the detonation of the first atomic bombs and the use of carpet-bombing to terrorize and kill vast numbers of civilians. It was a war fought in all theatres, with shifting allegiances. The German–Soviet alliance was to be short-lived as Hitler extended his lines of communication and fatally took on the Russian Bear and its cruel winter. As with Napoleon, Hitler's downfall proved to be the Russian Front.

For the free world, it was a close call. The Germans nearly won the day and conjecture as to the state of the world we would today live in had they prevailed is too horrendous to contemplate.

Japan too was only finally defeated without the loss of millions in a full-scale invasion of its islands by the use of the new super weapon – the atomic bomb.

The shape of our modern world has been largely the result of the geopolitical alliances and rebuilding efforts based on a variety of ideologies since the end of World War II.

Communism proved a failure and was finally discarded by the Soviet Union in the 1990s and in all but name by China in the early 1980s. It highlighted to great effect the relative performances of the 'capitalist' economies of Western Europe, the Americas and Japan against those of Russia, China and their satellites up to the point of abandonment of their flawed ideology. That abandonment now provides the basis of China and Russia's renewed growth, with China by far the most important of these in terms of re-entry into the global economy. As readers will now be aware, a recurring theme of this book is the effect that China's growth will have on the future of the world, along with other seismic shifts in the global political landscape.

Genocides and the Nazi Holocaust

The Holocaust is the most famous, or infamous, of a large number of genocides which have taken place in history. Mankind's record in treating their own species as they themselves would wish to be treated is woeful. Whole populations, once comfortably living side by side with neighbours of different ethnicity or religion, have been wiped out or severely depleted by genocides. These have taken place against backdrops of brutality and violence alien to those of us currently living in what the author Michael Moore calls the 'comfortable world'.

The Holocaust represents one of the worst and most concentrated of such events. During World War II, about 6.5 million Jews were killed by the Nazis, totally devastating the established Jewish communities of Russia, Poland and Lithuania. In those countries, the survival rate was less than one in a hundred. It was the first genocide to employ industrial methods and state bureaucracy to systematically destroy an innocent population. In addition to the Jews, who were easily identified by their distinctive culture and language, other 'nonconformist' groups (such as gypsies and homosexuals) were also targeted and exterminated in death camps; most notably Auschwitz/Birkenau, Treblinka, Belsen and Dachau.

The Nazi view of this mass extermination was based largely on a twisted interpretation of the science of heredity known as 'eugenics'. The eugenics movement started in Great Britain and its founder Francis Galton (1822–1911) was a follower of Charles Darwin and his survival of the fittest thesis (he was also his half-cousin). Galton was also the inventor of the fingerprinting system but it is for eugenics, which subsequently evolved into an evil science, for which he is best known. The word 'euge' means 'well done' in Greek. Eugenics became Galton's term for improving the quality of the human race and it was a science that gained popular as well as academic appeal in the UK and in the US.

AP Tredgold, a British eugenicist, argued in the early 1900s that Britain would be better off with the painless termination of the lives of 80,000 'imbeciles'. The Rockefeller Foundation in America devoted huge sums to eugenics and the principal beneficiary of this, the Cold Spring Harbour Station for Experimental Evolution, advocated that 'defectives' should not have their lives prolonged by unnecessary medical intervention.

These ideas seeded, and grew into the evil plant which thrived in Nazi Germany. The view that 'dead weight' people could not be carried by society then expanded to enforced sterilizations (they happened even in the United States). It then transmuted to justify the extermination of the Jews – who were certainly not a 'feeble' race and not one that would have fallen under Galton's original theory. But the Nazis used the theory to fit their own monstrous intentions.

Prior to and since World War II, there have been numerous other genocides, all brutal, inhumane and senseless. In 1915 over a million Armenians died at the hand of the Turks. Rwanda in Africa has been driven by continuous tribal savagery between the Hutus and the Tutsis, and since the 1990s well over a million people have lost their lives. Maoism in China and in particular the Cultural Revolution resulted in millions of deaths in that country in the period following the end of World War II. In 1971 about 2.5 million Hindus were slaughtered in East Pakistan. The Serbian atrocities in Bosnia and Croatia in the 1990s are but further evidence of a base tribalism which is a continued feature of mankind's behaviour. Atrocious actions by one set of people against another, usually by the stronger majority against a relatively defenceless minority, can be expected to continue until the final moments of man's existence.

The use of the Jews by the Nazis as a rallying point for their own cause is typical of how genocidal behaviour arises. The Nazis demonized the Jews throughout the 1920s as responsible for Germany's economic problems. In 1933 when the Nazis came to power they immediately started destroying Jewish communities. By the outbreak of World War II, ghettos for Jews had been established and by 1941 the 'Final Solution' was put into play. Albert Speer (Hitler's chief architect from 1933 to 1945) said, 'The hatred of Jews was Adolf Hitler's driving force and central point. Perhaps even the only element that moved him.'

Hatred for others because of their perceived differences thus becomes a political tool, one which can rapidly lead to violence and death of its targets.

In more recent times, mass migration into European states at a time of economic uncertainty could well result in the victimization of these migrants in the event that the coming economic problems of the West lead to serious social unrest.

North Africans, Turks, East Europeans, Arabs, Afghans and others could become the unfortunate bogeymen of the hate-filled masses. A society facing a depressed and unstable economy, fuelled by a sense of superiority, could result in the demonization of any of the above-mentioned ethnic minorities, perhaps even turning to violence as a means to vent frustrations.

A Holocaust refugee remembers

The following is a personal account of a World War II Holocaust victim – Susan Bluman, born 1920 in Warsaw, Poland – and her struggle to flee from the Nazis.[1]

'So finally, when we finally got to Vilna we were happy to get there because here we had the opportunity to get to the consulate and embassies who were representing most of the countries in the world. And we were just going from one consulate to the other, to the embassies, begging, and telling them about our tragic situation. And no one would pay any attention to us. No one wanted us. We were just rejected by all the consulates, by all the embassies.

'We were desperate, absolutely desperate. We didn't see any hope, absolutely no hope. We just … we were a people with no land, nobody to turn to. And then we heard about Chiune Sugihara, by hearing about other refugees going to his consulate and getting a transit visa, if … if you had a visa, Curacao visa, which is one of the small Dutch islands in the Caribbean. The problem was that I did not have a passport, so my husband had then difficulties putting me on … me on his passport. And then by the time we had all those formalities, the Dutch consul, which was an honorary consul, he already left the city. So we went to the consulate of, the Japanese consulate. And it was my husband who got to see Mr. Sugihara. And he told him about what … what was happening to us. And he already knew about it from other refugees. And despite that we did not have a visa to get somewhere – because transit visa is only to get you somewhere – Consul Sugihara granted us this wonderful visa for life, this transit visa.'

Moving on from war – other lessons from the past

Past financial bubbles and their aftermath

Guess what? The old saying that 'a fool and his money are easily parted' is true. More money has been lost by suckers than can be counted. And people keep on lining up to lose more. Unlike with wars and political events, we can be sure that the key types of financial scams that have occurred throughout the modern age will happen again, as sure as the sun sets. And the best way to lose your money is to get sucked into a so-called 'bubble'.

Bubbles in the financial world reoccur time after time for one simple reason – human greed. Throughout history, entire populations have taken leave of their senses to join financial bandwagons promising, but seldom delivering, expanded wealth. Bubbles have occurred in all sorts of investments, from tulips in Holland in the 1630s (see section on tulips, below) to Internet stocks in world markets in the 1990s. The first property bubble is thought to have taken place in Athens as far back as 333 BC.

Charles Mackay in his celebrated book *Extraordinary Popular Delusions and the Madness of Crowds* (1841) depicts specific manias such as the South Sea Bubble in England (1711–1720), when huge savings flows were channelled into a fraudulent company whose shares were traded in London. Equally celebrated bubbles have occurred in the US market in the 1920s, in Japan in the late 1980s and, of course, the bubble of the Internet era running from the summer of 1998 to an apex in March 2000. In that bubble, literally hundreds of billions of dollars of savings were wiped out.

Investment bubbles seem to follow a pattern: reasonable growth in share prices or other asset prices, followed by a dramatic acceleration leading to perverse valuations. Sensible investors who typically stay clear of bubbles are quite often the ones sucked into them in its end stages. The biggest losers in the Great Depression were those who thought share prices were attractive because they had already fallen by 20, 30 or even 50%. When prices of financial and real assets really go down they absolutely collapse – and then continue falling, typically in a slow grinding spiral that squeezes the last optimists into capitulation. Then and only then is it time to buy.

Major speculative bubbles have usually been related to the introduction of a new technology with apparently unlimited potential. Thus the opening up of US territory by the building of railroads in the 19th century set the scene for vast speculation, leading to bubbles which in turn led to boom/bust conditions for almost a century. The 1920s saw the same pattern in the US with the introduction of utilities for electricity, gas and water. Ambitious valuations were applied to what were essentially mundane businesses.

The most recent obvious bubble, the Internet bubble, is possibly the one in which the most extreme and absurd overvaluations occurred. At its peak in 2000, Yahoo!, the Internet portal, was valued at just under $145 billion! Sam Zell, the noted US investor, tellingly wrote at the time of so-called 'replication risk.' He suggested that if a rival spent just a fraction of the then valuation of Yahoo! in cash it could easily replicate and exceed what Yahoo! had achieved. So why was Yahoo! supposedly 'worth' $145 billion in the stock market? The madness of crowds!

In the late 1980s, Japan's cumulative 40 years of rapid expansion led to an excess of savings, which was channelled into the stock market and into property. The artificial restrictions of share supply in Japan by the then prevalent system of cross shareholding between members of the same industrial grouping led to absurd levels of valuation being attained. In property, prices rose to levels where it would sometimes take families three generations of projected earnings to pay off mortgages. The effect of the Japanese bubble bursting in 1990 is well documented. Even today, the stock market is only about a quarter of its peak levels, real estate values are down some 60% and the economy remains mired in a deflationary standstill with no end in sight.

Investors' memories tend to be short and greed is ingrained into the nature of man. The fallout from the US technology bubble of the late 1990s will persist for a long time to come. The financial scandals which have emerged in recent years – Enron, Arthur Anderson, WorldCom – are but symptoms of the unwinding of the process. Policy makers rarely step in to stop a party once it has got going. Japan's central bank, for instance, knew that it had a bubble on its hands for several years before it acted.

Alan Greenspan, Chairman of the Federal Reserve famously spoke of 'irrational exuberance' in the US four years before its peak, and did nothing to stop it. Professor John Kenneth Galbraith in his book *A Short History of Financial*

Euphoria wrote that 'you should always have your suspicions aroused when you hear someone saying we have entered a new era which justifies the price increase and ignores the speculative element.' The champions of the 'this time it's different' lobby – Abby Joseph Cohen of Goldman Sachs for instance – did incalculable damage to US savings by the ludicrously overoptimistic pronouncements in the late 1990s.

Today, in the United States and in several other countries in the richer 'bloc', another mania has surfaced: that of real estate. The US real estate market in particular has been very robust in the past few years, along with that of the UK. In both markets, 'equity release' (where mortgages are increased by homeowners to provide debt – secured against rising home values), have been key drivers of consumption. Recent, albeit modest rises in interest rates are a strong signal to all speculators in property that they should get out *now*.

Real estate is shaping up to be yet another bubble primed for bursting and the fallout from its demise will be particularly painful, particularly in the US and the UK, where house prices appear to have sky rocketed in recent years. The ratio of mortgage repayments to salaries is unprecedented; the relative pricing of property (i.e. real estate as compared to other assets) has become ludicrous; and the fact that mortgages are being refinanced to serve as a kind of automated teller machine (ATM) by many people to provide fuel for personal consumption.

A mania over tulips

Tulips, as anyone with a garden knows, are flowers grown from bulbs. Tulips first arrived in Europe from Turkey in about 1600. The Dutch in particular immediately took to this exotic looking flower and developed a huge array of types in differing colours and shapes.

Tulips are today quite inexpensive, perhaps US 20 cents per bulb. But back in the 1630s, Holland was in the grip of a mania for the tulip; a mania that would eventually become as all-consuming as any investment mania in history.

Tulip bulbs became tradable items, bought and sold in exchanges rather similar to stock exchanges. Between 1634 and 1637, people abandoned their jobs to grow and trade tulips full time. The original 'Bourse' (the European name for a stock exchange) developed because much of the tulip trading in Holland took place in the offices of the Dutch noble family, van Bourse.

One particular bill of sale for a bulb, the 'Semper Augustus', indicated that a Dutchman paid 'two wagon loads of wheat, four loads of rye, four oxen, eight swine, twelve sheep, two hogsheads of wine, four barrels of beer, 1,000 pounds of cheese, a marriage bed with linens and a sizeable wagon'. For ONE bulb!

Entire businesses, farms, houses and anything else was swapped for tulip bulbs. Credit expanded. No heed was paid to those who foresaw disaster.

The crash came swiftly and was painful. The Dutch government in April 1637 decreed that tulips were to be paid for in cash, not with IOUs or credit. Tulips were no longer acceptable as collateral for loans. The subsequent implosion of the market bankrupted a large number of businesses, financial institutions and individuals. The country's economy was so devastated that the Dutch Navy had to be cut back because the funds to pay for it did not exist. New Amsterdam, now New York, was seized by the British without a fight because the Dutch didn't have an army to defend it!

The mania that Dutch tulip speculation represented is easily identified:

1   Everyone is doing it. *Group reinforcement is important to sustain and feed manias.*
2   Not being part of something. *People feel left out if they are not part of the major economic event, i.e. property, the Internet, etc.*
3   Bigger fool than I theory. *Or pass the parcel! Surely I won't be the last one holding the baby?*

Does all this sound remarkably similar to the Internet bubble of the 1990s?

The Great Depression – the biggest lesson of all for modern-day investors

Apart from the Civil War, no other event in United States history has had a greater effect on individual Americans than the Great Depression of the 1930s. It permanently changed the character of the nation.

In response to an era of overproduction, which ironically was the result of much increased worker productivity, a new invention came into being in the United States to generate sales – buying goods on credit. As a result, the 1920s saw the introduction of buying on so-called 'instalment plans', allowing Americans to get hold of newly developed modern conveniences of household appliances. This credit-buying spree led to an overheated economy, based on a foundation of rapidly rising debts.

The Great Depression is the period of history that followed 'Black Thursday', the stock market crash of 24 October 1929. This stock market crash was one side-effect of the ending of the credit-fuelled excessive growth of the US economy.

The events following the stock market crash in the United States ultimately triggered a worldwide depression. This led to deflation and a huge increase in unemployment and underemployment.

The market crash in the United States was the proverbial straw which broke the camel's back in an already shaky world economic situation. Germany was suffering from hyperinflation and massive devaluation of its currency, in large part due to the excessive reparation terms imposed on it post World War I. In addition, many of the Allied countries of World War I were having serious problems paying off their huge war debts. In the late 1920s, the US economy at first seemed immune to the troubles being faced by other major nations, but by the start of the 1930s it became alarmingly clear that the US was highly interconnected to other nations' difficulties and was not going to escape a serious downturn. And this downturn was like none other in modern history – its extent took everyone, including pessimists, by surprise.

The Great Depression was made worse by two policies pursued by the United States government. The first was a tight monetary policy, where the Federal Reserve deliberately restricted the money supply – indeed the Federal Reserve tightened the supply of credit at just the wrong time for the economy. The second factor to exacerbate matters was a reversion to protectionism, evidenced by the introduction of the Hawley-Smoot Tariff Act, which raised tariffs on many imports in a misguided attempt to protect local producers that were being hurt by foreign competition.

In retaliation, many other countries also raised their tariffs, badly hurting those United States businesses which depended on exports. This led to a chain reaction of tariff increases, fragmenting and seriously damaging the world economy.

Herbert Hoover was the President of the United States when the depression started. He attempted to improve the situation with a number of ultimately futile measures. One of the major problems he and his administration faced was deflation, which meant that the currency people kept in their pockets could buy more goods tomorrow than it could today. Thus, there was no incentive for consumers to spend beyond what they needed for immediate use. This resulted in over-saving (see the section on Japan on p. 115). The other was that there had been no oversight committee of the stock market or other investments, and with the collapse, many of the stock and investment schemes were found to be either insolvent or outright fraudulent.

Unfortunately, many banks invested in these schemes, which precipitated the collapse of the banking system in 1932, followed by the Gold Reserve Act in 1934. Under this Act, the Federal Reserve acquired all the gold reserves in Fort Knox. In addition, Americans who owned gold were told, under penalty of felony, that they had to turn in all their gold coins to the government or the Fed. So, as an aside, never trust a government with your finances – and when you buy gold coins, as we will recommend, don't advertise the fact to the world (or indeed to anyone!).

Historians of that era cite the maldistribution of wealth as the chief cause of the Great Depression. What this meant was that as industrial and agricultural production increased, the proportion of the profits going to farmers, factory workers, and other potential consumers was far too small to create a market for the goods they were producing.

Even in 1929, after nearly a decade of economic growth, more than half the families in America were too poor to buy the cars and houses and other goods that the industrial economy was producing. Too poor in many cases to even buy adequate food and shelter. As long as corporations continued to expand (their factories, warehouses, heavy equipment, etc.) the economy remained buoyant. By the end of the 1920s, however, capital investments had reached a state where there was excess capacity and excess production. In addition, there was a serious lack of diversification in the economy of the 1920s; it was excessively dependent on construction and automobiles. Once these began to weaken, there was not enough strength in other sectors of the economy to take up the slack.

In 1932 Franklin D. Roosevelt was elected President to replace Hoover. With unemployment at near 25% of the workforce (up nearly 10 times in just three years!), he initiated a number of government programmes to increase liquidity and provide jobs, which were jointly called the 'New Deal'.

Roosevelt's first major action happened on his first day in office on 5 March 1933 when he declared that all banks would take a four-day 'bank holiday'.

This meant closing all US banks and freezing all financial transactions in order to stop the run on bank deposits. When banks were finally allowed to open on March 13, depositors found that they would never again be allowed to withdraw the gold that they had deposited. This confiscation of wealth substantially reduced the rate of bank closures.

Between 1933 and 1939, federal expenditure tripled, and Roosevelt was criticized for turning America into a socialist state. But the cost of the New Deal was insignificant when compared to that of World War II. War spending eventually cured the depression, pulling unemployment down from 14 percent in 1940 to less than 2 percent in 1943 as the labour force grew by 10 million. The war economy was not so much a triumph of free enterprise as the result of government deficit spending stimulating economic activity.

There are some worrying similarities between the Great Depression and the current state of the economy: excess capacity of goods, maldistribution of wealth, unprecedented levels of consumer debt, deflationary pressures, war deficit spending to stimulate the economy and the introduction of tariffs to protect local industry.

Carmen Carter remembers the Great Depression[2]

In 1929 Orlo and I had been married two years and had a year old son, Douglas. We were just nicely getting started in the turkey raising business on his parents' farm near Bridgeton (Michigan). We had about a thousand young turkeys that spring and we bought feed on credit during the growing season and paid for it when we sold the turkeys at Thanksgiving time.

But that year was different. The newspapers were full of news about banks closing, businesses failing, and people out of work. There was just no money and we could not sell the turkeys. So we were in debt with no way out.

But when we read about the bread lines and soup kitchens in the cities, we felt we were lucky because we raised our own food. Our house was rent-free, just keep it in repair. Our fuel, which was wood, was free for the cutting. Then our second child, Iris, was born and our biggest expense was doctor bills. However, this too was solved when our doctor agreed to take turkeys and garden produce for pay.

About that time my husband and a friend started operating a crate and box factory near Maple Island. After expenses they were each making about a dollar a day. Food was cheap.

Coffee was 19 cents a pound, butter 20 cents, bacon the same, with a five pound bag of sugar or flour about 25 cents.

Gasoline was five gallons for a dollar so for recreation we would get into our 1926 Overland Whippet and go for long rides. We also had an Atwater Kent radio we could listen to when we could buy batteries for it.

Orlo finally got a job as a mechanic at a garage in Grant. He earned $15 a week and for us the Depression was over. But it taught us to really appreciate what we had.

Learning from the 1987 stock market crash – quite recent, but easily forgotten.
The 1987 crash resulted from a surplus of optimism and an absence of fundamental underpinnings to what had become extremely expensive stock market valuations which on its first day, 19 October 1987, wiped 23% off the Dow Jones Industrial Average. The key symptoms of the overvaluations prior to the crash were:

1 deteriorating US current account deficit,
2 very low dividend yields on stocks,
3 very high price–earnings ratios,
4 weakening US dollar,
5 rapidly increasing US interest rates, and
6 rising gold prices.

All of the above factors, which contributed to the US stock market crash of 1987, the worst in US history – yes, even worse than that of 1929 – are present today. The only one that has been lagging in terms of development, though starting to move in an adverse way, is US interest rates.

There are three reasons to worry:

1 the great bond market rallies of 2002 and early 2003 are being deflated by the realization that foreigners are less interested in US assets than they once were;
2 the recognition of truly terrifying federal, state and trade deficits; and
3 rapidly emerging credit difficulties in the US financial system.

All the other factors that contributed to the 1987 crash are today very much in evidence. By any reckoning, including dividend yields and price–earnings ratios, US stocks cannot be considered to be anything other than expensive. The US current account deficit is today far bigger than it was in 1987, the dollar is generally weakening, and gold prices have been rallying for some time. Certainly, none of these factors bode well for the stock market, and we maintain the view that any rallies that occur in the US stock market are likely to be short lived-blips in what will be a very protracted bear market.

The crash of 1987 was one where the losses were relatively quickly recovered. Circumstances for the US today are very different to what they were in 1987. Most economic indicators are less positive and the outlook for corporate profits much less secure.

Crashes, however, only really occur at the top of a major bubble and the continuing correction of US and other global stock markets' values is likely to be more gradual and prolonged than one which takes a few days.

Bear in mind (pun intended) that the Dow Jones in September 1929 peaked at 381.2 and reached a low of 41.2 in July 1932. The modern Dow's highest close was just under 11,723 on January 14, 2000. Since 2003, the Dow has been in the 10,000 to 11,000 range, which is not far off its all-time high. If an equivalent fall were to occur, which we are not by any means forecasting but it is certainly something that could happen, then the Dow would need to fall to 1,267! Food for thought for investors who remain bullish in these times. Remember, falls in financial asset prices will be brutal and much, much worse than anyone can currently imagine.

Examples of failed nations and empires – more lessons from a dismal history

Those who think that governments are trustworthy need their head examined. Fundamentally, politicians have a unique loyalty, and that is to their own preservation as people of power. Of course, it is a bit of an exaggerated generalization but the point we are making is that you should not trust a government with your finances and your future. Investors who put money into countries with particularly bad or untrustworthy governments be warned.

Argentina's 'take it or leave it' default on its international debt, effected in 2005, was one where foreign investors were bilked out of about two-thirds of their money. This is a perfect example of how governments can and do cheat investors.

Argentina, and several other countries, are regular offenders in walking away from their international, as well as domestic, obligations. After the latest fiasco, the Argentine government actually partied and boasted about the fact they had stitched up yet another lot of foreigners – and this time for nearly $100 billion. The sad thing is that more fools will probably come along and give them even more money – and for sure they will lose a lot of it sometime in the future.

Of course, many other countries will do the same thing, especially as economic times get tough. Do not invest in emerging market debt at this stage of the economic cycle. And don't invest in the debts of nations which already have a huge burden of obligations – that includes the US, most European countries and quite a few others.

Argentina – riots in the streets

Argentina gained independence from Spain in 1816. It is a country rich in natural resources but its economic growth has not been able to match expectations in recent decades. It is a country rife with corruption, cronyism and a dishonourable sense that the outside world owes it a living.

At the turn of the 20th century, Argentina was one of the world's wealthiest nations, but corruption, military rule from the mid 1970s and the economic turmoil that began in 2001 left Argentina financially on its knees.

The chain of events that led to the eventual collapse of the economy was a long time coming and started to unfold in March 2001, when a series of economy ministers resigned over internal disagreements in reform measures. In June, the country announced that it had swapped $29.5 billion of debt and was deferring $7.8 billion in interest payments to the following year. The local stock market reacted by hitting a 28-month low in July 2001, followed by the slashing of Argentina's credit rating by the three ratings agencies.

The desperate and draconian measures undertaken by the Argentine government quickly eroded what little investor and consumer confidence there was and, in November 2001, Argentines withdrew $1.3 billion from their bank accounts. As a result, in the following month, bank withdrawal restrictions were placed on consumers. The International Monetary Fund (IMF), however, declared itself not satisfied with the reform measures and refused to release any additional aid. As a result the country defaulted on $132 billion in loans, making it the largest state bankruptcy in history.

In 2002 a new budget was eventually reworked and presented to the IMF, which agreed to a delay in a substantial loan repayment due in January 2002. The budget was not popular with the people and Argentina had to announce a state of emergency as rioters took to the streets, protesting against the austerity measures proposed by President la Rua and Mr Cavallo – up till then, the acclaimed Finance Minister – who then promptly resigned.

At this stage, the Argentine peso's ten-year peg to the US dollar was abandoned (one peso was equal to one US dollar) and in February 2002, the peso was floated. Naturally, the exchange rate plummeted and inflation rose rapidly. The situation continued to worsen and, in April, all banking and foreign exchange activity was suspended. By June there were further riots in the streets of Buenos Aires as the unemployed became desperate.

By the middle of 2002, things started to calm down and a new equilibrium exchange rate was reached. But as a result of the default and the devaluation, economic output fell by a sixth from the previous year and unemployment remained high at over a fifth of the workforce.[3]

In November 2002, Argentina defaulted on another $800 million debt repayment to the World Bank, having failed to re-secure IMF aid. Additionally, the World Bank stated that it would not consider new loans for the country.[4] In September 2003, Argentina missed yet another $2.9 billion payment to the IMF.

IMF stringency was overruled by the G7, somewhat worried about kicking the country while it was down, and as a result a portion of Argentina's debts were rolled over, leaving the country relatively stable but impoverished. There, despite glimmers of revival in economic activity, it is likely to stay for some time.

So Argentina, once the pearl of Latin America, is a pariah state. Unlike Russia, which was able to recover from its own series of defaults quite quickly post-1998, Argentina does not have abundant oil and its structural problems are greater even than those of Russia. Furthermore, Argentina's intransigent attitude to those who hold its debts has hardly endeared it to the world financial community.

Overall, foreign owners of Argentine debt have had to swallow losses of over 90%. And now, although Argentina is enjoying what in economic parlance is called a 'dead cat bounce' as its economy crawls off the bottom of the gutter, it is very unlikely to secure the credit it will need for sustained economic revival – although no doubt in the future a cadre of new idiots will emerge to lend to it. The moral is: either possess something that everyone wants (i.e. Russia has oil and gas) or pay your debts. Better still, don't borrow.

Unlike many countries in the Third World, Argentina has only itself to blame for its difficulties. Many developing countries were lent money inappropriately and will struggle to repay it under any circumstances. Argentina was relatively developed and fully aware of the consequences of its borrowing. It will now pay the price for its fecklessness. That price will be restricted access to credit for some time to come.

Zimbabwe – microcosm of a less-developed world being left behind

How corruption, absolute power and xenophobia destroy economies and lives
Zimbabwe has an estimated population of 12.9 million,[5] down from the 14.5 million it once had prior to its economic collapse. The life expectancy of a man and a woman is 34 and 33 respectively and the average annual income is $480. Since the land troubles erupted, estimates of hyperinflation have ranged anywhere from 100 to 600 percent. Some experts describe it as the world's fastest collapsing economy. A more complete picture of misery and waste of human life and potential cannot be found anywhere else. To make matters worse, a third of the population either has AIDS or is HIV positive.

Formerly a British colony named Rhodesia after its founder, Cecil Rhodes, Zimbabwe gained independence in 1980. Over the past two decades, under the appalling misrule of President Robert Mugabe, Zimbabwe has made its terrible fall to its current crisis.

Its main problems, which are in part replicated throughout many areas of the developing world, particularly Africa, are:

- unresolved land reforms,
- a rampant AIDS problem,
- a collapse in law and order,
- food shortages, and
- an economic crisis, with little or no capital investment and an inability to pay for imports or to borrow internationally.

Zimbabwe has come under the international spotlight in recent years following the high profile 'land seizures' of white-owned farms. This came about as a result of the rejection by the electorate of a new draft constitution in February 2000 which was to give President Mugabe and his henchmen almost unlimited power.

The failure of the referendum on the constitution prompted the so-called 'war veterans' (those who had supposedly been involved in the struggle for independence) to act. They, together with working class and rural landless dwellers, occupied almost all white-owned farms. These farms had formed the backbone of the agricultural economy and their devastation has made the economic situation even worse.

The government, complicit in this occupation, refused to compensate the white landowners, delegating that obligation to its former colonial ruler, Great Britain.

In March 2002 President Mugabe was re-elected in a rigged election. Yet despite many nations' expressions of outrage, no substantive action against him was taken. In November of that year, the Agricultural Minister, Joseph Made, declared the land-grab over, the government having seized a total of 35 million acres from white farmers.[6]

This case depicts how a once relatively prosperous nation has been reduced to poverty in a period of only 10–20 years, largely because of total and utter government mismanagement. Interestingly, because Zimbabwe is deemed to have little or no strategic value to the major powers (for example, oil), intervention in its affairs has been little or none.

The rise and fall of empires – the disintegration of the Soviet Union

Lesson to be learnt: if you run a poor economy then sooner or later your empire will collapse. When change comes, there's opportunity

One certain feature of history is that there is no such thing as the status quo. In the words of the historian Edward Gibbon: *'Empires rise and fall like billows.'* He was right: Rome, Greece, Egypt, Persia, Carthage, Turkey, Spain, Britain, France, Germany and Japan – all of them once had empires and all of their great territories and systems of government are now long gone.

The United States is the imperial force of the modern world, and usually, it has been a force for good. But US hegemony will pass also, and the first cracks in its power are already appearing.

The most recent empire to crumble is of course that of the Soviet Union, and its particular sphere of influence has now almost vanished outside Russia proper.

The seeds of the destruction of the Soviet Empire are already planted and growing in the fertile lands of Pax Americana – economic instability, overstretched international obligations and domestic social difficulties. Come the end of the American empire, a new world power will rise from the East and that power will be China. China is already the world's sixth economic power and likely to be its largest within twenty years.

The Soviet Union's disintegration is the most recent example of a failed imperial ambition and the Soviet demise is instructive for those of us who see dangers in the present world order. In December 1991, the Soviet Union suddenly split into fifteen separate countries. The United States, which had successfully engaged the Soviets in an arms race, which the latter could no longer afford, rejoiced in the triumph of capitalism over communism. Just prior to its collapse, the Soviet Union was spending 15% of its total economic output on arms, twice the percentage devoted to military expenditures in the US. This overspending on the military meant that the domestic economy became badly neglected. Widespread problems, including unemployment or underemployment, alcoholism and a decaying infrastructure resulted.

The Cold War, the dominant international point of tension in the post-World War II period, was over by 1991 and the Soviet Union imploded. The whole global political and economic landscape was radically altered almost overnight.

The Soviet Union, which was in territorial terms approximately the same size as pre-Revolutionary Tsarist Russia, had attempted to create a monolithic state in a vast country with an array of widely differing peoples and living conditions. More than 50% of the population of the Soviet Union were non-Russian and the twin liberalizations of 'glasnost' (or freedom of speech) and 'perestroika' (economic reform) allowed ethnic minorities to gain a taste of independence. Up until that point many ethnic minorities had been repressed by an often cruel communist regime. Now, for the first time, they could express themselves, and they did so by demanding autonomy. These liberalizations, glasnost and perestroika, were the result of the rise to power of Mikhail Gorbachev, the Soviet Union's last leader. Once the genie was out of the bottle, it proved impossible to return it.

The first to make the transition to autonomous rule were the Baltic States – Estonia, Lithuania and Latvia. Then Armenians in Nagorno-Karabakh (part of Georgia) demanded the right to join the Republic of Armenia. Despite resistance to these secessionist moves by the Gorbachev government, nationalist movements were soon at work in Moldova, Ukraine, Belarus and the Central Asian republics.

Despite a coup attempt in August 1991, which was overturned by the intervention of Boris Yeltsin and the army, the pace of change quickened. Popular demand for democracy meant that Gorbachev's position proved untenable and he resigned. By January 1992 the Soviet Union was formally abolished and the old Russian Empire had been finally laid to rest. Over 300 million people had lived in the Soviet Union and its lifespan had ended after seventy-five years.

While the imperial presence of the United States is at least much more subtle than that of previous empires, it too is coming to the end of its hegemonic role as the world's only superpower. China's rise to global dominance is more than simply hype in the media and shall become evident in our lifetimes.

*part*FIVE

Financial Survival Guide

Preserving your wealth in the coming economic turmoil

There is no doubt that we are heading into an extremely difficult period. People who think that the status quo will continue, i.e. comfortable lives supported by familiar institutions (jobs, banks, the State, and pension schemes), are in for a rude awakening. How bad things will get is impossible to determine – but for sure it's not going to be easy.

Now is the time to think rationally and to prepare ourselves for this difficult period ahead. It's always easier to get things right when there is still time for reflection, when panic has not yet set in, and when we are among the few who are taking appropriate action. We have the luxury of time today, but perhaps not tomorrow.

You certainly don't have to be rich to benefit from this advice. We provide a guide for people of all incomes and levels of wealth. If you have trouble with excessive levels of debt – and a large number of people do – you don't need to panic yet. Just follow the practical advice we offer and you could be back on the right track. In this part of our book, we highlight the steps you can take to protect your financial purchasing power – ultimately what is important in an economic sense.

Before we get into the details of our 'how to' section, let's talk about the concept of money. Everyone knows what money is – or at least thinks they do. But one of the key features of our thesis is that money has become so diverse in its forms, so susceptible to the many winds that blow its value around, that the old-fashioned concept of money – a piece of paper, a coin or a credit to spend in return for goods – is outdated. We need to look at the history of money to understand what it is today.

Money – a brief history

The evolution of money into its multifarious forms is important, because one of the reasons why we are in such a mess today is that money has become a catch-all phrase for a bewildering array of credits and currencies. As a result, what we regard as money is no longer the safe haven it once was. The loss of purchasing power should be instructive to all our readers. For instance, the British pound has lost more than 99% of its purchasing power in the past 150 years and the pre-glasnost Russian rouble has lost all of its purchasing power. Do not trust conventional forms of money to preserve your wealth; be pragmatic when it comes to how you hold your money and consider holding other forms of wealth as a hedge against the continuing devaluation of money. Governments today are just as capable of 'clipping the coinage', albeit in more subtle ways than earlier issuers of currency.

So what is money, then? Surely everyone knows what money is, or thinks they do – it's inescapable in the modern world, even to Trappist monks and to other recluses. But not everyone understands the evolution, importance and the differing types of money, and how money shapes the world we live in.

Money has been referred to as the lubricant of life. It acts as a reference by which mankind's social status is measured and it is a preoccupying force in the modern world. Money first emerged as a means of effecting trade in about 9000 BC, although not in the forms with which we are familiar today.

Cattle, then crops and later cowry shells were used for exchange. They became prevalent as forms of 'money' because they were more convenient alternatives to bartering (the direct exchange of goods and services), and were relatively easy to transport.

As time went on, money took the form not only of shells, but of beads, coins, paper and ultimately of credit held in banks and other financial institutions.

The word *pacare* in Latin is the root of the modern word to pay. *Pacare* literally means to placate or pacify, which, in part, money was used to do. Indeed, salt was used as a form of payment in the Roman Empire – and from it we derive the modern word 'salary'.

In Greek and Roman times, gold and silver coins were used to finance military campaigns. Alexander the Great spent half a ton of silver a day in his campaigns in Asia (almost as much as was wasted on the recent film of the same name!). In the Roman Empire, almost all silver output was used to run the army, particularly in the wars between Rome and Carthage. As Roman Emperors ran out of money, they began to debase the coinage – clipping coins at the edge, using inferior alloys, and making coins smaller. This of course resulted in inflation (too much money chasing the same number of goods). As inflation took hold in Roman times, so did measures to try to control it. Diocletian was the first Emperor to introduce a system of budgets and controls of prices.

The next great developments in money and its uses occurred in England during the reign of Ethelred, when substantial amounts of coinage were minted to pay off the Viking invaders from Denmark (Dane geld). This didn't work, which just goes to show that paying off blackmailers has never been a good policy.

Ethelred's predecessor, Aethelston had also introduced a unified national currency, marking the start of over 1000 years' continuous use of the pound as the British currency.

Other key English monarchs involved in the development of modern currencies included William the Conqueror, who introduced taxes to prevent debasement of the currency – he has a lot to answer for in this respect. Taxes became particularly well organized at the time of the Crusades when Henry II introduced formal military taxes known as 'scutage'. This money was paid to 'soldiers', so described because they were paid in 'solidus' – otherwise known as the 'King's shilling'.

The Spanish Conquests of South and Central America led to a huge increase in the production of silver and gold, much of it destined for China, which by the mid 1600s was the world's largest economy (and it's well on its way to resuming that position today). China, in time, became an economy highly dependent on South American silver production. As bullion supplies gradually began to falter, a massive recession ensued, leading to the collapse of the Ming Dynasty.

The use of cheques and the development of banking, as now known, came about as a result of the English Civil War of 1642–1651. This war broke out because of Parliament's refusal to recognize the King's right to levy taxes without its permission. Charles I then seized the Mint in 1640, where coins were produced, and as a result people with gold and silver increasingly stored their bullion in safes in the workshops of 'goldsmiths'. These goldsmiths therefore effectively became bankers – and thus modern British banking was born.

A system developed whereby customers of goldsmiths would issue instructions to pay money to other customers by way of 'cheque'. Goldsmith receipts were also used as pieces of evidence that customers could pay their bills and these very quickly developed into bank notes.

As nations increasingly took control of and standardized their units of currency, or money, the minting and purity of money became national monopolies. Typically, paper money was backed by, and convertible into, bullion. This in earlier periods was silver, and from the 1800s onwards became gold.

By 1900 all major countries, including the United States, had adopted the gold standard and, excepting the period of World War I, this was maintained right through to the Great Depression. In 1931, however, all the British Commonwealth (with the exception of Canada), as well as many other countries, abandoned this gold standard. The US was the last major nation to come off the standard in 1973 and by then the US dollar was the most widely circulated international currency.

With banking systems from the 1960s onwards becoming more sophisticated and electronic transmission growing to be a feature of international trade, intangible, non-paper or so-called 'potential' money assumed greater and greater importance. Today, currency in direct circulation (i.e. notes and coins) is only a small part of the total amount of 'money' in most major economies.

If you would like to learn more about money, you can download an excellent free booklet entitled *What Has Government Done to Our Money?* by Murray N. Rothbard at the the Ludwig von Mises Institute (http://www.mises.org/money.asp).

History lesson over. Let's move on to why you bought this book – how to prepare yourself for what is coming.

The essentials

The first and most important thing you can do to sort out your finances and to be prepared for the rough time ahead is to lessen your exposure to debt. There is an old saying that a dollar of debt can sink a ship – and it is true. Being unnecessarily committed to debt repayments could potentially scupper your ship.

Dealing with debt

The least good thing that can happen to anyone as we go into this period of considerable difficulty is to have too much debt. It is important that everyone realizes just how insidious and dangerous debt is. In the event that our forecast comes true – and clearly we believe that the facts point to just that (or we would not have written this book) – the people with substantial debt will be the ones to be the most severely punished. This is because in a deflationary environment, asset prices fall, and as asset prices tend to support debt, it becomes harder and harder for people to support their borrowings. It becomes more difficult for them to repay the principal as well as the interest that accrues on every sort of debt.

Furthermore, many people will likely lose their jobs in the future we are depicting, giving them little or no income – income that is needed to service debt, i.e. to repay the debt and to pay the interest on it. Remember that unemployment in the United States and elsewhere went up by a factor of between five and ten times during the Great Depression, and the wages of just about everybody left in the workforce were put under severe pressure. We think that it is highly likely that something similar will happen this time around.

Failure to service debt is likely to mean the loss of the underlying assets, typically houses or cars. Since house prices will fall in most rich countries, this may mean that the forced sale of the home will realize less than the amount of debt outstanding, leaving the householder in negative equity and facing bankruptcy.

So the first and most important thing investors can do is to pay off their debts. Start with credit card debts; almost certainly these will carry the highest rates of interest of all debts outstanding.

'Special offers' with low interest rates will only last for a short period and are generally to be ignored. Credit cards are for some people a means of addiction to consumption and one which will ultimately lead to problems. Pay off credit cards as soon as possible. There are so many credit cards in circulation in the richer nations that their use has for some become one of pure circularity, i.e. using one card to pay off another. Anglo-Saxon countries are those most addicted to credit cards. In the UK there is approximately one credit card for every member of the population, whereas in France there are hardly any at all outstanding. The US has a high penetration of cards also and there is a reason for this as we will explain later. Credit cards are highly profitable to the companies that issue them.

If you have to have credit cards, use them wisely. Only use them as debit cards. In other words, pay the outstanding balance in full by the due date of the statement every month. This may be easier said than done, we realize, but some simple steps can assist in the process. One of them is the act of planning and budgeting.

You need to think of your household finances in the opposite way to how most governments think of their finances – think prudently. Governments think nothing of living off credit, and we have written at length in this book about debt accumulation by rich nations. You, however, cannot accumulate debt that way. The government of any country tends to be the borrower of last resort. It can print money at will and it can borrow at the expense of all other borrowers – for a period, at least. You cannot print your own money, nor can individuals normally issue their own bonds. So, while you can borrow, you do not have the same means of repaying as a government. So, just because the government lives on credit is not a good enough reason to follow its example. Budget, budget, budget!

The other thing you need to do to free yourself from debt is to sell any assets you may have that leave you financially exposed. This is to ensure that you have zero secured debt. Secured debt is where one or more of your assets are used to support the debt. This is known as recourse debt (see sidebar below). It is the type of debt to which you are potentially most vulnerable in a severe economic downturn.

It is very important to remember the following: never ignore your debts. Don't borrow to purchase something whose life is less than the debt, for instance a vacation, an expensive spa treatment or a pair of fashionable shoes. Debt doesn't go away because you forget about it. Borrowing more money to pay off your loans is a bad idea. Debt consolidators that offer to 'clean up' your debts are typically a bad idea too, since the fees they charge, the interest rate they add and the time that it will take to pay them off will almost certainly be more onerous than if you had left your existing debts in place.

If you are overwhelmed by debt, make a list. Put them down in order and be honest with yourself. Prioritize those that are most important to your way of life – in other words, put debts related to your house first, then those related to other things last. Remember that if you have used 'equity release' as a form of procuring money, your house will be at risk against those types of debt too. Other forms of debt that you really need to pay include electricity, gas and other utility bills. In addition, local property or council taxes is high up the list of priorities. Failure to pay them can typically result in some fairly hefty consequences.

In almost all countries, there are organizations, some quasi-governmental, that will assist you with your debts if it all gets too much and you can't work out how to get through on your own. Call them or go and see them. We cannot be as specific as we would like in this book because we cannot assess every single case; others can, but you have to go and visit them.

Debt

- **Recourse debt** – *a bank or other lending institution can come after the assets used to secure the debt in the event you do not properly service the debt.*

  *If you have non-recourse debt, check very carefully that indeed this is the case. Some debt is backed by personal guarantees which are just as onerous as asset backed debt – and may be worse, because the bank can come after **all** of your assets and not just the one for which you took out the loan.*

- **Non-recourse debt** – *a bank or other lending institution has no right to your assets in the event that you do not pay off the debt. This is very rare, so for the majority of people the best thing to do is to work very hard at repaying debt. But if you are lucky enough to have no recourse debt this is the **last** debt you should repay because in the event of your inability to pay, the bank or lending institution can go whistle for its money and might as well make wallpaper with the relevant documents.*

Credit cards – the worst kind of debt

Mr Frank McNamara has a lot to answer for. In 1950, he founded the Diners' Club – an organization that initially allowed diners to pay in about 20 restaurants in New York with a piece of plastic. Pretty soon, that plastic became usable in other establishments and by 1958 the Diners' Card was being challenged by the new American Express card. Neither of these two pioneering cards were credit cards – they had to be paid off in full every month. The first true credit card was issued by the Bank of America in 1959 and, as the saying goes, the rest is history.

In just half a century, credit cards have become a huge part of the lives of many people in richer nations, and a dangerous part at that. Credit cards are typically very expensive and even 'rate shopping' can be a hazardous game, i.e. looking for special deals on credit card interest. This is because not repaying the debt back on the due date can result in massive charges.

Well we've made our point, so what do you do with your cards?

Tackling your credit card debt should be the first thing you deal with in your financial survival plan. If you cannot just cut up your cards and throw them away, here are ten things you can start with to regain control of your credit card debt and reduce interest charges and other fees:

1 If at all possible, pay off all credit card bills each month on time to avoid late fees and interest charges.

2 If you currently have a credit card balance that you cannot afford to pay off in full, transfer your existing balance to an interest-free credit card.

3 Never buy anything on a department store card – the interest rates are astronomical, typically double that of a normal credit card.

4 Never use your credit card for a cash advance. Cash advance fees make a lot of money for card issuers – at your expense.

5 Dispose of all cards in you possession that charge an annual fee unless you can pay the annual fee with the card's point scheme or unless you can truly justify the added value you receive for paying this fee.

6 Set up a standing instruction to pay at least the minimum balance every month so that you will never be charged late payment fees.

7 Never accept unsolicited increases to your credit limit. Simply call your card centre and ask them to reverse the unsolicited limit increase should this happen.

8 Always make sure you know your cards' annual percentage rate as this will bring to your attention how much money you are actually wasting by servicing the debt.

9 If you really cannot pay off your credit card debt right away, at least make sure your debt from credit cards and personal loans never exceeds 20% of your income. This is a guideline percentage – it is a reasonable figure for most people but adjust it according to your circumstances. The basic point is that credit card debt is not good debt. Think why banks and credit card issuers can advertise so lavishly to seemingly offer you such marvellous credit card deals – they do it because the little bits of plastic are very profitable for them.

10 Stop making purchases with your credit card(s) while you are repaying your credit card debt. If you must buy using plastic, use a debit card, which is almost identical to a Visa/MasterCard credit card, but the money for each purchase made is deducted directly from your bank account. That way, you will get out of the bad habit of spending money that you have not yet earned.

Remember, using credit cards as a form of revolving credit is a mug's game – don't be seduced by ads offering low interest rates or no interest on transferred balances. This is only useful if you can pay off the balance in full before the interest free period lapses.

Do not take this lightly; credit cards are poisonous to your long-term financial health. They are the equivalent of drugs being sold as sweeties at school gates and should be avoided at all costs. Lecture over on this one, but please take our advice! Use them as debit cards by arranging to pay off the entire balance at the end of every month or don't use them at all.

Property

Since the bursting of the stock market bubble in 2000, property appears to have taken over as the 'must-have' and 'safe' investment. Property prices in the West have climbed to record levels as a percentage of household incomes. Many investors have been so excited by this 'new' investment vehicle that they have bought multiple properties, often they buy-to-let.

Unfortunately, we believe that property prices have reached unsustainable levels in many Western countries, particularly in the Anglo-Saxon economies, and will consequently need to undergo serious price adjustments before reaching a new level. Although we are not alone in our belief, many homeowners and investors choose to believe that their properties are safe investments and they will continue to appreciate and outperform inflation. Believe this at your peril.

Worst affected will be property owners who are highly geared or leveraged, i.e. those who have a mortgage(s) of over 80% of their property value. It is these property owners who would do best to either pay off a large part or all (if possible) of their mortgage. Failing that, the best option is to sell the property and rent until the market has readjusted. We explore each of these options below:

Paying off your mortgage
If you have a mortgage, examine closely whether or not you can liquidate other assets such as bank balances, shares, bonds, etc. to repay it in part or in full. Mortgages will become very expensive in real terms in the coming economic downturn. This is because despite the fact that interest rates will remain low in nominal terms, the real cost of the mortgage debt will be high as house prices fall.

Here is an example of what could happen if you currently have a mortgage on your property or properties:

Consider a house worth $1 million today – perhaps yours? If a mortgage is currently outstanding on this house of, say, $500,000, your net equity in the house is $500,000, i.e. $1 million minus $500,000.

In other words, this $500,000 is what you would get, minus commissions, fees, etc. if you wanted to and were able to sell your house today.

Now suppose the house's value falls to $500,000 (and please do not dismiss this hypothesis as it is very likely that house prices will halve or more in rich countries); your net equity of the house will fall to zero!

The tragedy of it is that the homeowner could end up paying a mortgage of $500,000, which perhaps you can no longer afford, especially if household incomes fall. This mortgage will be on a house that effectively belongs to the bank! In other words, the home owner has gone from having 50% equity in the house to 0%, while still under the same mortgage payment obligations.

Now you may think that this example cannot happen in real life, but this is exactly what did happen in Hong Kong. This large scale and recent example of the 'negative equity effect' crippled many owners.

In order to buy a residential property in Hong Kong, banks typically required a down payment of 30% to obtain a mortgage (this has since been relaxed somewhat), which many people had to work hard to pull together given the very high property prices for much of the 1990s, when this particular rot began to set in.

After 1997 and the handover of Hong Kong back to China by the British, property prices in Hong Kong started falling sharply, in some cases by more than 60%. As a result the sad mathematics of this was that those who bought houses at the top of the market – and there were many – were left with a negative equity of 30%.

If we insert numbers into an example, it is easier to explain the financial consequences of this: suppose that a homeowner living in a place now worth $500,000 is still paying a mortgage of $875,000 – that's $1,250,000 (original value) minus the $375,000 (30% down payment). That means the homeowner is in negative equity in the amount of $375,000. Ouch!

This demoralizing situation leaves people slaves to their mortgages for most of their working lives, and those are the lucky ones that still have a job.

For too long we in the West have lived with the illusion that property is a rock-like investment that never or only temporarily goes down. The reality is that property is anything but stable over a very long period of time. Property is an economic good like any other, subject to wild swings in prices, both real and nominal. The difference between property investment and others is that (1) we tend to live in our properties and (2) we tend to borrow a substantial part of the purchase price. This means that when property prices rise, everything looks good because we make more money than we would if we were just buying a good for cash; but when property prices go down the reverse is also true (although often forgotten), and financial misery sets in.

So why make a financial loss off your property? If you can't afford to pay off a large portion of the mortgage, you need to sell your property/properties, or a fate similar to our Hong Kong example described above could await you.

If you can't or don't want to sell – one thing you can do is to shop around for a better deal on your mortgage which is almost certainly likely to be your largest debt. In the shorter term we think interest rates will go up – so in most economies we think you will be better off with a short term fixed rate mortgage. In other words, if you can get a deal on a two-year fixed rate (that is, constant interest rate) mortgage then you should take it. Thereafter, we believe that interest rates will fall, as the world adjusts to very strong deflationary pressures. Under those circumstances, you want to roll your two-year fixed rate mortgage – assuming you can afford to pay it – into the best possible variable rate mortgage. When you change mortgages look for the following:

1 Minimum amounts of charges for 'arrangement' (just another form of contribution to bank profits in most cases!).
2 Valuations on the property should in the best case be paid by the new bank that you are moving the mortgage to, including legal fees.
3 Do not increase the size of your mortgage as you change it.
4 A mortgage where there is no penalty on early repayment. This is unlikely on a fixed rate mortgage but should be absolutely normal on a variable rate one.
5 Do not be browbeaten into buying mortgage insurance. This is a scam normally and is not worth buying. It makes money for the bank and rarely for you.

In the unfortunate event that you go bankrupt, it is not the end of the world. But you will have to sell off most of your possessions to pay debts; you will be highly constrained in terms of future credit. You will have difficulty in being a company director for some considerable period of time, depending on where you live. It is not an action to be taken lightly.

Selling your property and renting

If you are fortunate enough to be able to sell your house while you are in positive equity, then you will need to rent a new home to ride out the storm. You will be able to buy houses at much lower prices (perhaps even half price) in the coming years in countries such as the United States and the UK, and in the meantime you will have cash to deploy. Surely this makes economic sense? So what's stopping you? The inconvenience of moving? A reluctance to believe that prices can go down as well as up?

Call a few real estate agents about your house. Don't be concerned if house prices have already fallen a bit – they are going to fall a lot further.

Of course, many people have attachments – sentimental or otherwise – to their homes that make them very reluctant to move. But remember that houses and flats/apartments are only material possessions that are easily replaced. In the rich West, particularly in the US and in the UK, house prices have significantly outperformed inflation and most other asset classes in terms of price performance. This will come to an end in the coming great depression.

When deflation sets in, as recent examples in Japan and Hong Kong show, house prices fall faster than other assets, leaving householders severely exposed. If you are reluctant to sell because prices have already fallen slightly from their highs, you may end up being a forced seller further down the line – a far worse fate.

This is particularly so with people who have bought second, third or even more homes to let out. Rents will fall, vacancies will rise and asset prices will fall, and those with multiple homes supported by mortgages will be hardest hit.

You need to take action. Do not be a rabbit frozen in the financial headlights! You'll end up in bankers' stew and that's not much fun.

If you are fortunate enough to have no mortgage on your home and are not interested in selling your home for a financial gain, then you have the luxury of being able to make that decision.

Now lets look at the hard facts concerning property: we believe that in Anglo-Saxon markets – principally the United Kingdom and in the United States, but also in certain other overheated markets, e.g. Australia, New Zealand, Canada, Hong Kong, China and Singapore – prices of residential real estate could fall by over half from current levels. In the United States, as we write, real estate prices remain relatively robust; in the United Kingdom and in Australia they have begun the early stage of a long meandering decline. In all instances, investors, owners and anyone else interested in capital preservation should get out – and fast. This is by far the best advice we can give you as readers – because for almost everyone, real estate, in the form of their own homes, is their largest investment. In Anglo-Saxon economies there is a misguided view that people who live in houses on which they have a mortgage 'own' their homes – they don't. The financial institution that lent them the money owns the house or apartment until such time as the mortgage debt is discharged.

So the frisson of excitement that 'homeowners' get when they survey 'their' property is a misguided one. Now it is true that in most nations there are tax advantages to owning property. It is also true that property is the only asset that you can 'gear' or 'borrow' against in large fashion. But of course, you should never invest just because of tax reasons. And gearing, as we have demonstrated, works both ways. Be borrowed at a time of falling prices, reduced job prospects and higher interest rates and you are well and truly up the proverbial creek, without a paddle.

Yes, we know that real estate has been a good investment for as long as just about everyone can remember, but that does not make it a good one now. In all the markets we have mentioned above, we strongly suggest that, if you can, get out, the sooner the better.

Back to basics: budgeting

The lesson here is very simple: don't spend more than you earn.

Sounds fairly obvious, but the spiralling debt figures in the Rich World indicate that a lot of people live beyond their means. If you are one of those people, you need to change your spending habits.

Start by taking a piece of paper (or you can do this on a computer spreadsheet) and write out carefully every single recurring expenditure you make. You can use the budget sheet we have prepared in the appendix as a guideline.

Now, put a line through all expenditures you really don't need to make. What like? Well, magazine subscriptions, cable or satellite TV, health club memberships, restaurant trips, or anything else that is discretionary and which prevents you from balancing your own personal budget.

Once you have balanced your budget – at least on paper – start thinking of further ways of cutting back, because you now need to start saving! Without savings you will be in a very awkward situation.

OK, maybe you already have big savings and substantial assets – so this bit doesn't apply to you. But if you don't, then you need to start saving now.

Next, determine how much money you have coming in and how much debt you have outstanding. The top priority is to pay off debt, especially credit card debts.

By the way, one very good form of saving is to pay off debt. It's the same thing as saving and it will be to your advantage. We promise you.

If you have to buy something, only buy non-food items during sales. Chances are you don't really need to make that purchase anyway. Resist advertising; resist blandishment from shop assistants and the lure of fashion. Your peers won't be able to eat their expensive shoes or their iPods once their credit cards are all maxed out. If you don't actually have the money for something, don't spend.

Your pension

Your pension is a critical part of your investment portfolio. You must ensure that your pension is suitably protected from any violent financial shake-ups. If you don't, you may find that you can no longer retire. And don't expect the State to provide you with a pension (see the section on pensions on p. 73) as State pension schemes in the West will be radically reformed over the next few decades.

So, what do you need to watch out for so that your pension stays with you until you are ready to retire? Certainly diversification is key to minimizing the risk profile of your pension. Let's go over a few points that you need to be cautious of.

Don't put all your eggs in one basket
Do not use your personal income to invest in the same company that pays you your salary, unless you are awarded options or stocks for free. If you break this rule and your employer gets into financial difficulties, the company share price will likely fall and you may also lose your job at the same time, resulting in a loss of income and a substantial loss to your pension/savings. Enron and WorldCom are classic examples of just that.

Find out the state of your corporate pension scheme
There's no denying it, most corporate pensions are in a mess and severely underfunded. If you work for an airline or for an automaker, you are almost certainly working for a company that may not be able to afford your pension. Almost all companies in these sectors have severely underfunded pensions.

Take United Airlines, for example: its employee pension plan is underfunded by over $8 billion and this amount of money is proving to be an albatross around the company's neck as it struggles to turn itself around. (It may or may not be around by the time you read this book.)

The failure to have fully funded pension schemes is impacting many major, international corporations' profits, as they have to make large contributions to their pension fund to make up the shortfalls.

Additionally, most corporations have had to revise downwards their assumed pension rates of return by 1–2%, which in the longer term means more contributions out of profits to reach retirement targets, i.e. to pay out their retirees.

But aren't these pensions insured? Well, yes and no. They are partially insured, but there's a catch: in the US, the insuring body, the Pension Benefit Guarantee Corporation, insures pensions up to a maximum of $45,000 per year. So if you thought that your corporate pension plan was fully secure, you would have been correct provided that you weren't expecting a pension of more than $45,000 per year. This may come as a shock to some of you.

Create your own pension scheme

Of course, there are many of us in the Rich World who don't work for corporations with pension schemes and we have to figure out a way to pay for our retirement on our own.

Suppose a 30-year-old man in the United Kingdom (but roughly equivalent figures apply in most rich nations) is looking to retire at the age of 65. If he currently has an annual income of £20,000, he will need to put aside £260 a month to fund a pension of a similar amount. That is 15.6% of his gross income – a very significant amount.

In the case of a 40-year-old man, this monthly contribution would need to rise to £450 – a staggering 27% of his gross income. Not an easy stretch when you factor in taxes, mortgage, utilities, car payments, credit card payments, tuition fees, feeding the family, etc. Finding this extra cash is simply not realistic for many.

In most cases in rich countries, the State also provides a pension. In the case of the UK, the maximum pension entitlement only comes to £75.50 per week for a single person or £120.70 for a couple, which is a shade over £6000 a year – hardly a comfortable retirement package. In the United States the figure is approximately US$14,000 per annum per individual – again not a king's ransom and not much above the poverty line. So once again we stress: don't rely on the State for your pension (unless you can live off £75.50 per week!).

If you have one already, take control of your pension scheme
If you can get cash out of your pension scheme without significant penalty, take the money out of it and put it to work elsewhere. If you owe money, the best thing you can do with this pension money is to use it to pay off your debts – there's no point in having a pension that's earning you 5–10% per year if you're paying 20% per year in interest on your credit card balance.

Keeping money in a pension scheme leaves you exposed to several risks:

- The company providing the pension scheme may well go bust or run into financial difficulties. Many companies in the West have underfunded pension schemes. This means that they owe money to their pensioners in one way or another. This will lead to serious problems in the event that the company finds itself in financial difficulties (see the Pension Burden section on p. 73).
- The insurance company or other providers of pension schemes may run into trouble due to insolvency. Yes, this can and does happen: for instance Equitable Life, a British life assurer/insurer and the oldest mutual insurance society in the world finds itself today in severe difficulties and has been unable to meet its pension obligations in full. This is because Equitable Life guaranteed returns to certain policyholders, guarantees which it was subsequently unable to meet in the context of falling interest rates and declining stock markets. More or less the same thing happened to all of the Japanese life insurance companies. Do not depend wholly on financial institutions for your long term prosperity! The pensioners of Enron will be ruing the trust they put in their employer for a long, long time.
- The managers of pension funds almost always slavishly pursue a policy of being partially invested in shares, bonds and property. In the coming economic hardship this will not be a good strategy and will severely limit the ability of these pension schemes to pay out to pensioners/retirees. Far better for individuals to take their own money out of pension schemes if they can, and deploy them in a safer manner. Some of the ways in which this can be done are discussed below.

Similarly, if you have insurance policies which you can cash in, withdraw all or as much of it as you can without being heavily penalized. Use the proceeds to pay off debts first.

Diversification is key to financial longevity

'Betting the farm' is a sure-fire way to end up singing for your supper. Never have all of your assets in one investment or in one place – without a diversified approach to your finances, you may well be a goner.

Diversification doesn't mean having two mortgages or three credit cards – that's like having three poisons in your system when the big crunch comes. Diversification means taking our advice, based on your own circumstances, and having a prudent mix of assets to see you through difficult times.

Some gold, some local and foreign currency and some deposits – those are the essentials. The mix that's right for you is discussed later, but if you genuinely 'mix and match' your investments you will be in a safer place, so don't just hold two tech stocks or invest in three government bonds.

'Mixing and matching' may mean that you will miss out on the 'big one' – the stock or property deal that might be the 'once-in-a-lifetime chance' (we've all heard that one before). Miss out on it. Not only are once-in-a-lifetime deals the specialty of investment hucksters, but they rarely ever pan out.

Won't you feel safer with a well-balanced defensive mix or 'portfolio' of investments to see you through the coming difficult times?

Cash and foreign currency

Selling your home and paying off your debts will hopefully leave you with some cash. What should you do with this cash? It doesn't matter whether you are rich or poor or somewhere in between. This bit is *really, really good advice.*

First, sell your US dollars. The US dollar is heading for a dramatic fall. In our opinion, in order to make any dent at all in the US current account deficit, the US dollar needs to fall by about 50% against other major world currencies. And that is despite the fact that it has fallen a fair way already.

We live in an interdependent world which relies on trade for a large part of its 'livelihood'. To facilitate that, currencies have to be traded to pay for goods and services bought from other nations.

When you go on vacation overseas you often have to buy the local currency to get around. When you buy a Japanese TV someone has had to make a currency conversion on your behalf – selling your currency to buy Japanese yen to pay for the TV. Of course, this is a simplistic rendition of what really happens in life – but sometimes the simplest things are not that obvious.

If there is one dominant theme in this book it is that the era of US economic ascendancy is coming to an end. This may be a good or a bad thing – we don't know and frankly it doesn't matter to those of us pursuing our purely selfish economic interests. We do, however, want you to take advantage of this trend and the best way to do so is to remember that US dollars will shrink and continue to shrink in absolute and relative value.

There is only one way that the United States can pay off its accumulated debts – and that is to effect a devaluation of its currency. This is going to happen, as sure – in economic terms – as the sun rises on a daily basis. The question is when and by how much. What does this mean for anyone with money, debts or sense? It means sell your US dollars and hold something else. We'll get on to that point in greater detail in a moment.

If you can, borrow US dollars, especially at fixed long-term low interest rates, and hold other, stronger currencies on deposit. If you have a mortgage on a property outside the US, see if you can obtain a US dollar mortgage for it. If you borrow US dollars, the value of that borrowing will go down in time, along with the US dollar – and you will have to repay less in real terms.

In this context, investors should also consider selling British pounds since many of the same characteristics that plague the US are apparent in the UK. For instance, a widening trade deficit, a widening fiscal/budget deficit, excessive levels of personal and mortgage debt, and excessive central government spending. The pound will therefore fall against other major currencies, with the exception of the dollar.

Which currencies to hold?

Although both the Eurozone and Japan have problems, the relative performance of their currencies is likely to be good for the next few years against both the US dollar and the British pound. So, depending on where you live and how accessible these currencies are to you, consider holding a mixed basket of the following currencies:

- euros;
- Japanese yen;
- Australian dollars;
- Swiss francs;
- for more exotic or richer investors who can find ways of doing so, hold some Asian currencies especially:
  - yuan (renminbi), the Chinese currency;
  - Singapore dollars;
  - Malaysian ringgit;
  - Thai baht;
  - Korean won.

  These Asian currencies are very likely to rise in value against the US dollar. Most banks in the rich West will allow clients to hold currencies other than their home currency. Talk to your bank about this.

Do not be tempted with Asian currencies like the Philippine peso and the Indonesian rupiah. These countries are too corrupt and volatile to be havens for safe money. Do not be too concerned about interest rates.

So to recap: if you are not in a position to repay any mortgage on your house and you live outside the US or a US currency area, ask if your bank will change your current mortgage for a US dollar one. It will be very much to your advantage to do so.

If your property is in the US, the best thing you can do is to sell it, take the net proceeds of US dollars and use them to buy a basket of the currencies we have listed above. This isn't a political statement – it's just plain economic sense.

Gold, silver and diamonds

What is evident from the brief history of money we outlined earlier is that money is just a commodity like any other. Its value rises and falls according to the relationship of supply and demand. Its supply is largely determined by governments, but its demand, or rather the way in which people treat money (save, spend, hoard), is another key factor. The way in which we as individuals treat our money is going to be critical in the coming ten years or so.

Having diversified your cash holdings in some or all of the currencies we listed above, you need to hold some precious metals:

Gold

The Greek poet Pindar described gold as 'a child of Zeus; neither moth nor rust devoureth it; but the mind of man is devoured by this supreme possession.'

In a deflationary environment, which ultimately (although, confusingly, not immediately) we will face, gold and its allies will retain their value. Gold will continue to benefit from growing scarcity, physical beauty and of course the metal's indestructibility.

In the current economic and political climate, there are a number of factors that will lead to continued rises in the price of gold.

Gold, in our opinion, has just begun a major bull market. The metal is universally recognized as a store of value; it is portable, a feature especially useful in times of crisis; and per ounce it has high value. This means that a great deal of wealth can be transported with little effort and space.

At a time when the US dollar is clearly under pressure, as a result of the double deficits and debts of the United States – trade and budget deficits, and public and private sector debt – gold will likely price in inverse relation to the dollar's fall.

China's increasing appetite for gold will add significantly to international demand. Central banks such as the Bank of England have been sellers of gold for some time, but that overhang in the market will come to an end. Gold discoveries and mining are absolutely not keeping pace with rising demand for the metal, in part fuelled by demographic factors, including the large increase in the world's population in the past fifty years. In general, we do not regard gold as being a top investment when times are good – it tends to be a fallow one, earning no interest. But we are not in good times, and so gold must be a part of any sensible investor's portfolio. Throughout recorded history, gold has been a refuge in times of crisis.

The first reported discovery of gold took place around 6000 BC and it was being used in Egyptian adornments as far back as 3000 BC. The first use of gold as a form of money was apparently in Western Turkey around 700 BC.

A pound coin in the United Kingdom in 2004 had less purchasing power than a penny in 1880 (there were then 240 pence to the pound). In three generations the Chinese currency has been wiped out six times, and the German currency twice. No wonder gold is regarded as a safe haven!

As early as 1792, the US Congress measured the dollar in terms of gold and silver, adopting a so called bi-metallic standard, gold then being valued at $19.30 per ounce. By 1973 a series of small devaluations in the value of the dollar relative to gold had pushed its price to $42.22 per ounce, but shortly thereafter the so-called gold standard came to an end. The dollar and the gold price were allowed to float freely and the US dollar ceased to be convertible into gold. In that year gold rose to $120 per ounce and by 1980, in a frenzy of speculative buying, it reached $850 per ounce. It has not yet ever regained that level. However, we are now in a new era of dollar uncertainty and although gold currently stands at a fraction of its peak price, it is absolutely not whimsical to suppose that it could recover to that peak price and beyond over the next few years.

Gold has many amazing qualities, making it the most precious of the widely traded commodities. It is malleable and as little as one ounce can be hammered into 100 square feet. It is ductile – a single ounce can also be made into a thread of about 50 miles long. Gold is heavy, with a specific gravity of 19.3 times an equivalent volume of water. It is estimated that all the gold mined in history is equivalent to only one oil tanker full – about 120,000 metric tonnes. Gold supply only increases by about 2% per annum.

Our recommendation is that every investor seeking to preserve wealth and to maintain flexibility in times of crisis should have a store of gold coins (Australian Nuggets or South African Krugerrands by preference). Gold coins come in a variety of sizes but the most recognized and easily traded is the one-ounce coin which typically sells at or just above its gold content value. Gold jewellery will typically have little value beyond that of its melted down gold content and that is why our strong preference is for coins.

Even though the world no longer operates on a gold standard, the real value of gold is the same today as it was at the turn of the 20th century and during the Great Depression. Over long periods of time, gold retains its value.

British people might also consider buying British Sovereigns and Britannias. These are capital gains tax free and this may be worth considering for British taxpayers who don't mind paying a slight premium to secure the tax benefit. For more information, visit http://www.taxfreegold.co.uk). Gold coins can also be bought through any bank and through reputable coin dealers. Avoid the Internet to buy coins. Go get them yourself and don't lose them on the way home!

Silver

Silver also offers huge potential as an investment and store of value. It is less portable and inherently less valuable but is commensurately cheaper and has even greater price upside than gold.

Silver currently sells at a much smaller fraction of its all-time peak price than gold, enjoys continuous and growing industrial demand and is rumoured to be the subject of market manipulation to lower the price artificially.

As its price begins to rise, this manipulation could well work in reverse as those who have 'shorted' their positions (i.e. sold silver they do not own) scramble to cover them and push the price of silver even higher.

If you are wealthy(ier), buy silver through a reputable metals broker who can hold it for you. Alternatively buy silver futures. Silver is too heavy to store in bulk at home and it is better to own it through a reputable proxy, one that you are sure will not go bust and where the metal is held in a segregated account. Futures accounts are simple to open and the 'margin' required to buy silver in the futures market is relatively small. But please remember that we are talking of precautionary investments here – not ones to make you wealthy; so keep the amount you have exposed to futures (i.e. the total amount of the futures contracts you are buying) to no more than 15% of your net worth.

Diamonds

Diamonds are a much more controlled market, because of the intervention of the Central Selling Organization, an arm of De Beers, the world's largest diamond company. This organization seeks to match supply and demand and to match market anomalies. Diamonds are portable, tangible and compact. However, they are not homogeneous like gold or silver and come in different grades, which require expert assessment. They are not as exchangeable or as tradable as gold or silver.

Bonds

Purchase short dated (i.e. early maturity) government bonds of countries which are unlikely to default (major rich Western nations, excluding the United States where there is a significant currency risk and ditto the UK). Recommendations would include the bonds of major European nations, Canada, and possibly Japan (though it is building up a huge stock of public sector debt that may be hard to repay). Make sure these bonds are of short dated maturities (i.e. the date on which they are repaid) – no more than three years – and do not put too much of your portfolio of assets into them – perhaps up to 15% of the total.

Do not hold corporate debt or bonds, as many companies will go bankrupt during the coming great depression. Every single company is vulnerable; think of how many of the blue chips of the 1920s are still around today. Not many.

Investment accounts

Do not hold any surplus cash with stockbrokers or investment banks because it is quite likely that some of them will go bust, even those in major nations. Ensure that any shares or bonds that you hold with brokers are held in segregated client accounts so that, in the event that the institution does go bust, you get your shares back. Check this by writing the institution a letter. Do not be afraid to press this point: make sure that they give you total satisfaction that they separate your assets from theirs. Ensure that that they cannot lend, pledge or in any other way create a lien over your shares.

Unless you are financially sophisticated, do not invest in derivatives of any kind, i.e. no options, no futures (the exception is silver), no contracts for differences (CFDs) and no spread bets. More money has been lost this way than in all the casinos of Las Vegas put together. And by financially sophisticated, we mean professional, not just someone who scans the business pages every day. Remember that one of our central worries is the extent of banks, brokers and other financial institutions to so called CDOs (collateralized debt obligations), baskets of bonds and loans. There are literally trillions of dollars in instruments like these and one day a 'black hole' will emerge in which these poorly understood risks will blow up in the face of their creators. Don't get sucked into this black hole by engageing in dodgy trading yourself.

Liquidate any mutual funds or stocks as equities/shares will not do well in a depression. The exception to this is well-performing and well-managed funds investing in gold and silver mining shares. Even here make only small investments and take advice from a reputable financial adviser as to which ones to invest in. If you want to invest directly in a gold mine, go for a blue chip – Newmont Mining, a US listed stock with the ticker symbol NEM is one of the largest mining companies in the world, well run and very sensitive to a rise in the price of gold.

Outstanding liabilities

Taxes

Make sure that you are fully paid up in terms of tax liabilities. Sadly, as the famous phrase goes, the only certain things in life are death and taxes. The taxman in every country always counts as a so-called 'preferred' creditor, in other words, he/she gets their money first. Argue, dispute and question the amount, yes – but give them what's theirs because otherwise you will be hounded.

Monthly obligations

Unless you already have substantial savings and earn much more than you spend every month, you need to watch the outgoing pennies. That means cancelling any unnecessary subscriptions to clubs or similar associations as these will be a drain on your finances when the depression comes. You may not even realize it, but you might be subscribing to magazines on long-term direct debits/payments that you haven't read in a long time. Check all your accounts and cancel that subscription to *Knitting Weekly* or *Truckers Monthly* that you don't need and don't read. More seriously, you might be double paying for certain types of insurance – perhaps your personal insurance overlaps with your company insurance – check that you are not. Do you really need that club or gym membership? When was the last time you went? If you are not going at least once a week, then you are not benefiting from being a member.

In general terms, do not pre-pay for any services as the providers of these may go bust, leaving you out of pocket (e.g. tuition fees, long-term member-ships, deposits, etc.).

If you pay alimony every month, consider settling with a one-off lump sum payment. Alimony is a form of long-term debt and you know our thoughts on debt!

More sophisticated/adventurous investors

If you really want to capitalize on the low US interest rates and the falling US dollar, see if you are able to borrow in US dollars and hold the proceeds of your borrowing in, say, Japanese yen, or one of the other Asian currencies we listed earlier. You will be able to pay back the loan you took out and enjoy a substantial surplus over the next few years. If you're not entirely convinced by our argument, let us remind you again that Warren Buffett, the world's most successful investor, is holding non-US dollars for the first time ever.

If you are looking for investment or new business ideas with growth potential for the 21st century, consider the following:

- The world's 'traditional' energy sources are under pressure because (a) as the developing world's economies grow, their demand for energy will grow with it (that is why China is now the world's second largest importer of oil after the US and (b) the introduction of the EU Emissions Trading Scheme in January 2005, and the ratification of the Kyoto Protocol in February 2005, will mean that corporations and countries alike will be pushed to reduce their greenhouse gas emissions in an effort to fight global warming (much of greenhouse gas emissions come from power stations and the transportation sector). This trend will do two things:
  1 it will continue to squeeze prices of energy sources, particularly oil and gas; and
  2 it will further encourage the private and public sector to find alterna-tive, sustainable and non-polluting sources of energy – look at hydro-electric power, wind power, tidal power and solar power – although the

latter so far has been expensive and rather limited in its power genera-tion abilities.

- Without a doubt the most precious commodity in the world is water. After air, it's probably the thing we take most for granted. However, as we dis-cussed earlier in the book, the world's population is still growing, particu-larly in the developing world. The additional water that will be required for drinking, sanitation and watering crops will put an additional strain on the already limited water supply. This trend will motivate industry to come up with better and cheaper ways to:
  - catch and store water;
  - purify/desalinate water;
  - recycle water; and
  - develop crops that require less water to grow.

Business owners

If you own your own business, assume as a rough rule of thumb that volumes of business will be down by 25% or more in the coming economic downturn, and cut staffing levels accordingly. As difficult as this may be, you would be wise to do this sooner rather than later. Order books will evaporate and very soon you will regret not taking action. The first cut should and must be the deepest. It's not your fault we are going into recession – let staff know that you have to let some go now to preserve the jobs of the others later on. Use the opportunity to get rid of deadwood.

Of course, not every business will be affected and some businesses cannot af-ford to let anyone go at all. But as examples, construction companies, catering companies, financial advisory businesses, shops selling specialty or upmarket merchandise, hire businesses, car dealerships, cleaning companies, public rela-tions businesses – will all suffer grievously in the years ahead. Take pre-emptive steps now. Manufacturers in the rich West will already have read the writing on the wall and it may even have included their bankruptcy – but if you are still in business, continue to cut costs – it's the only way you will survive.

If your business owns its own office space/building, sell it and put the net proceeds on your balance sheet. Rent something similar. Do not enter into any long-term contracts. Don't hold off on selling the office – there is no time like the present. Remember, what we are trying to do is to preserve liquidity and create every opportunity for cash.

Don't be a victim

Avoiding scams

Scams are closely linked, and are often members of the same family as investment manias. Scams, or the intentional defrauding of investors in schemes of little or no merit, are as old as human history.

One early recorded scam was the famous 'South Sea Bubble'. The South Sea Company was formed by John Blunt in England in 1720. Its declared purpose was to fund the British national war debt, which at that time stood at the then enormous sum of £31 million.

The company's business was to be in wool and cotton and its principal markets were Latin American countries. An improved political climate between Spain and Britain, which had hitherto been old enemies, would apparently allow the South Sea Company to prosper, according to its promoters.

The original shares were issued at £130 each. By the time Parliament had approved it, they had risen to £300 each. Hundreds of people, from King George I downward, subscribed to the stock. Only 10% was required as a down payment, with the rest due a year later. The price of the shares eventually peaked at £1000 per share. The company meanwhile had done absolutely nothing except print share certificates and of course, as is normal practice in a scam, only its original investors and promoters benefited.

A prospectus or selling document issued about the same time by a similar company had simply said that its intended business was to carry out 'an undertaking of great advantage but nobody to know what it is.' These sound a little too similar to documents issued during the Internet bubble.

Scams can take many forms. Other scams promoted around the time of the South Sea Bubble included (i) a wheel of perpetual motion; (ii) the transformation of quicksilver (mercury) into a malleable precious metal; and (iii) the importation of jackasses from Spain. Yes, really!

Although, as the centuries have unfolded, investment scams have generally become more sophisticated, the basic principle that they rely on, i.e. a sucker is born every minute, is unchanged.

Others include the Florida real estate scam of the 1920s (unusable land in the Everglades sold to northern investors), rare stamps in 1979, and (yes, in many ways a scam) Lloyds insurance underwriting in 1988, and all have made beggars out of thousands of gullible people.

The most common form of fraud in the Internet age is the securities-based scam. These, state regulators estimate, cost US investors alone billions of dollars a year. Such things as promissory notes, prime bank schemes, and viatical settlements (interests in the life insurance policies of supposedly terminally ill people) are prime areas of fraud.

Investors should be particularly aware of the following types of potential fraud:

1. *Affinity group fraud.* This is where the members of a group, e.g. a religion, are targeted using the bond of trust that exists in such associations to run off with the savings of other members. This can be anything from making off with the money for the Christmas party to much more sophisticated propositions.
2. *Promissory notes.* Short-term debt notes issued by obscure or even non-existent companies promising high returns – perhaps 15% per month – with little to no risk. It has been known for the scam artists in these cases to even engage in prayer with their victims to gain their trust! If someone offers you these types of return, they are almost certainly trying to defraud you. Beware!
3. *'Ponzi' schemes.* They are the legacy of the early 20th century Italian immigrant to the US, Charles Ponzi, and are one of the most common forms of fraud. They are basically variations of pyramid investment schemes where the high returns promised to investors come from the capital provided by new investors to the scheme. The only people to make money on these sorts of schemes are the promoters – everybody else loses. Period.
4. *'Viatical settlements'.* These were conceived as a way of helping the seriously ill to pay their bills and represent a purchase of a share in the death benefits from insurance or other assets of a terminally ill person. They are

always risky investments – no one knows when someone will die for sure – and should be avoided at all costs.

5 *Prime bank schemes.* These abound in the US and in Japan and supposedly allow investors access to huge returns through the investment portfolios of major banks. They are almost always fraudulent and are certainly not promoted by the major banks themselves.

6 *Internet fraud.* From the 1950s onwards, so called 'boiler room' operators, often located in lightly regulated countries, would target American and European investors with stories of untold wealth to be made in 'penny' or low priced stocks. These 'pump and dump' operators have now moved in large part to the Internet, and are routinely disguised as people who provide 'advice' in Internet chat rooms. Be wary of such 'advice' on penny stocks on the Internet – it is almost certainly worth avoiding!

Here are some important guiding principles for investors to remember when considering whether an investment could be a scam:

1 If it sounds too good to be true, it almost certainly is!
2 We live in a low interest rate world. People promising high yields with no risk are lying.
3 Beware particularly of viatical (big word, big losses) settlements, oil and gas investments, equipment leasing schemes, affinity fraud, penny stocks, anything to do with annuities and farming schemes.
4 And finally, if in doubt, don't do it!

Identity Theft – more common than you think

Do not view identity theft in a light-hearted way; according to a study commissioned by the financial industry,[1] 9.3 million people were victims of this crime in 2004 in the United States alone, and a similar figure was reported for 2003.

In order to protect yourself from this fraud, it is best to acquaint yourself with the different types of identity theft. The most common ones are listed below:

- *Credit card fraud* – purchases made without the knowledge or consent of the authorized card-holder; this is happening more and more and with greater sophistication.
- *Phone or utility services fraud* – where either of these services are set up under the victim's name.
- *Bank fraud* – which could either be unauthorized withdrawals from the victim's account or where an account is opened under the victim's name and fraudulent cheques are cashed.
- *Loan fraud* – where any sort of consumer loan is obtained in the victim's name.
- *Employment related fraud* – where back office employees such as temps or janitors take advantage of sensitive information on employee desks and computers – easy to do if you are not careful about applying passwords etc.
- *Government documents or benefits fraud* – where the victim's social security number or driving licence is obtained. Benefits fraud is where government benefits are obtained fraudulently by claiming to be the victim.

There are a number of risk-reducing measures that can be taken to reduce the chances of falling victim to identity fraud, some of the main ones are outlined below:

- Do not give out sensitive information over the phone (especially information that pertains to your identity) unless you are familiar with the person with whom you are speaking and the organization which they represent.
- Do not give out your credit card information over the Internet unless it is a trusted and secure site (look for the padlock which appears at the bottom of the browser to signify that the site is using data encryption).
- Consider taking out identity theft insurance which insurers such as AIG are starting to offer at a nominal annual fee.
- Make sure you destroy all credit cards, bank and other sensitive information before you throw it out. Buying a paper shredder is one way to destroy sensitive data on a day to day basis. Alternatively if you have a large quantity of documents that you wish to dispose of, you can either burn

it in the yard, or you can engage the services of a document destruction company.

- If like most of us you store sensitive information on your personal computer and are connected to the Internet, it is highly advisable to install a firewall to prevent unauthorized access to your computer. For additional diligence, turn off your computer whenever you are not using it. Furthermore, use a file shredder to permanently delete all unwanted files on your computer. Simply pressing the 'delete' button on a computer doesn't delete files. Get something like CyberScrub from www.cyberscrub.com and use it often.

- Change your passwords and PINs regularly and keep them in a safe place.

- Do not leave personal information lying around your work place as it may be taken or copied by anyone who has access to your office, from colleagues to janitors; this happens a lot so don't think it won't happen to you.

- Subscribe to a service that sends you a report of your credit rating regularly, or check your credit rating yourself once or twice a year as this way you will be able to see immediately if someone has taken out a loan, etc. under your name. Have a look at any of the big three credit rating/scoring agencies: Equifax, Experian and Trans Union Corporation. This service is available to residents in selected countries, including the US and the UK. The URLs of these companies are:
  - Equifax: www.equifax.com
  - Experian: www.experian.com
  - Trans Union Corporation: www.tuc.com (US only)

Other useful information

Be aware of what is going on in the world around you

By this heading, we're not talking about football scores or celebrity gossip here, enjoyable though they may be. We're talking about broad economic trends and their consequences. Make an effort to read and to at least partially absorb economic commentary in the business section of your newspaper. Don't believe it all, but at least get a sense of what is happening in the big world out there.

If you want some good regular reading, *The Economist* is an excellent weekly publication, offering a summary and analysis of key issues in the world economy. See how to subscribe by visiting their website: www.economist.com.

Also, it is worth checking out www.dailyreckoning.com, a useful guide to financial protection. We also suggest the *Financial Times* (www.ft.com), the *Wall Street Journal* (www.wsj.com) and *Money Week*, a UK publication (www.money-week.com) for those with more time and/or in-depth interest.

This material should give the reader a sense of what is happening beyond Main Street or the High Street. Whether readers agree with the commentary and analysis or not, information is power and this will help you make better-informed decisions.

How banks and other lending institutions make their money

This may seem obvious, but banks make money in a fundamentally simple way. On the one hand, they pay depositors as little interest on their money as they can get away with and, on the other hand, they charge borrowers as many fees and as much interest as possible.

'Free' services, such as ATM withdrawals, cheque books and direct debits are all designed to keep deposits in for the lowest possible cost. Quite often 'special deals' on interest payments for mortgages and other loans have caveats, contained in small print attached to the attractive big print, i.e. they are of limited duration or extent or they just don't apply to you.

Naturally, banks make money in other ways as well – playing stock markets, trading 'derivatives' and other fancy footwork (sometimes tripping up on the moneyed dance floor). But basically, banks make money in the simple old-fashioned way – they pay little and charge a lot.

Now, we'll keep saying this until we are blue in the face … debt is going to be a big problem for many people in the difficult period ahead, so be aware of what you are paying for and how much you are paying.

Preferably, as we emphasize again and again, get rid of or reduce your debts, particularly those related to short term credit (i.e. those pesky plastic cards or personal loans). Watch what the banks are charging you; does the small print all seem a bit small, does all the technospeak of your bank seem a bit dazzling – it's because they want more of your money than you would really like to give them if you knew how much they were really taking. Wise up, shop around, read the documents, shop for banking services like you would for a car – review, inform yourself and choose price and quality.

Choose your banks carefully

There is an old expression that banks are 'as safe as houses'. Well, if we are right, houses aren't going to be that safe in the future – and nor will some banks.

In certain cases, banks based in the rich nations are highly exposed to houses of all types – or at least to real estate – because a lot of their lending has gone into property.

What happens if householders can no longer pay off their mortgages, or landlords of commercial buildings are unable pay back debts because tenants can't/won't pay? Who foots the bill then? The answer is the banks which lent the money in the first place. This is because although banks tend to have juicy margins (remember the difference between what they pay for your deposits and what they lend them out at minus their costs), these are quickly eroded if the borrowers won't or can't pay.

In a recession or depression this can become a very difficult situation for banks, even if they have made substantial 'non-performing loan' provisions, i.e. deducted from revenue the anticipated cost of borrowers defaulting.

If property prices fall sharply and unemployment and business failures rise sharply, then banks can and will get into serious trouble. This is especially the case if they have highly leveraged balance sheets, in other words, they have lent out far more money than they have in deposits.

Although in the US and in the UK, as well as in other rich nations, there is some depositor protection, this tends to be highly limited. Please refer to the next section on credit ratings, which are not infallible, but are a useful guide to the good, the bad and the ugly among the banks which are offering you their services.

We would suggest dividing your monies on deposit – and remember, try to arrange to place them in 'hard' (non-US dollar) currencies – into three or more portions and place them in three banks rated 'A' or better. Do not be embarrassed if your deposits are not large – at least you are fortunate enough to hold cash, unlike those who did not sell their homes and have no savings.

Ask the bank if you don't know what its rating is and get its answer in writing.

Make sure that you are dealing with the parent company of the bank involved, not just some subsidiary or affiliated company that the parent could walk away from if the subsidiary gets into trouble. This is important and again is something you need to check.

Rating agencies – boring but important

Ratings are in essence measurements of the financial health of institutions that borrow money. These can be corporations, governments or banks.

There are three large rating agencies: Fitch, Moody's and Standard & Poor's. The ability of a bank or corporation to meet its payment commitments in full and on time depends on the institution's financial standing. The agencies assign ratings to help investors compare the relative risks of investing. Ratings are extremely important in determining at what rate of interest banks or corporations borrow money at, and what their general credit standing is. This affects the willingness of individuals and companies to do business with them. Rating agencies are highly profitable businesses, but subject to potential conflicts of interest. Their fees are mostly paid by the companies or countries that want to get their debt rated – and therein lies an obvious potential conflict! Rating agencies have been, and no doubt will be again, wrong on several major defaults. If management of bad companies is skilled at lying and fiddling the books, they will probably find a way to do this. So the views of rating agencies are useful as a guide, but should not be taken as written in proverbial stone.

Table 5.1 shows the two grades of ratings: investment grade and speculative grade.

Table 5.1   How rating agencies grade financial institutions

Fitch	Moody's	Standard & Poor's	Ability to meet financial obligations
Investment grade – range			
AAA	Aaa	AAA	Highest, extremely strong
BBB	Baa	BBB	Adequate
Speculative grade – range			
BB	Ba	BB	High degree of uncertainty
C	C	C	Very vulnerable

Source: Long term ratings from Fitch, Moody's and Standard and Poor's.

Table 5.2 shows examples of ratings assigned by the three rating agencies to a sample of the leading financial institutions.

Table 5.2   How some leading financial institutions are rated

Bank Name	Fitch	Moody's	Standard & Poor's
Bank of America	AA	Aa2	AA-
Citigroup	AA+	Aa1	AA-
JP Morgan Chase	A+	Aa3	AA-
Deutsche Bank	AA-	Aa3	AA-
Dresdner Bank	A+	Aa3	A+
Lloyds TSB Bank	AA+	Aaa	AA
Royal Bank of Scotland	AA	Aa1	AA-
Abbey National	AA-	Aa2	AA-
HSBC	AA	Aa2	AA-
UBS	AAA	Aa2	AA+
Credit Suisse	AA-	Aa3	A+
Credit Lyonais	A	A1	A
BNP Paribas	AA	Aa2	AA-
Societe Generale	AA	Aa3	AA-
ING Bank	AA-	Aa2	AA-
ABN AMRO Bank	AA-	Aa3	AA-

When investors are considering doing business with a bank, a brokerage or buying bonds issued by governments or corporations, they should check the rating of the institution with whom they are proposing to engage.

In an economic crisis, institutions with poor ratings will be more likely to fail. Though ratings are by no means infallible as a guide to the financial health of institutions (for a long time Enron had a good rating, as did WorldCom), they are absolutely worth consulting. Investors can find this information easily on the Internet at either of the following websites:

- http://www.standardandpoors.com
- http://www.fitchratings.com/

It should also be noted that rating agencies can and do get things wrong – Enron had a strong rating sometime before it went spectacularly belly up. Agencies tend to react to events – and of course if companies are deliberately falsifying their accounts, there is generally not much an agency can do about it.

Readers should be aware that banks in major countries are increasingly making money from less secure sources – so called 'proprietary' trading (operating like a big hedge fund, in essence), 'sub prime lending' (trailer park and pawnshop lending) and the financing of heavily borrowed (or 'leveraged') takeovers. This last – fuelled by the so called 'private equity' boom – has grown exponentially in the last few years. The idea is for funds to buy cash-generating or asset-backed companies using lots of debt – often provided by banks – and then to improve the performance of the underlying companies.

The trouble is, like all good things, it has become very popular indeed and has led to some frankly risky deals being done. In the event that our economic forecasts come right, a lot of the emperor's clothing in these deals will have been stripped bare. And the now highly prosperous banks of the West will have their smiles wiped off their well-fed faces!

That is why, dear reader, we urge you not to put your money – your hard earned money – into just any old bank. Look at its ratings, look at how much exposure your bank has to the key areas of risk ahead – housing, takeover deals and proprietary trading, and place your money in the safer ones.

In general also, spread your deposits around several banks – taking advantage of whatever deposit insurance is offered by your government.

For instance, if the government guarantees 'X' in the event of a bank failure, place the relevant amount – 'just under X' – into as many banks of apparent quality as you can. That way the government will carry the can in the event that one or several of them go bust. But of course governments also can and do default, so you need other strategies to make sure that you preserve your purchasing power. Hence the need for hard assets, which we discussed earlier.

Counterparty risk

This has nothing to do with festivities of any type, or indeed of any revolutionary political movement, but it is important nonetheless. Counterparty risk is the risk that the people you do financial business with go belly up or have some other problem. Of course, that wouldn't matter if you owed them money, but it will certainly matter to you if they owe you money or hold assets on your behalf.

What sort of institutions are we talking about? Well just about all of those that handle money in any kind of way, on your behalf. Just pause a moment to think about the sort of counterparty risks you as an individual run today. Do you own mutual funds or unit trusts? Do you own stocks? Do you have a pension plan, an IRA or a 401k plan (in the US) or the equivalent in another nation? Do you have a life or auto or household insurance policy? Have you got a prepaid membership for a long period with a club of some sort? Have you got deposits tied up with utility companies? Every one of these constitutes a counterparty risk.

Now, it is our belief that a number of financial institutions in the Rich World will go bust in the coming difficult period, and if they do they might take wads of your cash with them. So take our advice on the subject.

We have already written of the perils of having your money in one bank or credit institution and of not carefully vetting the creditworthiness of that institution. However, the same applies to insurance companies, stockbrokerages, pension providers and anyone else you do financial business with. You need to ask them two questions each, and don't be afraid to do so, because if the shoe was on the other foot, they would be looking into your credit history.

The first question is:

Dear Sir/Madam

Do you separate your money from that of your clients?

(In other words, in less polite words, do you keep my money separate from yours so that if you go bust I don't go down with your sinking ship?)

And the second is:

Dear Sir/Madam

Please provide me with your latest credit rating and the comparitive position of your company in terms of financial strength with other companies in your industry.

If the answers to these questions are not forthcoming or don't sufficiently reassure you, don't do business with them.

The reason why these questions are so important is that it is our firm belief that at least one major investment bank will go bust in the next few years. Should this happen it could drag the savings of millions of people down with it or alternatively leave people with their savings frozen for a long time while the mess is sorted out.

Don't let that happen to you. Investigate, prepare and diversify.

*part*SIX

Timeframe and Summary

The uncertain future

As you may have already concluded, our book does not depict a positive picture for the rich Western nations in the coming years. We have analysed many influencing factors, particularly the global economic and political situation, as well as reviewing the lessons that history has taught us, and that is our conclusion. Those people who know us don't regard as us natural pessimists and we don't think of ourselves as such either. But we have to face facts: these are dangerous times and we want to be as prepared for them as we reasonably can be. We too want to live long lives and get through the coming difficult period.

No doubt there will be many commentators who will not agree with us, but time will reveal all. Remember how anyone who criticized the ludicrous valuations of Internet companies were ridiculed and accused of 'not getting it'. It is only in hindsight that the follies of Internet investors are so obvious. There will be those who describe our attempts as facile and scaremongering. They will deride us over our economic analysis and perhaps our checklists which appear to some to be survivalist and extreme.

There are plenty of doom and gloom forecasters who predict a far bleaker future for the world than we do. They contrast much more starkly with those who believe that the world is currently going through a golden age and the current situation is just a blip that will soon correct itself.

We neither subscribe to this extreme pessimism nor to false optimism but we are of the opinion that even the best case scenario for the rich West is a gloomy one – though not an irretrievable one. Our outlook is not based on any form of astrology, crystal ball gazing or analysis of prophecies of the likes of Nostradamus.

Our view of the near future can be summarized as follows:

- Severe dislocations will start to appear in elements of major industrialized nations. German unemployment will rise further; US unemployment will also rise, as will the rest of Europe and Japan. Deflation will spread throughout the West.
- Despite attempts by the Fed and other central banks to maintain healthy economic growth, Western economies will go into deep recession resulting in wide-scale calls for protectionism of domestic industries.
- The dollar will be subjected to increasing downward pressure. Foreigners will be reluctant to hold US dollars thereby exacerbating the problems faced by the US economy.
- In the meantime, al-Qaeda and other terrorist threats will rear their ugly heads every once in a while, denting the already fragile consumer confidence.
- North Korea and Iran will continue to engage in brinkmanship, which could lead to further global instability.
- By 2006 or 2007, all these factors will lead to deepening recession and, in some nations, depression, elevating levels of unemployment and bankruptcy to the point where pockets of social unrest become a serious threat to civilized order.
- Immigrant populations in industrialized nations will be at increasing risk from xenophobia and racially motivated attacks.
- In certain parts of the world, social unrest and disorder will lead to strikes (for France this may not be something new), interruptions of supplies and possibly power failure.
- The homeless or dispossessed will be everywhere and eventually their despair will lead to widespread crime, looting and violence which the authorities will struggle to contain.
- In a worst case scenario, a breakdown in power will affect hygiene standards and medical care will become patchy. Disease may become more prevalent. Pandemics in the West will be likely and many could die from illness and malnutrition.

Possible scenarios

In this section we hypothesize how events might unfold in a step by step sequence of possible events, each incident having one or more knock-on effects (see Figure 6.1).

Of course it's impossible to predict the actual chain reaction, but regardless of the forecast circumstances, the end result comes out as disturbingly similar.

To make the event tree even more realistic we have thrown in some additional incidents that might take place in an unconnected fashion, destabilizing the world even further (these 'random' events are indicated in shaded balloons).

You can reformulate this exercise yourself: start with the dollar's collapse as the trigger event, which, as we have explained ad nauseam in this book, is

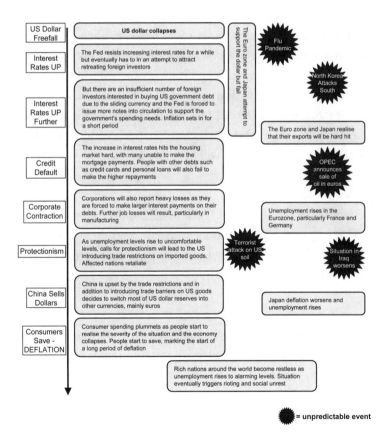

Figure 6.1 How world events may unfold

an inevitable event for an indebted nation with a larger-than-wallet spending habit.

Then see if you can come out with a scenario that has a more positive result – we couldn't!

This suggests to us that it doesn't really matter how the events unfold, the outcome will be similar – high unemployment, social tensions/unrest and deflation.

Alternative outlooks: the futurists

At this point, we thought it would be useful to include the opinions of some independent futurists, i.e. 'gurus' who specialize in analysing trends and making predictions about how our lives will be in the future.

Obviously there is no certainty about what the future truly holds, but certain trends are undeniable; the 'art' or particular angle of each of these futurists is how to interpret these trends to paint a picture of what lies ahead.

Each of the three futurists we review depicts a somewhat similar outlook to that of ours, but perhaps over a more distant horizon and without considering geopolitics, which is an area that we have particularly focused on.

We believe that there are two tiers of future to consider: one is the coming economic collapse of the 'Rich World', which will happen within the next few years; the other is more long-term and will be influenced by:

1 global power plays;
2 the consequences of the ageing and increasing population; and
3 environmental factors, such as global warming and dwindling natural resources. These factors will impact our living conditions as well as our supplies of food, water and energy.

Gerald Celente
Our first futurist, Gerald Celente, is the author of *Trends 2000*[1] and the founder of the Trends Research Institute. Mr Celente points out that the convergence of globalization and computerization has dramatically shaped the principles of economics. He uses five 'O's to summarize his picture of the 21st century:

- Overproduction: there are more products and services available world-wide than can ever be consumed.
- Overcapacity: there is a glut of advanced facilities and excess service capabilities to supply the world marketplace with more than can ever be consumed.
- Open markets: in the borderless new millennium marketplace, products and services flow freely, unbound by the old economic channels.
- Overpopulation: in the multinational bazaar, companies will freely exploit the 6-billion-plus labour pool, without regard to geography.
- Online: a planet full of browsers is weaving its way through the web, forging the connecting link in the new millennium's economic chain.

Mr Celente concludes that these 5 Os will result in lower wages and a prolonged period of low inflation, possibly even deflation – two predictions that we too are making in this book.

Peter Schwarz
In 2003, veteran futurist Peter Schwarz[2] published a book entitled *Inevitable Surprises*. The highlights of his vision of the future are:

- People are living longer, are healthier, and either want to work or cannot afford to retire so they will have to keep working.
- Migration levels will continue to climb, mainly those from poor nations seeking new and better lives in the West, particularly Asians and Hispanics in the US and Muslims in Europe.
- The eventual return of the economic boom as a result of greater productivity, better communications and globalization. The next 3–4 years might be so-so, but growth will take off towards the end of the decade.
- Sources of conflict will rise out of a disorderly world (parts of Latin America, Central Asia and Africa) and tensions will mount as the rest of the world tries to contain the United States (as per the invasion of Iraq) – as the rogue superpower – making the rules but not abiding by them.
- Terrorism will continue and can never be fully eradicated.
- We could already be at the start of a new wave of scientific discoveries, such as alternative sources of energy and applications of nanotechnology.

- New diseases (such as SARS) may spread rapidly across the world and will be hard to control.
- New technologies will help clean up pollution as fossil fuels are replaced.

Daniel Burrus

Daniel Burrus is considered one of the world's leading technology forecasters and business strategists, and is the author of *Technotrends*.[3] Mr Burrus differentiates between hard trends and soft trends – and does so as follows.

Hard trends are concrete and verifiable. They are based on the scientific study of tangible, physical, existing items in our world. For example, studies of the ageing population of the US have revealed very accurate hard trends. People are tangible and their age is measurable, leading to more accurate forecasts over time.

Soft trends contain possibilities. These are usually in the form of best case/worst case scenarios and the predictions that are made are as a result of public opinion surveys, news events that show a pattern, shifts in popular culture, and anecdotes. They can also be based on the extrapolation of numerical patterns.

One significant hard trend with far-reaching consequences, Mr Burrus points out, is the ageing of the baby boomer population in the US. Its impact on the US and the rest of the world will catch people off guard. In the US alone, there are over 80 million baby boomers (people born between 1946 and 1964) – their societal impact cannot be ignored and Mr Burrus breaks down this impact into four points:

- *Historic wealth transfer.* The parents of baby boomers, who literally created the modern economy as they left the farm and moved to the city for higher paying jobs, are entering their 'mortality' age. As they die, they bequeath their estates to their offspring, resulting in the biggest transfer of wealth in history.
- *Stock market dive.* Today, the oldest baby boomers are in their mid-to-late fifties. Looking ahead ten years, these baby boomers will start to retire. As millions of boomers begin to retire, they will be shifting their money into a retirement portfolio, pulling much of their money out of aggressive growth and growth stocks, and getting into conservative stocks and bonds

that pay dividends and interest. Will this only happen for a few years and then growth stocks will be popular again? No, he says. This is not very likely as hard trends show us that there was a baby bust after the baby boom, so there are not enough people to make up for the shift in asset allocation that will take place. What about the children of the baby boomers? It is true that the baby boomers' kids will just be entering their investing years and will find some very good prices, but when young people begin investing, they usually do not have large amounts of money to begin with.

- *The ageing of industrialized countries.* The majority of the industrialized world also has an ageing population, with Japan leading the way. This will propel this hard trend even further. The areas of the world that are made up of predominantly young people are economically undeveloped, and it will take time for them to contribute to a revival in global stock markets. This hard trend tells us that by the end of this decade and well into the next decade, stocks will be in for a rough ride.

- *Many boomers won't retire* – either because they cannot afford to or because they can but won't in order to keep themselves active and to give themselves a sense of purpose.

Prophecies of Edgar Cayce – unconventional, yet deadly accurate

Edgar Cayce was one of America's greatest psychics and at the time was world-famous. He was born on a farm in Kentucky, USA, in 1877 into a strict Protestant Christian family. His psychic abilities were not discovered until he was in his twenties, when he agreed to be hypnotized as a final, and successful, effort to cure a medical condition.

Also known as the 'Sleeping Prophet', Cayce found that he had prophetic abilities. By lying down, closing his eyes and folding his hands over his stomach, he was able to put himself into some kind of self-induced meditative state. While in this deep trance he was able to answer any question put to him with an uncannily high degree of accuracy.

Among his many prophecies, none are more relevant today than his prediction of the coming economic collapse and subsequent depression. Cayce believed that economic depression cycles take place every 25 years[4] and that the next depression or severe recession is due in 2006 or 2007. He rightly predicted a great crash in 1929 after a long bull run and spent the preceding two years teaching his clients how to exit from their investments. In 1928, he predicted the

Dow Jones would fall after hitting a high of around 385 – on 1 September, 1929, the Dow hit a high of 386 and the following month, on 'Black Thursday', the Dow lost 300 points. Cayce made 63 general economic predictions in all, and only 4 of them were incorrect, which means that the objective accuracy of his predictions was 93%[5] – all the more reason to take what he had to say seriously!

Table 6.1 illustrates how past recessions and depressions have indeed taken place every 24/25 years, thus highlighting the inevitability of our first 21st century recession or, worse, depression.

Table 6.1 Cayce 24/25 year economic depression cycle

Interval in years	Cayce bottom	Recorded bottom	Note
25	1783	1784	Recession
25	1808	1808	Depression
25	1833	1837	Bank crisis
25	1858	1858	Depression
25	1883	1883	Depression
25	1908	1908	Depression
25	**1933**	**1933**	**Great Depression**
24	1958*	1958	Eisenhower recession
25	1982*	1982	Reagan recession
25	**2007**	**??**	**Next recession or depression**

* Recessions took place without an actual contraction of the overall economy.
Source: *The Coming Economic Collapse of 2006*, Michael Wells Mandeville.

Summary

Although much of the writing was already on the wall, the trigger event that marked the turning point for the worsening economic and political times will appear in the history books as the September 11, 2001 terrorist attacks on the World Trade Center in New York and the Pentagon in Washington DC. In a sense, this is analogous to the assassination of Archduke Franz Ferdinand in Sarajevo in 1914. This assassination directly triggered the Great War and a chain of events that affected the world's politics and economics for the following 70 years. The punitive sanctions imposed by the Allied victors after World

War I contributed to the rise of Nazism, which in turn led to World War II. Similarly, the events of September 11, 2001 will prove to have been a watershed in the affairs of countries in North America, the European Union and the developed Asian world.

The world economy is not yet in depression but in our view there is an increasing chance that it will move into this state. Already, pockets of deflation – a precursor to depression – are making themselves apparent. Since the bursting of Japan's economic bubble in 1990, the country continues to suffer from declining prices. Other examples include the world's technology and telecommunication industries: massive overcapacity in what have now become commoditized products – personal computers, mobile phones, fibre optic cabling, to name but three – have experienced (and will continue to experience) downward price pressures.

Of course there are also, confusingly, pockets of inflation in the modern world: commodity prices have been rising rapidly in recent times, partly as a function of the decline in the US dollar, the currency in which commodities like steel, copper, oil and gold tend to be denominated, but also because of China. China is at the stage of its economic development where it is a huge importer of basic commodities and its influence in world markets for these products is enormous. But there is another and more potent side to China's growth: its ferocious ability to compete in world export markets with lower and lower prices. This means very simply that inflation will not be an issue in major economies for the foreseeable future, despite the massive injections of liquidity that have taken place in the early part of the 21st century.

Industries subject to mounting Chinese competition – white goods (household appliances), toys, textiles, electronic products as examples – will atrophy in coming years in the rich, industrialized nations. Most of them simply cannot compete with lower Chinese labour costs. In addition, as China develops a larger domestic market it will gain economy of scale advantages over richer Western nations and over Japan.

The much more rapid pace of technology transfer between nations, partly due to the Internet, will mean that the gap between Chinese technical capability and that of, say, the US will narrow rapidly. The 'gap narrowing' will be much quicker than, for instance, the narrowing of the gap between the German and British economies in the second half of the 19th century.

It is not unlikely that, within ten years, China will be a major player in personal computers, cars, steel and chemicals, rivalling the output levels of Europe and of the US. Indeed, it is instructive to note that IBM recently sold its PC operations to Lenovo, a Chinese manufacturer. IBM just can't make them cheaply outside China any more! This process of technology transfer is of course aided by the flagrant flouting of rules on intellectual property which occurs in China – copies of literally all goods abound, including many that are indistinguishable from the original.

We believe that the further and relentless downward pressure on prices will lead to calls for protectionist barriers to be raised once again in rich, industrialized nations. If such short-sighted thinking comes to pass as policy – and history is littered with examples of such nonsensical economic theory being put into practice – the effects will be devastating: unemployment will rise still further in countries such as Germany, France, the US and Japan and thereby lay the foundation for social unrest. It is not far-fetched to suppose that 1930s unemployment levels (over 25% at that time in the US) could return to major nations. This would have obvious and disastrous consequences for social order, not to mention the added burden of an already severely indebted government. The link between economics and politics will then once again become evident as newly impoverished countries turn to extreme political creeds to find some way out of their deep problems. Already the European Union has an average rate of unemployment of around 9%, and undoubtedly, this will rise further.

Of course, there are differences between the 1930s and the current period, but it does seem that it will be hard for governments in the major industrialized nations to reverse the trend towards depression. The traditional tools available to governmental institutions are no longer easy or effective options: the Federal Reserve in the US cannot re-inflate the economy through further credit creation, and with interest rates already very low and inflationary pressures at work, the Fed cannot cut rates to stimulate the economy. Indeed, the official inflation rate for the US in 2004 was 3%, yet the Fed Funds Rate stood at only 2.25% at the end of that year, meaning that the real funds rate is still negative. A more realistic figure for inflation is closer to 6% if house price inflation is included (this for some reason is not considered when calculating the Consumer Price Index, or CPI). This figure of 6% is an alarming level of inflation indeed, and a warning to all that interest rates will have to rise to at least this level to curb inflation.

Many economists argue that a 'neutral' funds rate is around 2–3% above the inflation rate, so it should be no surprise to anyone to see the Fed Funds Rate climb to the 5% range over the near to medium term, and that is a conservative forecast. But it's not just rising inflation that is pressuring the Fed to raise rates, there is also mounting concern over the perceived creditworthiness of US government debt as the structural debt imbalances of the US become more apparent.

The devaluation of the US dollar against other currencies has commenced but the Fed still needs to raise more cash to plug the hole in the government's deficit spending: raise interest rates too little and the Fed will not attract enough buyers, an increasing number of whom are reluctant to invest in a falling currency; raise rates too much and the domestic housing market could implode. The Fed is caught between the proverbial rock and hard place (see Figure 6.2).

Consumption has been the driving force behind US economic activity. This is because of the Faustian pact that the US has seemingly entered into with Asian economies, in particular China. This has enabled the US and China to grow at illusory and unsustainable rates. This pact is really quite simple: take our 'paper' (i.e., debt in the form of Treasury bonds and bills) – says the US to its Asian counterparts – and this in turn allows the US to carry on buying Asian

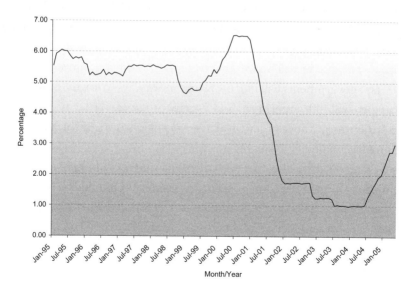

Figure 6.2 The US federal funds rate
Source: Federal Reserve Board.

goods it cannot pay for in full with other goods. In return, the Wal-Marts and other emporia of the United States can continue to be filled with the output of Asia's fast growing manufacturing sector. Indeed, 5% of China's entire national output is now exported directly to Wal-Mart.

If we believe the lessons of economic history – and we should – this cannot go on for long. The scale of involvement of Asia's central banks in the national debt of the US is now so large, and the destruction of the US manufacturing industry so rapid, that the nexus will break – and break soon.

Central governments have at their disposal the use of tax cuts and spending on large-scale public works to keep their economic 'shows' going. However, almost all the governments of major industrialized nations are constrained by the fact that these particular shows have been going on for a long time. As a result, the ability to go out and borrow on an even grander scale just isn't there any more. As far as this golden period is concerned, the Fat Lady is about to sing.

It is an economic truism that as modern economies falter, tax revenues decline. This is because profits and incomes are lessened in sluggish or weak economies. However, at the same time, governments faced with such circumstances need to spend more, as increasing numbers of people claim welfare or unemployment benefits. This widening divergence between falling revenues and rising demands on central governments' resources will be an increasing feature of the next few years. It is a vicious cycle which is hard to break, and one for which traditional so-called Keynesian economics can offer no structural cure. For us as individuals – probably ones who work for a living – this bodes ill for our futures. We will be working to support more and more people who don't – and governments will find more and more ways to tax us to enable this. This in turn will stifle enterprise. Not a pretty prospect.

So, is there any chance of a revival in economies despite the bleak backdrop which we have painted? Probably not.

As we stated earlier, the effects of the stock market bubble bursting at the beginning of the century, a longer term deflation compounded by the September 11 terrorist attacks on the United States, combined with an addiction to debt will cause a long period of, at best, sluggish performance and, at worse, depression. And don't think it will all be over in a flash. This isn't some passing rain shower, mildly inconvenient; it's a full-on hurricane and only a fool won't batten down the hatches to deal with it. After all, it took three decades after the crash of 1929 for the US stock market to recover its highs of the late 1920s.

Certainly the massive injections of credit into the US economy, in particular after the bursting of the Internet bubble and the events of September 11, 2001, promoted rapid growth in the US – at least on a temporary basis. Think of this liquidity injection as a kind of sugar high, munching on a bar of chocolate – euphoric for a short while but then leading to lethargy and sluggishness.

The US and its rich allies have had their highs and are starting to come down from it, and no amount of money printing, or so-called 'pump priming', will now work.

What, then, are the ingredients for a healthy global economy? There is little doubt that peace, stability and the absence of trade barriers are key factors in creating global economic growth. Today, the world is a long way from achieving the first two, and the third – barriers to free trade – are beginning to creep up.

The issue of trade is fundamental to our negative outlook. The deterioration in the US trade deficit is now giving serious cause for alarm. It runs at around US$1.5 to US$2 billion a day and the financing of this is largely taking place by the very people selling Americans the goods that are being imported in record quantities. This daily build-up of deficits in the United States' external position is leading to a rapid accumulation of foreign reserves (primarily US dollars) for countries such as China and Japan. It is leaving their central banks with substantial holdings of US dollars and US government securities.

If these central banks were to get it into their heads to sell even a relatively modest portion of these holdings, there could be disastrous consequences for the dollar's international value, which has already been sliding against all major currencies for some time. Should the US dollar continue to slide (and it will), it could lead to a dramatic price fall in US government bond prices – and conversely a very big rise in interest rates. These higher interest rates will choke the US economy, already fatally overburdened with debt.

Modest growth in European economies has been offset by apparently rapid growth in the United States and China which together have been gorging on the credit bubble that has fast built up in the world's major economy. The use of tax cuts and deficit financing, as well as a fast-and-loose monetary policy by the US authorities, are the principal reasons why things don't seem half as bad as they really are.

It is quite evident to us that the buoyant post World War II era in major industrialized nations has now ended. Occasional bursts of optimism characterized by stock market rallies and sighs of relief all round should be regarded for what they are: false hopes in a gloomy period in world economic history.

No, we are not saying that we are all going back to riding in carts, sitting in darkened rooms and eating swill! But we are entering a difficult period of readjustment where easy lives in the West will be turned upside down and the 'normal' rules will be challenged. This period will be characterized by a gradual but unremitting decline in the growth of world economic output, made worse by rising unemployment and the reintroduction of barriers to trade. This rising protectionism is a major warning sign to the authors of this book. It shows that the lesson of history has not been fully or even partially learnt. Free trade is a positive for economic growth.

The world economy is much more interdependent than at any period in its history and a reversal of the free trade practices of the past fifty years will have dire consequences for all of us. But it does seem that the barriers are slowly going up and that even the apparently savviest of people (such as Warren Buffett) are preaching dark-age economics.

Many of the readers of this book will be living in the 'comfortable world' of the rich nations club. The developed world population alive today has lived through fewer hardships than any of its forefathers. Our most recent global war ended well over 50 years ago, World War II. As a result, many in the rich part of the world have simply not lived through periods of real hardship and cannot relate to how quickly lives can be devastated by conflicts that spread. History frequently repeats itself though, particularly so when we neglect to learn from the lessons of the past. Granted, the repetition of history will not be exact – its form may even take us by surprise – but the repetition of disaster is coming soon.

In our modern, busy lives, we take our most fundamental needs for granted: our safety, our water and our food supply. In contrast, these represent daily challenges for most of the people living in the world today. As a consequence, Rich World troubles have developed around superficial layers of angst; we have become too self-obsessed, making issues of relatively trivial matters. This will render the coming hardship even more devastating for those physically and mentally unprepared.

So that is why we wrote this book. It does not purport to be a geopolitical masterpiece, nor does it offer solutions to the world's problems – though many of those solutions are obvious. For instance, why doesn't the Rich World write off the debts of the poor or developing world, and transfer real aid to those most in need? Why do we in the Rich World continue to subsidize rich farmers when farming is one of the few areas in which the developing world has a comparative advantage, one that is destroyed by the effect of such subsidies? All of these aspirations of course are considered unlikely by man, and are dismissed as the ravings of hippies with guitars singing anthems to 'greenish' themes. The cynicism that greets such expressed hope of a better world is the enemy of safety and self-preservation.

The ingrained selfishness of the Rich World is one that will likely make moves to partially equalize the quality of life between Rich and Poor World almost impossible. Aid to poor countries now runs at only 0.2% of Rich World income and even that token amount is more than offset by the destructive effect of farm subsidies. If just 5% of Rich World incomes were devoted to the developing world, a large swathe of the problems that the world faces would at least be addressed in part. The gap between the rich and the poor sections of the world is one of the most destabilizing areas of the global landscape and serious efforts to reduce it would have a highly positive effect on the world as a whole. For instance, there would be a lessening of the economic pressures that have led to a rise in terrorism; there would likely be a lessening of tensions between Israelis and Palestinians, and a lessened urgency to the huge mass migration under way between Poor and Rich Worlds, much of it illegal.

The reality is that very little of this wishlist of obviously worthwhile aspirations will take place. Vested interests (such as the farm lobby of the Rich World) will make sure that it does not. So the realists among us had better recognize what is coming.

A full-scale recession, even depression, is imminent; the product of reckless spending and borrowing, particularly in the United States. The depression that is coming is the direct result of the 'living beyond means' mentality of much of the Rich World and will be exacerbated by a variety of factors which will produce a domino-like effect throughout the world. Certainly the irresponsible behaviour of the Fed hasn't helped matters: its maniacal printing of money in recent years will have two effects: first, it will continue to reduce the value of the US dollar and, second, it will ultimately lead to deflation, as economic structures crumble under the huge weight of accumulated debts.

The problem is that this deflation will likely be preceded by a period of inflation while all the surplus money being printed chases available goods. This inflation is unlikely to be long-lasting and not of huge significance, because China's emergence as a manufacturing superpower has had and will continue to have a tendency to keep final output prices down.

Within a few short years, however, the full effects of the consequence of reckless borrowings and deficit spending in the United States and elsewhere will be evident and deflation will set in. This deflation will happen even as commodity prices rise and as the US trade deficit balloons even further.

The weakness of the Eurozone model (see 'Eurosclerosis' section on p. 119) makes independent growth in the economies very unlikely.

The dependence of China on its mercantilist approach to trade as the principal engine of economic growth will lead to serious problems. The crisis will come as the US and other economies buy less of its goods, in part because the US dollar is about to suffer its worst collapse in value in recent history.

The threat of terrorism, which is certain to rear an even uglier head in the near future, will put further downward pressure on already weakened economies.

As unemployment rises, so too will the strain on government finances in the Rich World as welfare payments increase and tax revenues fall. These are already under considerable pressure so it is likely that ultimately governments will have to put up interest rates to be able to compete for loans. This will be a further blow to an already incipiently deflationary world economy.

How this will end is uncertain. But consider carefully that a new power is rising in the East – China. This country certainly has the capability of counterbalancing US hegemony in the relatively near future – especially if the US turns protectionist in its inclinations.

In the past, when one empire has been dominant another has risen to challenge it, always resulting in armed conflict. This type of destabilization of the current world order is a possible outcome of geopolitics in the next few years. It is for this and other reasons that the sensible reader will not delay in taking our advice. And get ready, we only have a few years at our best estimate. Action is required now.

To get the latest updates on surviving the coming economic turmoil, visit the authors' website: http://www.wakeupnewsletter.com

Appendix A – Budgeting Template

Household budget sheet

Monthly Outgoings	
HOME	
Rent	
Insurance	
Upkeep	
Local Taxes/Rates/Body Corporate Fees	
Management Fees	
TELECOMS	
Telephone	
Internet Access	
Cable TV	
ENERGY/WATER	
Electricity	
Gas	
Water Charges	
CAR	
Car Insurance	
Car Fuel (LPG, gasoline, diesel)	
Cark Parking/Toll Charges	
Maintenance	

OTHER	
Medical/Life Insurance	
Other Insurance	
Laundry/Dry Cleaning	
Subscriptions	
Club Memberships	
Non-Car Transportation	
Groceries	
Eye Care/Dental Care (not covered by insurance)	
DISCRETIONARY SPENDING	
Dining Out	
Entertainment (clubs, cinemas, etc.)	
Alcohol and Tobacco	
Vacation	
Shopping for Clothes/Shoes	
Purchases for the Home	
Other	
TOTAL OUTGOINGS	

Monthly Income	
SALARY	
ALIMONY	
CHILD SUPPORT	
OTHER	
TOTAL INCOME	
Debt	
MORTGAGE REPAYMENT	
CREDIT CARDS	
CAR LOAN	
PERSONAL LOAN	
STUDENT LOAN	
OTHER LOANS	
TOTAL DEBT	

Appendix B –
Being Prepared for a Worst
Case Scenario

S uppose our worst case scenario starts to look like it might come true. Recession lingers and turns to depression, large corporations are forced to make massive layoffs as they go out of business themselves, high unemployment leads to pockets of social unrest, supplies of everyday items become erratic, armed conflict in somewhere other than Iraq or Afghanistan erupts (perhaps Iran), leading to further economic jitters. Things could turn rather nasty and without much notice. Already, you will be in better shape than most if you followed the advice above, but if you wanted to be seriously prepared for an economic meltdown, we discuss what you need to do in this section.

No income

In a worst case scenario, it is very possible that you will have no job. In this case, you need to sit down and work out a budget of your monthly expenditures. How will you survive? Do you have at least 3 years' worth of money (in the form of cash, gold and liquid, safe investments)? How much could you get by on every month?

Emergency cash

At the time of the Great Depression and, more recently, during Argentina's financial crisis, banks were closed for a period of time. Assuming ATMs are out of cash as a result of all the panic withdrawals, how will you survive? Forewarned is forearmed. Make sure that you always have an emergency supply of cash under the proverbial mattress (obviously we don't mean this literally). Our recommendation is that you keep six months' worth of spending cash at home or in another safe place. Put it in your safe if you have one. Consider dispersing it in several places should your home get burgled (but don't forget where you put it!).

Physical assets – portable, useful stores of value

Should the local currency itself become almost valueless, you would be better off including some gold coins or equivalent to your emergency cash.

Consider this scenario: things go bad, you need to get out of town on the last bus/train/plane. Due to the general state of panic, the only way to get a seat is to pay over the odds – perhaps even a bribe. Is a handful of dollars going to do it? US government bonds? Share certificates? Forget it. In extremis, gold coins, bagfuls of silver or precious stones (although harder to authenticate on the spot). Archaic, outmoded – but this advice could save your life in a worst case scenario.

Essential consumables

Only a few years ago, in the United States, a panic overtook the nation as terrorist alerts were raised to the highest possible level; every store was cleaned out of duct tape, plywood board, bottled water and canned food as people sought to protect themselves against a variety of potential terrorist attacks.

Although the United States and other nations remain on high alert for terrorist incidents, the panic to accumulate what may be essential supplies appears to be over and people have reverted to their normal spending patterns (although we don't know when you are reading this book, so things may be different again).

As readers will know by now, we are not alarmist and advocating a backwoodsman style of life – but we do think that as part of financial survival you should start accumulating essential commodities now, in advance of what might happen in a variety of circumstances. Make a list of what you might need and get to work storing these things up. It is possible that these basic supplies will be unavailable once panic sets in.

Many of these items we take for granted but our lives would be a great deal more awkward if we had to do without many of them.

- A comprehensive survival handbook – we recommend the *SAS Survival Handbook* by John 'Lofty' Wiseman.
- Disinfectant, such as bleach.
- Toiletries such as toilet paper, sanitary pads, nappies/diapers, washing powder (including hand wash detergent), dishwashing detergent, toothbrushes and toothpaste, cleaning materials, cloths.
- A supply of batteries.
- A wind-up/solar powered/or at least a battery-operated radio.
- Water purification pills.
- A cool box.
- A wood-burning stove and supply of wood, and a place to store it and keep it dry.
- An axe for chopping wood.
- A pickaxe and shovel.
- A long hosepipe (for transporting water or perhaps fuel).
- An electric and manual drill with drill bits.
- A large supply of candles.
- String and rope.
- A sharp hunting knife.
- A quick-bonding adhesive, such as superglue.
- A full set of household tools – do not rely on electrical tools.
- A generator and a sufficient supply of fuel.
- Scissors.
- Needle and a selection of threads.
- Pens and paper.
- Warm clothing, sufficient for going outdoors during the cold season.
- Fire blanket.
- Fire extinguisher.
- Smoke hoods.

- Matches (waterproof), lighters, flints.
- A pair of binoculars.
- A pair of night vision binoculars.
- A reliable, long-life battery timepiece.
- Adequate supplies of key medicines and a good first aid kit.
- A large supply of bottled water for drinking and cooking.
- Canned foods with at least two years left before the expiry date, regularly replaced.
- Replacement contact lenses, glasses and a good supply of medicines that you take regularly.

No doubt you will have many of these items already, but make sure you get the complete list by purchasing the missing ones.

References

Duncan, Richard (2005) *The Dollar Crisis : Causes, Consequences, Cures*, John Wiley & Sons, New Delhi

Huntington, Samuel P. (1998)· *The Clash of Civilizations and the Remaking of World Order*, Simon & Schuster.

Klare, Michael T. (2002) *Resource Wars: The New Landscape of Global Conflict*, Owl Books, New York.

Shambaugh, David (2004) *Modernizing China's Military: Progress, Problems, and Prospects*, University of California Press, CA

Toffler, Alvin and Toffler, Heidi Adelaide *War and Anti-War: Making Sense of Today's Global Chaos*, Warner Books.

BBC News

The *Guardian*

The Economist

The *New Statesman*

Newsweek

The *Financial Times*

The *Wall Street Journal*

The Organization for Economic Development (OECD)

The United Nations (UN)

The Federal Reserve Bank

The Dow Jones Indexes

US Department of Commerce

Energy Information Administration (EIA)

CNN

The *South China Morning Post*

The Associated Press

Notes

Part One

1 Ken Dychtwald, *The Age Wave*, (www.agewave.com).
2 Population Division, DESA, United Nations (2002) *World Population Ageing 1950–2050*.
3 Michael Bickett, 'Japan fears for its centenarians' *Independent*, (2003).
4 Population Division, DESA, United Nations (2002) *World Population Ageing 1950–2050*.
5 Intergovernmental Panel on Climate Change (IPCC), *Climate Change 2001: The Scientific Basis*.
6 Environmental Defense – a leading US non-profit organization (www.environmentaldefense.org).
7 National Oceanic and Atmospheric Administration (NOAA), US Department of Commerce (www.noaa.gov).
8 http://www.climatehotmap.org.
9 Source: Gulf Publishing Co., *World Oil*, Vol. 223, No. 8 (August 2002).
10 Source: Gulf Publishing Co., *World Oil*, Vol. 223, No. 8 (August 2002).
11 PennWell Publishing Co., *Oil & Gas Journal*, Vol. 99, No. 52 (December 24, 2001).
12 United Nations Department of Public Information, *Water: A Matter of Life and Death* (December 2002).
13 Huntington, Samuel P. (1998) *The Clash of Civilizations and the Remaking of World Order*, Simon & Schuster.
14 Bongaarts, John and Bruce, Judith (1998) *Population growth and policy options in the developing world*, 2020 vision briefs 53, International Food Policy Research Institute (IFPRI), Washington DC.
15 United Nations Population Fund, *The State of World Population 2001: Footprints and Milestones: Population and Environmental Change*.
16 *Le Monde diplomatique, (The Politics of Hunger)*, Ignacio Ramonet, November 1998.

17 *New York Times*, 'Rich Nations Are Criticized for Enforcing Trade Barriers' Edmund L. Andrews. September 29, 2002.

18 J. Sachs and A. Warner, *Natural Resource Abundance and Economic Growth* (www.cid.harvard.edu/hiid/517.pdf).

Part Two

1 Blinder, Alan S., 'Keynesian Economics', *The Concise Encyclopedia of Economics*. Liberty Fund, Inc. Ed. David R. Henderson. Library of Economics and Liberty. 30 July 2005. <http://www.econlib.org/library/Enc/KeynesianEconomics.html>.

2 OECD Data. 'OECD Central Government Debt, International Comparisons – Data from 1980 Onwards.' 5 October 2004.

3 *The Economist*, 'Special Report – State Pensions in Europe', September 27, 2003.

4 *The Economist*, 'Work longer, have more babies', September 27, 2003.

5 Quoted in the *Guardian*, 'Europe's ageing population revolts at longer work and lower pensions', Ian Traynor and Jon Henley, June 11, 2003.

6 Board of Governors of the Federal Reserve System.

7 Board of Governors of the Federal Reserve System.

8 The Office of the Comptroller of the Currency (OCC), a bureau of the US Department of the Treasury.

9 Cambridge Consumer Credit Index, March 2004.

10 Administrative Office of the US Courts. In 2003, 1,625,813 people filed for personal bankruptcy.

11 Source: The Library of Congress Country Studies.

12 *The Economist*, 'China's Economy', November 15, 2003.

13 BBC News, 'China: the world's factory floor', November 11, 2002.

14 BBC News, 'China: the world's factory floor', November 11, 2002.

15 Sources: Ministry of Land, Infrastructure and Transport; Real Estate Information Network for East Japan.

16 *The Economist*, 'A survey of retirement', March 27, 2004.

Part Three

1. *Washington Post,* 'Iran's Nuclear Skeptics' by Ray Takeyh, April 25, 2003.
2. *USA Today,* 'Ex-CIA director says administration stretched facts on Iraq', John Diamond, 18 June, 2003.
3. An act or event that is used to justify war.
4. *Washington Post,* Foreign Service, June 11, 2003, p. A16.
5. *South China Morning Post,* 'PLA troupes to be cut from ranks of troops', September 2, 2003.
6. United States Department of Defense, DefenseLINK, American Forces Press Service.
7. World Bank published GDP data.
8. *The Economist,* 'Gate-crashing the party', November 15, 2003.
9. *The Economist,* 'Ready to roll (again)?' September 20, 2003.
10. *Guardian,* 'In India, it's service with a compulsory smile', Julia Finch, November 17, 2003.
11. *Financial Times,* 'Lessons of 1920 revolt lost on Iraq', Charles Clover, December 2003.
12. Source: Gulf Publishing Co., *World Oil,* Vol. 223, No. 8 (August 2002).
13. *Moscow Times* 'Putin: Why Not Price Oil in Euros?' Catherine Belton, October 10, 2003.
14. *Sunday Telegraph,* 'They're out of excuses, we're out of time', Con Coughlin, September 7, 2003.

Part Four

1. United Nations estimate published for 2004.
2. Taken from official State of Michigan website: http://www.michigan.gov.
3. CIA, *The World Fact Book.*
4. BBC News, The Events that Triggered Argentina's Crisis; Country Profile: Argentina.
5. The United Nations, 2004 figure.
6. BBC News, Timeline: Zimbabwe.

Part Five

1 Study conducted by Javelin Inc., a research firm. Study sponsored by CheckFree Services Corp., Visa USA, and Wells Fargo Bank, January 26, 2005.

Part Six

1 Celente, Gerald (1998) *Trends 2000: How to Prepare for and Profit From the Changes of the 21st Century*, Warner Books.
2 Schwartz, Peter (2004) *Inevitable Surprises: Thinking Ahead in a Time of Turbulence*, Gotham Books.
3 Burrus, Daniel with Gittines, Roger (1993) *Technotrends: How to Use Technology to Go Beyond Your Competition*, HarperCollins.
4 Mandeville, M.W. (2000) *Return of the Phoenix Book Two: The Great Breakup*, MetaSyn Media, 2000.
5 Mandeville, M.W. (2000) *Return of the Phoenix Book Two: The Great Breakup*, MetaSyn Media, 2000.

Index